DE PROPRIETATIBUS LITTERARUM

edenda curat

C. H. VAN SCHOONEVELD

Indiana University

Series Maior, 24

RUSSIAN CUBO-FUTURISM 1910-1930

A Study in Avant-Gardism

by

VAHAN D. BAROOSHIAN

1974

MOUTON

THE HAGUE · PARIS

LIBRARY OF CONGRESS CATALOG CARD NUMBER: 73-81271

Printed in The Netherlands by Zuid-Nederlandsche Drukkerij N.V., 's-Hertogenbosch

To Barbara, Daniel,
and Sarah

ACKNOWLEDGEMENT

The present study is a revised and significantly expanded doctoral dissertation prepared for the Department of Slavic Languages and Literatures, Brown University. I am deeply grateful to professors Sam Driver, Thomas Winner, and Henry Kucera who guided the dissertation and provided valuable criticism and counsel. To Professor Vladimir Markov I owe a special debt of gratitude for his wise suggestions, comments, and great encouragement. I extend heartfelt thanks to Professor Sidney Monas for his generous advice and encouragement. Professor Robert Short gave me valuable advice of the French Surrealists. I am grateful to Mr. John D. Wilson, President, Wells College, for a grant to cover the costs of preparing this manuscript. To the library staffs of Wells College, Pushkin House, Cornell University, Lenin State, Harvard Russian Research Center and the Majakovskij Museum libraries go my genuine thanks for their kind assistance. I am also very grateful to the International Research and Exchanges Board for a grant that allowed me to continue research on the Cubo-Futurists in Moscow and Leningrad in 1971. To many others who were directly or indirectly involved in the completion of this study, my sincere appreciation.

Four sections of this study, which correspond approximately to Chapter I and Part 5 of Chapter VII, Part I of Chapter VII, and Chapter IX, were respectively published in *The Slavic and East European Journal* (The Regents of the University of Wisconsin Press), *Russian Literature Triquarterly*, and *Problems of Communism*, to which I am very grateful for their permission to use materials.

Vahan D. Barooshian

PREFACE

This book is intended for Slavists and students and specialists of poetry, literature, comparative literature and those interested in Russian avant-gardism. It might best be described as an interpretive history and critical assessment of the poetry, theory, politics, psychology and achievement of Russian Cubo-Futurism, the major avant-garde literary movement in Russia of this century.[1] This study of Cubo-Futurism differs fundamentally from previous studies, which have been mainly quite general and/or theoretical, or chronological, descriptive and factual.[2] To determine the origins of the Cubo-Futurist movement, its salient features and its ideological orientation, this study analyzes the poetic theory and practice

1 Throughout this study, Futurism will be synonymous with Cubo-Futurism.

2 I refer primarily to the valuable contribution by Professor Vladimir Markov, *Russian Futurism: A History* (Berkeley, 1968), to which this study owes a certain debt. The present study deals with those aspects of Cubo-Futurism that appear to be most significant. It does not claim to be, as it were, a 'complete' history. A number of aspects and figures of the Cubo-Futurist movement not treated here are discussed in Professor Markov's history and will perhaps be topics of further research. While there are some inevitable similarities between Professor Markov's history and this study, there are basic conceptual differences in approach which far outweigh the similarities. Professor Markov's work, by his own admission, is primarily a descriptive and factual treatment of four Russian Futurist groups, their works, and critical works on them. This study deals *exclusively* with the Cubo-Futurist group (the most significant of the Futurist groups) in analytic and synthetic terms. Moreover, this study covers in considerable detail the actual poetry of the Cubo-Futurists, their postrevolutionary period rather extensively, their relations with the Italian Futurists and the French Surrealists. Professor Markov's approach to Futurism precludes these important and neglected aspects of Cubo-Futurism. Professor Markov notes in his introduction: "Even as a description, this study is only the first step; a discussion of postrevolutionary developments should be the second step. Simultaneously the role of Russian futurism in the larger context of Russian – and European – modernism should be clarified... Only after these studies have been written can one start meditating about the nature and meaning of Russian futurism" (p. x). Professor Markov's definition of the problems in the study of Russian Futurism thus clearly recognizes and justifies the necessity of other studies which will contribute to the search for a meaning of Futurism. To his pioneering work, the present study seeks to add in that search.

of five major Cubo-Futurists: Velimir Xlebnikov, Vladimir Majakovskij, David Burljuk, Aleksej Kručënyx and Vasilij Kamenskij. This approach seeks to reveal their basic assumptions, their specific methods, interests and contributions, the role and significance of each in the movement, and the relation of each to the poetic and artistic ambience of their time: Symbolism and Cubism. A discussion of the early lives of the Cubo-Futurists and the circumstances which led them to form or join the movement is also included. Thus, unlike other studies, the basic history of Cubo-Futurism will be seen through its *dramatis personae*.

The lack of interpretation of Cubo-Futurism has perhaps also been the major lacuna of previous studies. Zbigniew Folejewski appears to have had this clearly in view when he wrote that the "entire problem of the meaning of 'futurism' as conceived by him [Majakovskij] and some of his friends has to be investigated in a larger context than has been done up to now".[3] What is more, very little, if any, attention has been directed to the argument that Cubo-Futurism never abandoned the poetic and ideological principles that inspired the movement. Perhaps of equal importance is that the factors which made Futurism a viable, vigorous, and largely independent movement have remained unexplored.

Both before and after the Bolshevik revolution, Cubo-Futurism sought to create new literary forms and new means of expression. Majakovskij, Burljuk, and Kamenskij, who largely shaped the ideological orientation of the movement, made a conscious and consistent effort to find a new role for the artist in society. One can discern the practical premises of this notion in their efforts in the prerevolutionary period to bring their poetry and art to the streets, squares, and auditoriums, to yoke art and life. After the Bolshevik revolution, when Futurism expanded its ranks and gained new vitality and momentum, the notion of integrating the artist into society emerged with sudden and dramatic urgency and assumed a number of forms in the nineteen twenties. During those years, Majakovskij and Osip Brik made more determined efforts to realize that notion – to make the artist an active and leading participant in the life and events of his time. This notion of the artist's role in society appears to be a significant but entirely neglected aspect of Cubo-Futurism and is at the core of its only seemingly contradictory, vague, and confused literary theories in the nineteen twenties. It is from this perspective that the Cubo-Futurist movement takes on a consistency and meaning and

[3] Zbigniew Folejewski, "Mayakovsky and Futurism", *Comparative Literature Studies* (Special Advance Issue, 1963), 72-73.

logic of its own.

There are also two chapters which discuss and analyze the important relations between the Cubo-Futurists and the Italian Futurists and the French Surrealists respectively. The chapters seek to provide guidelines for further exploration of the phenomenon of avant-gardism from the viewpoint of comparative literature.

TABLE OF CONTENTS

Acknowledgement 7

Preface 9

Introduction: The Background of Early Cubo-Futurism in Brief Historical Perspective 15

I. Velimir Xlebnikov
1. Xlebnikov's Path to Futurism 19
2. Xlebnikov's Linguistic, Poetic, Mathematical and Historical Interests in Relation to Russian Symbolism . . . 23
3. Xlebnikov's "Žuravl" and Some Features of His Poetic Practice 29
4. Conclusion 34

II. Vladimir Majakovskij
1. Majakovskij's Path to Futurism 38
2. Majakovskij's Prerevolutionary Esthetics and Poetry . . 42
3. Some Aspects of Majakovskij's Poetry 56

III. David Burljuk
1. Burljuk and the Organization of Futurism 67
2. The Esthetics and Poetry of Burljuk 70
3. Conclusion 76

IV. Aleksej Kručёnyx
1. Kručёnyx's Path to Futurism 79
2. Kručёnyx: Theory and Practice of Trans-sense 1913-1928 82
3. The Critics of Kručёnyx's Trans-sense 91
4. Conclusion 96

V. Vasilij Kamenskij
1. Kamenskij and the Formation of Futurism 98
2. Kamenskij's Poetry: Theory and Practice 100
3. Conclusion 105

VI. Early Russian Futurism in Perspective 108

VII. Futurism in the Postrevolutionary Period
1. The Futurists and the Artistic Avant-Garde 114
2. The Creation of *Lef* and Futurist Theories 126
3. Criticism of the Futurists 131
4. The Crisis and Dissolution of *Lef* 133
5. *New Lef* and the 'Literature of Fact' 134
6. Conclusion 142

VIII. Russian and Italian Futurism
1. Some Similarities and the Problem of 'Influence' 145

IX. French Surrealism and Russian Futurism
1. Some Comparisons and Differences 153
2. The Surrealist Political Commitment and 'Proletarian' Literature 155
3. Conclusion 162

Bibliography 164

Index 172

INTRODUCTION: THE BACKGROUND OF EARLY RUSSIAN CUBO-FUTURISM IN BRIEF HISTORICAL PERSPECTIVE

During the first decade of this century, Russian Symbolism, strongly influenced by French Symbolism, dominated Russian poetry. While it was essentially a search for new forms of poetic expression, Symbolism also assigned itself a theurgic mission, attempted to discover new metaphysical realities and to effect an 'artistic' transformation of life which many Symbolists actually believed was close at hand. It is probably no exaggeration to assert that Symbolist visions of new orders to come, often opposed to the very reality in which the Symbolists lived, were a form of religious faith. Symbolism was in no sense a 'mass' or 'democratic' art; it was a highly suggestive and intellectual art intended for the trained and initiated reader. This feature of Symbolism is important for an understanding of the reaction against it by the Acmeist and Cubo-Futurist poets.

By 1910, Symbolism had exhausted itself: it had failed on its theurgic mission, lost its novelty and declined. The crisis of Symbolism, as one observer put it, was that it no longer believed that it could conquer and transform the world.[1] Symbolism, however, contributed significantly to the intellectual ferment, the artistic diversity and the vigorous, passionate, and almost desperate search for artistic freshness and innovation that characterized the *fin-de-siècle* in Russia.

In 1910, a critical appraisal of Symbolism and the nature and aims of poetry were made. New poetic groups gradually emerged. The first of these major groups was the Acmeists, of which Gumilëv, Gorodeckij, Axmatova and Mandel'štam were the leading members. Another member, Kuzmin, whose role in the Acmeist movement is not as substantial as claimed, appealed in 1910 in the (Acmeist) journal *(Apollo)* for "beautiful clarity". For Kuz'min, this demanded logical structure, love for the word,

[1] S. Adrjanov, "Kritičeskie nabroski", *Vestnik Evropy*, No. 10 (1910), 390.

and economy of means.[2] Acmeism, however, was not so much a reaction against Symbolism as a reform or reorientation of it towards material reality, clarity of vision, imagery and verbal design. The Acmeists valued Symbolism highly for its poetic achievements and for its liberation of poetry from the "Babylonian captivity" of civic duty that was characteristic of the nineteenth century. They believed, however, that mysticism, theosophy, and occultism had led the Symbolists into a *cul de sac* which threatened the further growth and development of poetry. In his programmatic article, Gumilëv, the founder of Acmeism, wrote that Symbolism had grappled with the "unknown", and with metaphysical problems which lacked solution. Gumilëv did not reject the "unknown", but viewed as the principle of Acmeism an awareness of it.[3] Gorodeckij, in his article, defined Acmeism in terms of painting: "The struggle between Acmeism and Symbolism, if it is a struggle and not the seizure of an abandoned fortress, is above all a struggle for this world, vibrant, colorful, having form, balance and time, a struggle for our planet Earth."[4] What united the Acmeists was a "common attitude towards the 'uttered word', and not style".[5]

A second major group undertook a much more radical reappraisal of Symbolism. It consisted of painters and painter-poets who had formed their own poetic circle. These artists decided to enter the literary field with the aim of reacting against Symbolism, which they considered wrongheaded and misguided in its philosophical and religious pursuits, odious, a "stagnant swamp", and "intolerably boring" as a whole.[6] They also wanted to react against what they considered the lifeless and abstract language of the Symbolists, and to reorient language to that of the street and daily life, to democratize poetry. As social exiles, political revolutionaries, poor, disaffected and almost starving, these artists saw in poetic and linguistic activity not only a means of self-expression, but also a means of expressing their discontent with society.

These artists anticipated the publication of a collection of articles and poetic works by which they would state their seeming reaction against Symbolism. One of the artist-poets, Vasilij Kamenskij, saw in the poetry

[2] Mixail Kuz'min, "O prekrasnoj jasnosti: Zametki o proze", *Apollon* No. 4 (1910), 10.
[3] Nikolaj Gumilëv, "Nasledie simvolizma i akmeizm," *Apollon* No. 1 (1913), p. 43.
[4] Sergej Gorodeckij, "Nekotorye tečenija v sovremennoj russkoj poèzii", *Apollon*, No. 1 (1913), 48.
[5] Sergej Makovskij, *Na parnase 'serebrjannogo veka'* (Munich, 1962), 217. See also Boris Èixenbaum, *Anna Axmatova: Opyt analiza* (Petersburg, 1923), 19-25.
[6] Vasilij Kamenskij, *Put' èntuziasta* (Moscow, 1931), 109-110.

of Velimir Xlebnikov what he believed to be a new poetic technique. Kamenskij eagerly suggested to the leader of the group, David Burljuk, that Xlebnikov join it and that his poetry be included in the collection for publication. After listening to Xlebnikov's poetry, Burljuk remarked that Xlebnikov was a "poet of genius". What Burljuk saw in Xlebnikov's poetry was an affirmation of Cubist principles: artistic creation is a deliberate distortion, not a reflection of reality, hence it affirms itself, and bears its own reason for existence. Poetry is not unlike a painting in that it is constructed of words which possess a self-contained reality. Poetry is not so much constructed of ideas as of words whose composition and arrangement are designed to evoke its content or 'idea'. The poet is thus a verbal engineer, as it were. These notions became the theoretical basis of Russian Cubo-Futurism.

In 1910, the group's publication appeared, entitled *A Trap for Judges (Sadok sudej)*. It contained poetry which was written on the reverse side of cheap wallpaper. Kamenskij notes that the wallpaper was a "mark of protest against luxurious bourgeois publications".[7] As for the poetry, Stepanov observes that almost all of it was a mixture of Symbolist and Decadent poets: Blok, Brjusov, Sologub, Rimbaud, Corbière, Maurice Rolland and others.[8] The contributors were Kamenskij, Xlebnikov, David, Nikolaj and Vladimir Burljuk, Elena Guro, Ekaterina Nizen and others.[9] They called themselves *budetljane* (i.e. 'those who will be'), a name coined by Xlebnikov.

Contrary to the expectations of the group, the publication received scant attention: the poets were relatively unknown, and failed to define the new poetic technique and to articulate the new poetic vision. The publication also met with hostile reviews. For example, Brjusov, the leader and organizer of Russian Symbolism, wrote that it was "almost beyond the limits of literature. The collection is replete with puerile escapades in bad taste, and its authors above all aim to shock the reader and to harass the critics (what is called *épater les bourgeois*)."[10] This

[7] Kamenskij, 113.

[8] N. Stepanov, "Biografičeskij očerk", in Velimir Xlebnikov, *Izbrannye stixotvorenija* (Moscow, 1936), 22.

[9] Vladimir Burljuk was a painter, as was his brother David, who also wrote poetry. Nikolaj Burljuk, Ekaterina Nizen, and Elena Guro were Futurist poets. The last began to write lyrical poetry around 1905. She was the wife of Mixail Matjušin, a musician, painter, and theoretician.

[10] Quoted in N. Xardžiev, "Kommentarij", in Velimir Xlebnikov, *Neizdannye proizvedenija* (Moscow, 1940), 420. See other reviews and comments on this page.

failure to receive favorable recognition did not, however, deter the determined David Burljuk from trying again.

In 1911, the group was armed with new talent when Vladimir Majakovskij and Aleksej Kručënyx joined it. Once again David Burljuk intended to publish polemical articles on poetry and painting, including the works of Xlebnikov, Kručënyx, and Majakovskij. Burljuk felt that the undertaking would be successful if he could achieve an alliance with a newly formed avant-garde group of painters, the Jack of Diamonds, which arose in 1910. Through this alliance, Burljuk hoped to found the new poetic movement on a broad base, to create a united front of poetry and painting, and to show the close relationship between the two. The Jack of Diamonds group refused, however, to participate in the polemical venture.

In December 1912, Majakovskij succeeded in persuading a private publisher to publish the collection of poetry and articles entitled *A Slap in the Face of Public Taste (Poščëčina obščestvennomu vkusu)*, which contained the famous Futurist manifesto that was influenced strongly by Italian Futurism. The collection captured the immediate attention of literary circles and was publicly ridiculed. Signed by Majakovskij, Xlebnikov, Kručënyx and Burljuk, the manifesto was disrespectful, arrogant, and designed, as most avant-garde manifestoes are, to outrage the sensibilities of its readers. Moreover, the manifesto suffered from a certain lack of clarity: it vented so much discontent that it failed to define its concrete and positive aims. It also failed to credit the Russian Symbolists with numerous experiments in poetic vocabulary. The notion of the "Self-sufficient Word" meant, in poetic terms, that experimentation with, and deformation of, the word is the primary end, not the means, of poetry.

I

VELIMIR XLEBNIKOV

1. XLEBNIKOV'S PATH TO FUTURISM

Velimir Xlebnikov was born in 1885 in the village of Tundutovo in Astraxan' Province. His mother had been educated as a historian, and his father as a scientist. The young Xlebnikov began to read at an early age and displayed an interest in languages and painting. He later wrote that, "during my years as a student, I thought about the regeneration of the language".[1]

In 1898, Xlebnikov attended the gymnasium in Simbirsk Province. A year later, after his family had moved to Kazan', Xlebnikov attended the gymnasium there. At this time, his interest in literature, history, and mathematics took shape. In 1903, upon completion of the gymnasium, Xlebnikov pursued mathematics as his major subject at the University of Kazan'. Xlebnikov once took part in a student demonstration of protest against the arrest, for political activity, of a student who subsequently died in a psychiatric ward. Although Xlebnikov had the opportunity to escape arrest, he refused to do so because he wanted "to answer" to someone. He was imprisoned for a month.

When Xlebnikov resumed his studies at the University in 1904, he began to read the Russian Symbolist poets and their literary journal *Vesy (The Scales)*. He wrote a number of works, one of which he sent to Gor'kij for criticism. According to Xlebnikov's sister, Gor'kij returned the manuscript with his comments; he apparently approved, "because Vitja looked proud and happy".[2]

In 1905, when he learned that the Japanese had ignominiously defeated the Russians in the naval battle at Tsushima, Xlebnikov became curious

[1] Velimir Xlebnikov, *Sobranie proizvedenij*, V (Leningrad, 1929-1933), 279. Henceforth, this edition will be referred to as SP.

[2] Quoted in N. Stepanov, "Biografičeskij očerk", in Velimir Xlebnikov, *Izbrannye stixotvorenija* (Moscow, 1936), 12.

about historical determinants and set himself the task of discovering "the laws of time" by investigating the nexus between mathematics and history.[3] He devoted most of his life to this investigation, and its implications for his poetry will be discussed below. Further, one of his early works, which is undated, was an account of the Tsushima battle; and it was most probably written in 1905. In this early poem, entitled "Byli vešči sliškom sini" ("Things Were Much Too Blue"), Xlebnikov introduced initially the theme of historical retribution, a theme which recurred often in his later poetry.[4]

In 1907, Xlebnikov began to write poetry under the strong influence of the Russian Symbolists, especially of Bal'mont, Vjačeslav Ivanov, Remizov and Gorodeckij. Most of Xlebnikov's early poetry reflects the idealization of primitive life and nature and interest in folklore and pagan mythological motifs that were characteristic of Ivanov's and Gorodeckij's poetry.[5]

A year later, Xlebnikov went to St. Petersburg with the intention of continuing his education there. Once he became acquainted in poetic circles, however, he lost his interest in formal education and failed to complete it.[6] Poetry and research in mathematics and history consumed his energies. One of Xlebnikov's close friends, Matjušin, has left us a description of Xlebnikov's personality and way of life in St. Petersburg:

> He was astonishingly silent and constantly in concentration... When spoken to, he would become embarrassed, and would softly whisper an unintelligible reply. In his association with his friends, he was extremely reserved, and became animated when there was discussion of a new publication and work as a whole... In his daily life, V. Xlebnikov was as helpless as a child and terribly absent-minded. For dinner, he would take a box of matches instead of bread; and when he left the house, he would forget his hat. His reticence and reserve often made us forget that he was in our midst.
>
> When working all day on an investigation of numbers in the public library, Xlebnikov would forget to eat and drink; and he would often return so exhausted and gray from fatigue and hunger, but in such deep concentration that it required an effort to tear him away from his calculations and seat him at a table [to eat].[7]

3 Xlebnikov, SP, II, 10.

4 For example, in "Gibel' Atlantidy" ("The Death of Atlantis", 1912), "Noč' pered sovetami" ("The Night before the Soviets", 1921), "Pračka" ("The Washerwoman", 1921), and "Nastojaščee" ("The Present", 1921).

5 See, for example, Xlebnikov's early works.

6 Xlebnikov (intermittently) studied biology, Eastern languages, and Sanskrit at the University of St. Petersburg until 1911, when he finally abandoned his studies.

7 Quoted in Stepanov, 18. See also L. Brik, "Iz vospominanij", in *Almanax s Majakovskim* (Moscow, 1934), 77-78, and Sergej Spasskij, *Majakovskij i ego sputniki* (Leningrad, 1940), 64-67.

In 1908, Xlebnikov met Vasilij Kamenskij, who was the editor of the journal *Vesna (Spring)*. Kamenskij was struck by Xlebnikov's talent and published his work "Iskušenie grešnika" ("The Sinner's Temptation"), whose major feature was neologisms. Through Kamenskij, Xlebnikov met the leading avant-garde painters, Matjušin and Kul'bin. Xlebnikov undoubtedly renewed his interest in painting. According to Denike, a professor at the University of St. Petersburg, Xlebnikov "found an analogy between his formal pursuits in the sphere of poetic language and the system of modern French painting".[8] In fact, Xlebnikov himself wrote that "we want the word to pursue painting boldly".[9] In a letter to Kamenskij in 1910, Xlebnikov spoke of "the right to use newly created words, to write with words of a single root...to paint by sound". He added that "we are a new kind of people-rays [ljud-ljuči] who have come to illuminate the world. We are invincible."[10]

Here one should note that Xlebnikov's syncretism reflected the strong experimental current of the period, and the search of many poets for new poetic forms and styles in the spatial arts.[11] In particular, the Symbolists' view of poetry as emotional activity led them to merge poetry with music.[12] Moreover, some poets of this period, such as Gumilëv, Gorodeckij, and Mandel'štam, explicitly looked to painting, architecture, and sculpture for principles or devices applicable to poetry in an attempt to merge them with it. Poetry was increasingly being viewed as a craft, as a structure.

In 1909, Xlebnikov met Vjačeslav Ivanov, who became "highly sympathetic" to Xlebnikov's "literary beginnings".[13] Prior to this meeting, Xlebnikov had written to Ivanov and said that Slavic languages should revitalize contemporary Russian.[14] Xlebnikov subsequently frequented Ivanov's famous "Tower", where philosophy, mysticism, anarchism,

8 Quoted in N. Xardžiev, "Majakovskij i živopis'", in *V. Majakovskij: Materialy i issledovanija*, eds. V. Percov and N. Serebrjannyj (Moscow, 1940), 381.

9 Velimir Xlebnikov, *Neizdannye proizvedenija* (Moscow, 1940), 334.

10 Xlebnikov, SP, V, 391.

11 "Forms and styles of the individual arts are often, and perhaps even always, determined by common interaction of the arts in a given moment. In this sense, syncretism lies in the nature of art as such, and is an organic phenomenon. One of the arts usually dominates over others, and is isolated from them, becoming characteristic for a given epoch" (Boris Eixenbaum, "Melodika stixa", in his *Skvoz' literaturu* [The Hague, 1962], 209).

12 Georgette Donchin, *The Influence of French Symbolism on Russian Poetry* (The Hague, 1958), 106.

13 Xlebnikov, SP, V, 286.

14 Xlebnikov, *Neizdannye proizvedenija*, 352.

poetry and religion were the frequent topics of discussion.[15] Although Xlebnikov considered Kuz'min as his teacher, Ivanov should probably be regarded as the dominant ideological influence on Xlebnikov.[16] Ivanov reinforced the East Asian, pan-Russian,[17] and prehistoric orientation of Xlebnikov, and inculcated in him the lofty notion of the theurgic mission of the poet and the notion of poetry as the 're-creation' or transformation of life. Further, Xlebnikov's use of archaic diction and folklore motifs was also influenced by Ivanov.[18]

In the autumn of 1909, Xlebnikov became acquainted with a group of young poets called the Academy of Verse, which was initiated by Gumilëv. It first began to meet at Ivanov's "Tower", where Ivanov gave lectures on versification and critical commentaries on the works of the young poets. In October, 1909, the group met at the editorial quarters of the newly created journal *Apollon*, with which it was associated. At this time, Ivanov, Faddej Zelinskij, and Innokentij Annenskij gave the poetry lectures. With Sergej Makovskij, Valerij Brjusov, Aleksandr Blok and Mixail Kuz'min, they were also members of the managing board.[19] Xlebnikov desired to ally himself with a group of poets so as to find an outlet for his works. He entertained high hopes of publishing in *Apollo*, and wrote to his mother that one of his works would be published in the February, 1910 issue.[20] However, while Ivanov and Kuz'min were sympathetic to Xlebnikov's work, Xardžiev observes, "the tendency toward innovation in the early works of Xlebnikov, with their orientation towards non-traditional [*nekanoničeskie*] genres of folklore poetry [*raešnik*, *bylina*] encountered the hostility of the majority of the members of the Academy of Verse".[21] Xlebnikov's hopes of publishing in *Apollo* were thus never realized.

Very shortly after Xlebnikov left the Academy of Verse in December, 1909, he met Kamenskij again, who introduced him to David Burljuk, who had recently formed his own poetic circle. It was then that he

15 According to Sergej Makovskij, *Portrety sovremennikov* (New York, 1955), 274, "almost all the young poetry of the time, if it did not emanate from Ivanov's Tower, at least passed through it..."

16 Kuzmin's influence on Xlebnikov was primarily in the sphere of colloquial speech and free verse. Vjačeslav Ivanov was also, for a time, Kuzmin's 'mentor'.

17 Xlebnikov considered Russia the capital of the world, and Moscow and St. Petersburg its two provinces. See Xlebnikov, SP, V, 291.

18 See I. Postupal'skij, "V. Xlebnikov i futurizm", *Novyj mir*, No. 5 (1930), 189.

19 Makovskij, 274-275, and N. Xardžiev, "Kommentarij", in Xlebnikov, *Neizdannye proizvedenija*, 419.

20 Xlebnikov, SP, V, 268.

21 Xardžiev, "Kommentarij", 419.

published his well-known "Zakljatie smexom" ("Incantation by Laughter") in *Studija impressionistov (The Studio of Impressionists)*, the main inspiration of which was Kul'bin. This work brought Xlebnikov immediate recognition. As we have already observed, in that same year he became associated with a literary group that came to be known as the Cubo-Futurists,[22] and published two other works in the ill-fated *Sadok sudej:* "Zverinec" and "Žuravl'".

2. XLEBNIKOV'S LINGUISTIC, POETIC, MATHEMATICAL AND HISTORICAL INTERESTS IN RELATION TO RUSSIAN SYMBOLISM

As a theoretician of Russian Futurism, Xlebnikov's linguistic experiments with *zaumnyj jazyk* (trans-sense language) fall into two basic categories: (1) the creation of neologisms from Slavic morphemes by analogy with other words, and (2) the creation of a universal language. Xlebnikov expressed his 'attitude toward the word' as follows:

> To find, without breaking the circle of roots, the philosopher's stone for transforming all Slavic words one into another – this is my first attitude toward the word. This self-contained word is beyond daily life and everyday uses. Having observed that roots are only spectres which conceal the strings of the alphabet, to find the unity of world languages in general, constructed of units of the alphabet – this is my second attitude toward the word. The road to the world of trans-sense language.[23]

With regard to the creation of neologisms (Xlebnikov's concern for a universal language will be dealt with in another context), Xlebnikov employed prefixes, suffixes, and infixes in the work that bestowed fame on him, "Zakljatie smexom" ("Incantation by Laughter"):

> Oh, laugh forth, laugh laughadors!
> O laugh on, laugh laughadors!
> You who laugh in laughs, laugh-laugh, you who laughorize
> so laughly, Laugh forth, laugh laugh belaughly!
> Oh, of laughdom overlaughly, laugh of languish laughadors!

22 There were four groups that comprised Russian Futurism: The Ego-Futurists, the Mezzanine of Poetry, the Centrifuge and the Cubo-Futurists. The Ego-Futurists were in the main concerned with the exaltation of the Self in poetry. The Mezzanine of Poetry and the Centrifuge wanted to "introduce more themes connected with modern city life" (Vladimir Markov, "On Modern Russian Poetry", in *Modern Russian Poetry*, eds. Vladimir Markov and Merril Sparks [London, 1966], lxiii). See also Kornej Čukovskij, *Futuristy* (Petrograd, 1922), 5–26, and N. Xardžiev, "Kommentarij: Zabytye stat'i Majakovskogo", in *Literaturnoe nasledstvo*, 11 (Moscow, 1932), 156.

23 Xlebnikov, SP, II, 9.

Oh, forth laugh downright laughly, laugh of super laughadors!
Laughery! Laughery!
Belaugh, uplaugh, laughikins, laughikins,
Laughutelets, laughutelets!
Oh, laugh forth, laugh laughadors!
Oh, laugh on, laugh, laughadors![24]

Related to this category were Xlebnikov's numerous creations of neologisms by replacing the initial consonant of a substantive with another consonant. For example, he would replace the consonant "k" in the word *knjaz'* 'prince' with the consonant "m" and create the word *mnjaz'*, which Xlebnikov defined as "thinker".[25] He wrote in this connection: "If we have a pair of words such as *dvor* and *tvor*, and we know of the word *dvorjane* [the noblemen], we can create the word *tvorjane* – creators of life." As to the significance of neologisms, Roman Jakobson writes that "an important possibility of a poetic neologism is non-objectivization".[26] A neologism does not necessarily evoke a definite object, although it can convey a meaning. Neologisms can also "enrich poetry in that [they]...create a euphonic effect...and produce an awareness on the part of the reader and compel him to think etymologically".[27]

Xlebnikov's linguistic experiments were designed to enrich poetic language and to expand the range of poetic expression. "Word creation", Xlebnikov remarked, "is the enemy of the bookish ossification of the language, and, inasmuch as this is supported by the fact that in the country...language is being created every instant...this right carries over into living literature".[28] The Russian Symbolists, to be sure, made numerous linguistic experiments, but only so as to lend their work a suggestive atmosphere, enabling them "to transcend the limits of reality", by means of vague hints and associations;[29] so that their experiments were "a means of materialization, of unveiling 'contacts with other worlds'".[30] To a certain extent, this may be said of Xlebnikov.[31] Unlike the Symbolists, however, Xlebnikov was concerned with linguistic

24 See Alexander Kaun, *Soviet Poets and Poetry* (Berkeley, 1943), 24.
25 Xlebnikov, SP, V, 232.
26 Roman Jakobson, *Novejšaja russkaja poèzija* (Prague, 1921), 47.
27 Jakobson, 44.
28 Xlebnikov, SP, V, 233.
29 V. Timofeeva, *Jazyk poèta i vremja: Poètičeskij jazyk Majakovskogo* (Moscow-Leningrad, 1962), 53.
30 V. Gofman, "Jazykovoe novatorstvo Xlebnikova", in his *Jazyk literatury* (Moscow, 1936), 228.
31 "You recall what freedom at times a misprint gives from this world" (Xlebnikov, SP, V, 233).

technique *per se*. His technique, moreover, was of "a rational and logical character", in part a conscious effort to create new paths to a scientific linguistic system.[32]

Passionately dedicated as he was to determining 'national destinies' and to the 're-creation' of humanity – both Symbolist notions – Xlebnikov set himself two basic tasks which claim brief discussion.

Curiously, Xlebnikov devoted almost all his life to research on numbers, and not to poetry. For Xlebnikov, history was not the result of the efforts of men to impose their will on events, or the result of human conflict, human interaction or human activities, but the result of mathematical laws or cycles; and Xlebnikov firmly believed that these were discoverable by, and amenable to, mathematical formulae. Xlebnikov simply could not live in an unpredictable and irrational and illogical world; and he was determined to discover "the rules to which national destinies are subject".[33] But where and with which event does one begin? Since there were no criteria for selecting historical events and for assigning significance or irrelevance to them, selection was perforce arbitrary. Xlebnikov therefore had to manipulate selected events until he reduced them to a scheme in which a number or formula appeared often enough to permit him to embrace other events. After years of lucubration,[34] intensive research in libraries and endless wandering about Russia in an effort to sense the rhythms of history, Xlebnikov discovered that three hundred seventeen (years) was the magic number that separated turning points in history. He concluded and predicted that the year 1917 marked "the fall of a state", which for Xlebnikov meant Russia.[35]

Xlebnikov's chronic obsession with, and perhaps mystical belief in, numbers as the magic key to the structure of history and reality are central to an understanding of his poetry. This obsession with numbers was poetically productive.[36] Poetry for Xlebnikov was often an outlet for, or the handmaiden of, his mathematical and historical theories, as well as a medium for their creative application. These theories not only shaped to a large degree his view of art as description of an historical era or event, but also enriched and informed most of his poetry; they shaped

32 Gofman, 228.
33 Xlebnikov, SP, V, 175.
34 David Burljuk notes that Xlebnikov "worked slowly, at night. He would get up about one o'clock in the afternoon". (Quoted in Xardžiev, "Kommentarij", *Neizdannye proizvedenija*, 480).
35 Xlebnikov, SP, V, 179.
36 Vel, "Xlebnikov – osnovatel' budetljan", *Kniga i revoljucija*, No. 9-10 (1922), 24.

its epic orientation and led Xlebnikov to explore specific periods of Russian and world history.[37] Markov points out that "There is more unity in Xlebnikov's verse than in his themes, which were as disorganized and varied as the reality surrounding him."[38]

Xlebnikov explored historical eras to escape from reality:

Mne, babočka, zaletevšej
V komnatu čelovečeskoj žizni,
Ostavit' počerk moej pyli
Po surovym oknam, podpis'ju uznika,
Na strogix stëklax roka.
Tak skučny i sery
Oboi iz čelovečeskoj žizni!
Okon prozračnoe "net"!
Ja už stër svoë sinee zarevo, toček uzory,
Moju golubuju burju kryla – pervuju svežest',
Pyl'ca snjata, kryl'ja uvjali i stali prozračny i žëstki,
B'jus' ja ustalo v okno čeloveka.
Večnye čisla stučatsja ottuda
Prizyvom na rodinu, čislo zovut k čislam vernut'sja.[39]

I, a butterfly, happened to fly
Into the room of human life,
To leave the imprint of my scales
On the grim windows, as the sign of a prisoner,
On the stern window-panes of fate!
So dull and grey
Are the surroundings of human life!
The transparent "No" of the windows!
I have already dusted my blue glow, the pattern of the dots,
The blue storm of my wing, the first freshness,
The dust has gone, the wings withered, transparent and stiff,
I wearily beat against man's window.
Eternal numbers knock from beyond
As a call to native land; the number is called to return to numbers.

Since Xlebnikov believed that the past would inevitably merge with the future, he also contemplated and explored historical eras to discover which era would merge with that future. "Carskaja nevesta" ("The Czar's

[37] In 1913, in the article "O rasširenii predelov russkoj slovesnosti", in *Neizdannye proizvedenija*, 340-342, Xlebnikov decried the narrowness of the territorial limits of Russian literature and called for the literary treatment of Poland, India, the era of Justinian I, the Balkans, the Urals, Siberia, the Russian battles of the fourteenth and fifteenth centuries, the life of the Jewish people, and medieval Slavic personalities. This was a small measure of Xlebnikov's historical interests.

[38] Vladimir Markov, *The Longer Poems of Velimir Xlebnikov* (Berkeley, 1962), 156.

[39] Xlebnikov, SP, III, 324.

Bride" 1908) deals with Ivan IV; "Vnučka Maluši" ("Maluša's Granddaughter" 1909) concerns the era of Prince Vladimir; "Lesnaja deva" ("The Forest Maiden" 1910) and "I i È" ("I and È", 1912) have their settings in prehistory; "Marija Večora" ("Marie Vetsera", 1913) is based on the suicide of the Austrian archduke Rudolf and his mistress Marie Vetsera in 1889, an event to which Xlebnikov seems to have attached considerable importance in constructing his mathematical theories of history. "Deti vydry" ("The Otter's Children", 1913), which Xlebnikov considered one of his greatest works and which has been regarded as one of the artistic syntheses of Xlebnikov's "mathematical explorations",[40] combines historical eras and introduces key historical figures: Marx, Justinian I, Darwin, Hannibal, Sten'ka Razin, Hus, Pugačev, Copernicus and others.[41] Stepanov perhaps rightly observes that Xlebnikov's "historical and philosophical hypotheses are not only the themes of his poetry, but also their semantic base [*kostjak*], which permeates all the imagery and themes".[42] This in part explains the plotless and fragmentary nature of Xlebnikov's poetry and accounts for the presence of historical data and numbers and mathematical formulae in his work. In "Gibel' Atlantidy" ("The Death of Atlantis", 1912), Xlebnikov pointed out the significance of numbers and their relation to events and nature. That Xlebnikov had Czar Nicholas II as "king" is conceivable:

> Poxody mračnye pexot,
> Kop'ëm ubijstvo korolja
> Poslušny čislam kak zaxod,
> Dožd' zvëzd i sinie polja.
> Goda vojny, kovry čume,
> Složil i vyčel ja v ume.
> I uvaženie k čislu
> Rastët, ruč'i vedja k ruslu.[43]

> The grim marches of soldiers,
> The murder of the king by lance
> Are subject to numbers, like the sunset,
> The rain of stars and the blue fields.
> The years of war, the coming of the plague
> I have added and subtracted in my head.
> And respect for numbers
> Grows, leading the brooks to the channel.

40 Vel, p. 22.

41 See Stepanov's extensive commentary on the historical sources which Xlebnikov used to write this work in Xlebnikov, SP, II, 311-316.

42 N. Stepanov, "Tvorčestvo Velimira Xlebnikova", in Xlebnikov, SP, I, 41.

43 Xlebnikov, SP, I, 94.

In "Čisla" ("Numbers"), Xlebnikov personified numbers:

> Ja vsmatrivajus' v vas, o čisla,
> I vy mne vidites' odetymi v zveri, v ix škurax,
> Rukoj opirajuščimisja na vyrvannye duby.
> Vy daruete – edinstvo meždu zmeeobraznym dviženiem
> Xrebta vselennoj i pljaskoj koromysla,
> Vy pozvoljaete ponimat' veka, kak bystrogo xoxota zuby.
> Moi sejčas veščeobrazno razvërzlisja zenicy.
> Uznat', čto budet ja, kogda delimoe ego – edinica.[44]
>
> I stare at you, O numbers,
> And you appear to me dressed like animals, in their hides,
> Leaning a hand on uprooted oak trees.
> You give the unity between the serpentine movement
> Of the universe's backbone and the dance of the shoulder yoke.
> You grant the understanding of the ages, like a quick grin.
> My eyes have now seen the meaning of things.
> To know what will I be when its dividend is one.

While the Russian Symbolists spoke of re-creating and transforming humanity 'artistically',[45] Xlebnikov attempted to achieve this *linguistically*. And this was his second major project: to create a universal language of consonants so as to restore the lost unity of men. Quite conceivably, Xlebnikov was prompted to this fantastic task by the human violence and carnage which he saw in history. "Trans-sense language is the embryonic future language of the universe. Only it can unite men. Rational languages are already disuniting men."[46] Xlebnikov believed that, in the state of primitive reality, men spoke one language, when "savage understood savage". Languages, however, "betrayed their glorious past" and began to "serve the cause of discord".[47] And Xlebnikov once asked: "What is better, a universal language or universal slaughter?"[48] To Xlebnikov's vision of universal harmony, this universal language was central. In "Ladomir" ("World Harmony", 1920) Xlebnikov spoke of remaking "the languages of the world into a unified language of mortals", and in his view the Futurists "had given their oath to destroy languages".[49]

Xlebnikov's idealization of, and intense yearning for, a primitive

[44] Xlebnikov, SP, II, 98.

[45] "The final aim of art is the re-creation of humanity" (B. Bugaev [A. Belyi], *Simvolizm* [Moscow, 1910], 10).

[46] Xlebnikov, SP, V, 236.

[47] Xlebnikov, SP, V, 216.

[48] Xlebnikov, SP, V, 266.

[49] Xlebnikov, SP, I, 186, 198.

world and a mythical universal language can be seen as a kind of corollary to the Symbolist ideas of Vjačeslav Ivanov and Belyj, for whom art and language were the key to some 'other' reality and a kind of religious activity, or at least a substitute for it. This intense longing may have been a form of escape from, and a negative protest against, reality. This at least was true of the Russian Symbolists.

3. XLEBNIKOV'S "ŽURAVL'" AND SOME FEATURES OF HIS POETIC PRACTICE

Before discussing one of Xlebnikov's works and some features of his poetic practice, it would be useful here to give a summary, however brief, of the Symbolist orientation of his poetry. Xlebnikov's poetry, rich in ideas and in mythological allusions, exhibits an extraordinary thematic and linguistic range. As noted, he has an abiding concern with historical eras and *dramatis personae;* he yearns for the past and antiquity, and is almost religiously devoted to the east. For Xlebnikov, poetry was not an end in itself, or a 'realistic' description of reality, or an obsession with the 'I', but a means of exploration and discovery of, and innovation in, style, language, and new forms. Because he saw poetry as a symbolic language and because of his supreme linguistic command, Xlebnikov often consciously eschewed logical or precise selection of poetic language. The notion of the 'right' word in poetry was alien to him as it was to many Symbolists. The operative principle in poetic word selection was often the 'wrong', or 'illogical', or 'trans-sense', or 'automatic' word. Hence the deformation of language and distortion of phenomena in his poetry. For poetry, in Symbolist esthetics, is the art of a seer who seeks analogies between things; it is an intellectual, cryptic, and elliptical art of words, a complex of sound relationships and their suggestive and evocative ability; it is an art which requires of the reader that he unravel or decipher its deliberate or calculated mystery. Some of these aspects will be seen in Xlebnikov's poetry.

One of Xlebnikov's early works, "Žuravl'" ("The Crane", 1909) will now be examined. The work appears to be a synthesis of the real and dream worlds. One may also consider it a surrealistic allegory. Gumilëv has remarked in this regard that Xlebnikov "is a visionary. His imagery is convincing by its absurdity, his thoughts by their paradox. It seems that he dreams his poems and then writes them down, preserving the entire incongruity of the course of events."[50] In the "Crane", the city of St. Petersburg revolts against man and is transformed into a crane. The crane evolves from an "iron hook" which "gallops along the river in a certain whirlwind". Chimneys become animate and "raise their necks". The crane takes on movement and begins to "rush toward things with hitherto unknown strength, like a prisoner who rushes to meet his beloved". The crane takes on further shape as the "iron and cunning chambers" of the city, "in a certain fierce fire, like a flame arising from heat", form the crane's legs. Then chimneys become animate and fly, "imitating the movements of a worm". Parts of trains form the crane's veins. Nature joins in the revolt as the railroads become uprooted by "the motion of pods ripened in the autumn". The crane then comes to wreak savage destruction on the city with the assistance of its inhabitants, who come to worship and offer sacrifices to the crane. Finally, the crane performs its ritualistic and grotesque victory dance, "like a savage over the corpse of a vanquished enemy", and disappears.

By equating the city with the grotesque, or by treating the city grotesquely, Xlebnikov was continuing the tradition of the Symbolists – especially Blok, Belyj, Brjusov – who treated the city in similar terms. They, too, saw the city as sordid and menacing. Moreover, by viewing the transformation of the city as inevitable – "according to some ancient design" – and by alluding to the evolutionary process of the crane – "And the hook forms the hand of the bird, a vestige of that time when it knew life as a four-footed animal" – the work may be considered as Xlebnikov's vision of the way mechanical civilization will fuse with "primitive" reality – the crane. Finally, the work may be viewed as nature's revenge upon urban civilization.

Jakobson has pointed out that "Žuravl'" is a 'realized' metaphor. The 'plot' of the work is to develop the primary metaphor – the transformation of the "machine", the city, into a "crane". Hence the double meaning of the word *žuravl'*.[51] Stepanov notes that Xlebnikov achieves the realization of the 'basic' metaphor by means of structural shifts, whose aim is to violate the usual correlation and static nature of things. 'Secondary' metaphors and similes contribute to the unfolding of the 'basic' metaphor.[52] For example:

[50] Quoted in A. Metčenko, "Rannij Majakovskij", in *V. Majakovskij*, ed. A. Dymšic (Leningrad, 1940), 16. Spasskij, 68, notes that at night Xlebnikov was often aroused from sleep by an idea and would rush to the table "in one leap" and write it down.
[51] Jakobson, 52.
[52] Stepanov, "Tvorčestvo Velimira Xlebnikova", 48-50.

Truby...dviženjam podražaja červjaka
The chimneys...imitating the movements of a worm

Most...podražaja dviženiju l'diny
The bridge...imitating the movement of an iceberg

Železnye puti...spletajas' zmejami v krutoj pleten'
The railroads...lacing like snakes into a wattle fence

K nemu sletalis' mertvecy iz kladbišč
I plot'ju odevali ostov železnyj.

From the graves the dead flew to him [the crane]
And covered the iron skeleton with flesh.

The poetic devices and themes in "Žuravl'" invite particular study, for they seem to constitute Xlebnikov's contribution to both the poetry and the prose of the 1920's. The work contains a number of Symbolist features: an aura of vagueness produced by the use of indefinite pronouns *(kakoj-to)* and by the work itself, which seems to require an imaginative effort to fill in, so to speak, the details; the "occasional passages of high diction", which are reminiscent of Vjačeslav Ivanov;[53] the use of colloquialisms, which has a great deal in common with Andrej Belyj's use;[54] and the use of sound repetitions that were cultivated by the Russian

[53] Markov, 61.

[54] V. Trenin and N. Xardžiev, "Poètika rannego Majakovskogo", *Literaturnyj kritik*, No. 4 (1935), 175. Belyj's relationship to Russian Futurism has been pointed out by a number of scholars and writers. Markov, 12, has observed that Belyj "not only influenced the futurists, or was influenced by them, but he also helped to develop futurism and, on a higher level, cooperated with it." Zbigniew Folejewski, "Futurism East and West", *Yearbook of Comparative and General Literature*, XIV (1965), 62, has labeled Belyj a "late symbolist who has certain features which are pre-futurist", one of which is "the idea of freeing the poetic word". Benedikt Livšic has suggested that Belyj broke Futurist ground when he wrote his *Symphonies* in 1902 (*Polutoraglazyj strelec* [Leningrad, 1933], 48). V. Asmus has observed with some justification that, of "the symbolists, no one did as much as Andrej Belyj to implant formalism in art, poetics, aesthetics" ("Filosofija i èstetika russkogo simvolizma", in *Literaturnoe nasledstvo*, XXVII-XXVIII [Moscow, 1937], 38). For Belyj, the poetic word was the key to a new poetic revival; he saw the "death of the word" as the decline of Symbolism, and saw in the creation of neologisms and new sound combinations the unveiling of the secrets of the poet's inner world. Via the word, the poet became a creator of reality: "The word creates a new third world, the world of sound symbols, by means of which the secrets within me of the established world *[položennyj mir]* are illuminated..." (Belyj, *Simvolizm*, 430). Belyj also noted that the creation of neologisms, "aimless play with words", regardless of their meaning, were expressions of man's struggle against the "pressure of obscurity" and a "hostile environment" (437).

Symbolists.[55]

Xlebnikov uses in "Žuravl'"[56] devices and themes that were perhaps peculiar to Futurism. First, the theme of the "revolt of things" to which Xlebnikov makes direct reference:[57]

Zlej ne byl i Koščej,
Čem budet, možet byt', vosstanie veščej.

Even Koščej was not more angry
Than will be, perhaps, the revolt of things.

Secondly, the emphasis on concrete phenomena is also a Futurist feature. Third, 'deformation of reality' is the device of 'making-it-strange', which is a 'semantic shift', a means of transferring an object to a "sphere of new perception".[58] Xlebnikov alludes to street-cars which form part of the crane thus:

Žukoobraznye povozki,
Kotoryx zamysel po volnam molnij sil grebët,
V krasnye i žëltye raskrašennye poloski
Ptice dajut stanovoj xrebët.

Beetle-shaped vehicles,
Whose aim is to sail over the lightning-charged waves,
Painted in red and yellow stripes
Form the bird's backbone.

Markov notes the appearance of 'wrong' words in Xlebnikov's poetry. This may very well be a literary device.[59] One of the cardinal features of Xlebnikov's poetry, the odd word creates 'strangeness' within a familiar context. 'Strangeness' may also be a way of arousing perception. For example, instead of the word "tears", Xlebnikov uses "devout dewdrops":

I s bogomol'nymi vdol' šček iz glaz rosami.

And the eyes shed devout dewdrops along the cheeks.

[55] V. Gofman, "Jazyk simvolistov", in *Literaturnoe nasledstvo*, XXVII-XXVIII (Moscow, 1937), 96-97.
[56] Xlebnikov, "Žuravl'", in SP, I, 76-82.
[57] The unfolding of this theme seems to have a similarity with Cubist principles: "Cubism is an art entirely concerned with interactions between different aspects: the interactions between structure and movement; the interaction between unambiguous signs made on the surface of the picture and the changing reality which they stand in for. It is an art of dynamic liberation from all static categories" (John Berger, *The Success and Failure of Picasso* [London, 1965], 59).
[58] Victor Erlich, *Russian Formalism: History – Doctrine*, 2nd, rev. ed. (The Hague, 1965), 176.
[59] Jakobson, 34.

Xlebnikov refers to fingers as "grass" in a striking metaphor:

Na kryše neboskrëbov
Kolyxalis' travy ustremlënnyx ruk.

On top of the skyscrapers
The grass of grasping hands fluttered.

Finally, there are a number of mythological and folklore motifs in the work which Xlebnikov used when treating contemporary themes: the sacrifices and prayers to the crane; the animation of inanimate objects; the allusion to Koščej,[60] and to the "stern and gloomy maidens who fly, tugging their garments, like melodies of the wind's forces".

To diversify his poetry, Xlebnikov used a 'cubist' device which afforded him maximum flexibility and variation – the shift. This may be characterized as a radical mixing of mutually exclusive poetic categories.[61] Xlebnikov deftly and successfully applied the shift to most of his poetry. That he borrowed this device from cubist painting is unmistakable.[62] It extends not only to the structure of the plot, as in "Žuravl'", but to meters,[63] tenses, rhymes, genres, and to levels of language.

According to Markov, "the salient feature of Xlebnikov's poetry is the mixing of traditional meters, with one meter predominant, usually iambic tetrameter".[64] While Xlebnikov initially mixed accentual and free verse in "Žuravl'", in many of his works he used iambic tetrameter as the metrical base and "violated" it by "constant metrical shifts".[65]

Xlebnikov's experiments with epic genres and his use of the 'didactic poem' link him with Lomonosov and Deržavin. One of Xlebnikov's major achievements was experimentation with his creation of new poetic genres, which were neglected by the Russian Symbolists because traditional genres suited their aims.[66] His most daring innovation was the 'supertale' which consisted of a cycle of works, such as tales, stories, poems, and mathematical, historical and linguistic treatises. "Vojna v myšelovke"

60 "In Russian folklore, a bony, emaciated old man, rich and wicked, who knows the secret of eternal life" (A. Smirnickij, *Russko-anglijskij slovar'* [Moscow, 1958], 730).
61 Markov, 107.
62 See Xardžiev, "Kommentarij: Zabytye stat'i Majakovskogo", 157.
63 "If the violences against the meter take root, they themselves become metrical rules" (Roman Jakobson, "Closing Statement: Linguistics and Poetics", in *Style in Language*, ed. T. A. Sebeok [Cambridge, 1964], 364).
64 Markov, 38.
65 For further discussion of this, see D. Tal'nikov, "Literaturnye zametki", *Krasnaja nov'*, No. 11 (1928), 222, and Markov, 135-136.
66 See Markov, 27-29.

("The War in a Mouse Trap", 1917), "Zangezi" ("Zangezi", 1922), "Carapina po nebu" ("A Scratch on the Sky", 1920) and others belong to this category. In "Deti vydry", also a 'supertale', Xlebnikov mixed prose, drama, poetry and narrative because one genre apparently could not embrace the extraordinary sweep of his historical interests. Xardžiev notes that Xlebnikov's mixing of genres stemmed from his "tendency to destroy the traditional framework of temporal arrangement and therefore to create multiple stylistic and thematic planes".[67]

4. CONCLUSION

In defining Xlebnikov's relationship to, and role in, Russian Futurism, one is faced with two complex questions: his participation in the writing of the 1912 Futurist manifesto and *The Word as Such*. As for the former, the commonly accepted view is that Xlebnikov took part in writing it.[68] The available evidence for this view is Xlebnikov's signature to the manifesto. The evidence against this view is also available, and merits greater consideration. Livšic remarks that he himself "was unsuccessful in eliciting from Burljuk" information as who drew up the manifesto. Livšic goes on to say that he "only knows that Xlebnikov had no part in it (it seems that he was not even in Moscow at the time)".[69] Šklovskij appears to suggest that Xlebnikov may have participated in the discussion of the manifesto, but that he was absent when it was written.[70] Markov notes that "It is now known that Xlebnikov did not actually participate in the manifesto of the *Poščëčina*, although he signed it."[71]

With regard to *The Word as Such* (1913), again the general view is that Xlebnikov wrote it in conjunction with Kručënyx. Xardžiev, however, notes that it "was written by Kručënyx".[72] This work was published with Xlebnikov's and Kručënyx's signatures, which appear to have been written by a single hand.[73] If Xlebnikov wrote the work with Kručënyx

[67] N. Xardžiev and T. Gric, "Ot redakcii", in Xlebnikov, *Neizdannye proizvedenija*, 11.

[68] See, for example, Renato Poggioli, *The Poets of Russia 1890-1930* (Cambridge, 1960), 256, and Johannes Holthusen, *Russische Gegenswartsliteratur 1890-1940*, I (Bern, 1963), 95.

[69] Livšic, 129.

[70] Viktor Šklovskij, *O Majakovskom* (Moscow, 1940), 69-70.

[71] Markov, 11.

[72] Xardžiev, "Majakovskij i živopis'", 392.

[73] See Velimir Xlebnikov and Aleksej Kručënyx, *Slovo kak takovoe* (Moscow, 1913), 12.

(who wanted to gain popularity for his linguistic theories by allying himself with Xlebnikov) one is puzzled by Xlebnikov's disparaging comment after receiving from Kručënyx for approval his *Declaration of the Word as Such* (1914). Contrary to Kručënyx's expectations, Xlebnikov remarked that it was "pale", and that he was "afraid of fruitless and abstract debates on art".[74]

In 1914, moreover, Xlebnikov wrote an unpublished 'open' letter in which he protested vehemently against the publication of his manuscripts by Nikolaj and David Burljuk without his permission: "...David and Nikolaj Burljuk continue to publish works which bear my signature, which are worthless and thoroughly garbled to boot."[75] In particular, David Burljuk was induced to take these liberties because he needed Xlebnikov's works and experiments to demonstrate to his critics that the Futurists were creating a new poetic language.[76] Perhaps Burljuk felt free to take these liberties since he was Xlebnikov's major source of financial support.[77] Markov notes that "Burljuk's praises [of Xlebnikov] seem a tactical exaggeration designed to show rival parties that the futurist movement possessed a genius, rather than a sincere tribute to Xlebnikov's greatness."[78] Consequently, "no Russian writer has ever been presented to the reader in such distorted works as Xlebnikov".[79] What is more, the preposterous notion took firm root that Xlebnikov's poetry never went beyond the pale of neologistic experiments.

Second, one finds it difficult, if not impossible, to see how Xlebnikov could embrace the notion of Futurism as the cult or the poetry of the city.[80] Tynjanov observes that "It is indeed no accident that Xlebnikov called himself a *budetljanin* (and not a futurist)..."[81] For Xlebnikov,

74 Xlebnikov, *Neizdannye proizvedenija*, 367.
75 Xlebnikov, SP, V, 257. David Burljuk notes that when Xlebnikov discovered that he (Burljuk) had published his manuscripts, "he became furious" and cried out: "You have murdered me" *[pogubit']*. I never wanted to show anyone my experiments." Quoted in N. Stepanov, "Ot redaktora", in Xlebnikov, *Izbrannye proizvedenija*, 475.
76 See V. Trenin and N. Xardžiev, "Retuširovannyj Xlebnikov", *Literaturnyj kritik*, No. 6 (1934), 145-147.
77 On Burljuk's generosity to Xlebnikov, see David and Marussy Burljuk, "Majakovskij", *Color and Rhyme*, No. 31 (New York, 1956), 27.
78 Markov, 11.
79 C. Vol'pe, "Stixotvorenija Velimira Xlebnikova", *Literaturnoe obozrenie*, No. 17 (1940), 35.
80 Both Majakovskij and Burljuk expressed this notion of Futurism. See V. Katanjan, *Majakovskij: Literaturnaja Xronika*, 4th ed. (Moscow, 1961), 56, Vasilij Kamenskij, *Žizn' s Majakovskim* (Moscow, 1940), 19.
81 Jurij Tynjanov, "O Xlebnikove", in Xlebnikov, SP, I, 19.

budetljanin may have served to distinguish sharply or adequately his particular world view from those of the Futurists. *Budetljanstvo* was "the study of the influence of the future on the past", a return to a primitive and timeless age in which man is wedded to the harmony of nature.[82] Third, Xlebnikov rarely read his poetry or appeared at the poetry readings of the Futurists, from the sheer fact that he was barely audible; and whenever he did, he would read several lines and abruptly conclude by saying "and so on".[83] Spasskij remarks that Xlebnikov "literally lived in train stations, getting off one train and waiting for another".[84] In Xlebnikov's absence, Majakovskij and Burljuk often read his neologistic experiments at their poetry readings. They seem to have used Xlebnikov's poetry as the theoretical foundation and banner of Russian Futurism, as an instrument, as "a polemical weapon in the defense of the new form".[85] Xlebnikov apparently allied himself with the Futurists because he essentially wanted to publish his works, to receive a certain recognition and for financial reasons.[86]

In conclusion, Xlebnikov was clearly influenced by, and was sympathetic to, the literary and art movements of his time – Symbolism, Acmeism, Cubism. Yet Xlebnikov also reacted against certain tendencies which he detected in literature and poetry. He was repelled by the despair and negation and melancholy in the works of Arcybašev, Andreev, Remizov, Merežkovskij and Sologub. Xlebnikov saw only "horror" and "death", not "beauty" in their works. For Xlebnikov, Russian literature affirmed nothing: Brjusov "cursed" the past.[87] As for the Symbolists as a whole, Xlebnikov considered them slavish imitators of Western Symbolism and therefore utterly devoid of national roots. By introducing it into Russia, the Russian Symbolists seemed to Xlebnikov to be feeding "poison" to Russian youth.[88]

Finally, Xlebnikov's life and work point to the conclusion that he

[82] Xlebnikov, SP, V, 174.
[83] Kamenskij, 60.
[84] Spasskij, 68.
[85] David Burljuk, "Tri glavy iz knigi 'Majakovskij i ego sputniki'", in *Krasnaja strela* (New York, 1932), 11.
[86] Livšic, 179, notes that at one Futurist reading of poetry, every time that Burljuk mentioned Xlebnikov's name, Xlebnikov would arise and bow to the audience. See also Xlebnikov, *Neizdannye proizvedenija*, 353. It seems that with the Futurists Xlebnikov perhaps felt a certain sense of recognition, identity, and purpose which he could not find with the Symbolists.
[87] Xlebnikov, SP, V, 180.
[88] See "Gibel' Atlantidy" in Xlebnikov, SP, I, 95, and Trenin and Xardžiev, "Retuširovannyj Xlebnikov", 145.

brought to fruition poetic and linguistic tendencies within Symbolism and gave new direction to them. His ultimate link with Symbolism appears to be that he saw in *numbers* reflections of the 'other' reality. Torn by the chaos, irrationality, human discord and violence of history, Xlebnikov dedicated his life to the discovery in language of conceptual structures that would unify men. Until his tragic death in 1922 of malnutrition, Xlebnikov remained totally and unflinchingly committed to the enchanting Symbolist notions of human solidarity and universal harmony[89]. In view of all his supreme efforts towards their realization, Xlebnikov was not cheated. For the epitaph on his coffin reflected his deepest and loftiest aspiration: "The President of the Universe" (a typically Symbolist gesture).

89 In this regard, Xlebnikov seems to have a good deal in common with Andrej Belyi. See T. Xmel'nickaja, "Poèzija Andreja Belogo", in Andrej Belyj, *Stixotvorenija i poèmy* (Moscow-Leningrad, 1966), 9.

II

VLADIMIR MAJAKOVSKIJ

1. MAJAKOVSKIJ'S PATH TO FUTURISM

Vladimir Majakovskij was born in 1893, in an obscure Georgian village near Kutaisi; his father was serving there in the civil service as a forest ranger. Despite the remoteness, the young Majakovskij did not lack cultural advantages. His father was a man of ready wit, and from him Majakovskij learned early to speak with effect. The mother had been educated; she read to her son daily and developed his interest in poetry and literature in general.[1]

In 1902, after the family moved to Kutaisi, Majakovskij attended the gymnasium there. Like many of his future colleagues, he showed an early interest in painting, which was his favorite subject. He would remain alone after classes to "paint various birds and animals with chalk" on the blackboard.[2] His sister relates that "he painted well, primarily from memory [and] ... would paint caricatures of domestic life".[3] This orientation towards caricature would later find expression in Majakovskij's poetry.[4]

In 1905, Kutaisi became a major center of student revolutionary activity and strikes as a result of the 1905 revolution. Majakovskij took active part in student demonstrations and discussions, and was to some degree involved in supplying weapons for the Social Democrats.

A year later, after the father's death, the Majakovskijs moved to Moscow. At the Moscow gymnasium, Majakovskij lost interest in his studies, but he continued to paint and became increasingly involved in a

[1] A. Majakovskaja, "Detstvo i junost' Vladimira Majakovskogo", in *V. Majakovskij v vospominanijax sovremennikov* (Moscow, 1963), 33.

[2] G. Bebutov, *Gimnazičeskie gody Vladimira Majakovskogo* (Tbilisi, 1946), 32.

[3] Quoted in V. Katanjan, *Majakovskij: Literaturnaja xronika*, 4th ed. (Moscow, 1961), 18.

[4] For a discussion of this aspect of Majakovskij's poetry, see V. Trenin and N. Xardžiev, "Majakovskij i 'satirikonskaja poèzija'", *Literaturnyj kritik*, No. 4 (1934), 117-139.

Marxist circle. While at the gymnasium, Majakovskij took an interest in poetry and wrote his "first half-poem" in an illegal student journal. He also wrote another poem a lyric for the same journal but, as he himself remarked in his autobiography in 1928, "I did not regard such lyrical poetry compatible with my 'socialist dignity' and abandoned it completely."[5]

In 1908, Majakovskij abandoned his studies and joined the Bolshevik party as a distributor of propaganda material. It may very well be that Majakovskij saw in Bolshevism or Marxism not so much a protest against the social order, as a kind of religious faith, a means of self-sacrifice.[6] In this connection, he took the name of "Comrade Konstantin" (Constantine) as party member, which strongly suggests that he desired to bring a new 'humanistic ethic' to the universe.[7] Majakovskij's 'humanistic' or 'revolutionary' mission as Comrade Konstantin, however, is intelligible largely in terms of the Symbolist tradition of poet-priest, not in political terms.[8]

Majakovskij was soon arrested for printing and distributing illegal literature. In 1909, his sister persuaded him to resume his studies as an artist at the Stroganov Art School. He was arrested once again shortly after he made application. In prison, he painted and prepared for his examinations. Probably disillusioned as a political propagandist, Majakovskij desired to turn to a vocation that would provide him with an opportunity for self-realization and self-expression. On release from prison, Majakovskij began to study painting. He was soon arrested again in 1909 for aiding the escape of political prisoners and was sentenced to prison for eleven months, some spent in solitary confinement because of his unruly and rebellious character. Boris Pasternak has left us with

[5] Vladimir Majakovskij, *Polnoe sobranie sočinenij*, I (Moscow, 1955-1961), 16. Unless otherwise stated, all citations from Majakovskij's articles and poetry will refer to this edition of his complete works, and will be indicated parenthetically in the text by volume and page number.

[6] Prince Evgenij Trubeckoj, a professor at the University of Kiev, noted in 1904: "I knew students who only read banned writings and formed their outlook in accordance with these because everything that could be openly published in Russia aroused from the start their distrust...revolutionary proclamations...replace the daily press...Marxism itself was taken up by our students as a sort of religious faith...a need for self-sacrifice, a yearning for martyrdom" (Quoted in Lionel Kochan, *Russia in Revolution 1890-1918* [London, 1966], 147). This observation may be applicable to Majakovskij.

[7] "One sensed in him [Majakovskij] that he was a man with a great destiny, with a great historic mission" (Kornej Čukovskij, "Majakovskij", in his *Sobranie sočinenij*, II [Moscow, 1965], 348).

[8] See, for example, "Cloud in Pants", and "War and the Universe".

a highly interesting description of Majakovskij's 'revolutionary' character:

Before me sat a handsome youth of gloomy aspect with the bass voice of a deacon and the fist of a pugilist, inexhaustibly, deadly witty, something between a mythical hero of Alexander Grin and a Spanish toreador.

One could see at once that if he was handsome witty, talented, perhaps supertalented, that was not the main thing about him; the main thing was his innate iron self-control, a kind of inherited principle of nobility, a feeling of duty which did not permit him to be different, less handsome, less witty, less talented.

And this resoluteness of his and his tousled mane of hair, which he kept ruffling with all his five fingers, at once made me think of a young terrorist conspirator, a composite image of the minor provincial characters in Dostoevsky's novels.

...Mayakovsky brought from the remote Transcaucasian forest district where he was born the conviction...that education in Russian could only be revolutionary.

To his natural attributes the young Mayakovsky added, in quite a wonderful fashion, an artistic disorder which he affected, and a rather coarse and careless ponderousness of mind and body, and rebellious features of Bohemianism in which he draped himself and with which he played about so tastefully. His taste was so mature and fully developed that it seemed older than himself. He was twenty-two, and his taste was, as it were, a hundred and twenty-two.[9]

In prison, Majakovskij read all the major authors of the day, whether Symbolist, Decadent, or Realist, including Gor'kij, Andreev, Bunin, Sologub, Blok, Belyj, Brjusov and Bal'mont. He also began to write poetry himself. Majakovskij filled a notebook with his poetic experiments; but he was forced to surrender it on being released, and it has not survived.

In his autobiography, he has, fortunately, left us with some idea of the nature of his readings and poetic experiments and his reasons for abandoning the Bolshevik party:

The most important period for me. After three years of theory and practice, threw myself into literary works.

Read all the latest literature. Symbolists, Belyj, Bal'mont. Analyzed formal innovations. But this was alien to me. Themes, images had no relation to my life. Tried to write just as well, but about other things. Discovered that it was impossible to write about the other. Came out stilted and banal. Like:

> V zoloto, v purpur lesa odevalis',
> Solnce igralo na glavakh cerkvej.
> Ždal ja: no v mesjacax dni poterjalis',

[9] Boris Pasternak, *I Remember: Sketch for an Autobiography*, trans. M. Harari (New York, 1959), 91-92.

Sotni tomitel'nyx dnej.

The forests were dressed in yellow and purple.
The sun played on church cupolas.
I waited: but days got lost in months,
Hundreds of wearisome days.

Wrote a whole notebook of such verses. Thanks to the authorities for taking it on release, or else I would have published it.

...If I remained in the party, I would have become an outlaw. To be an outlaw meant that I could not study. The alternative was writing leaflets all my life, uttering ideas from books which were correct, but not expressed by me. If what I had read had been shaken out of me, what would remain? The Marxist method. But didn't this weapon fall into the hands of a child? It is easy to be equipped with it if one deals with one's ideas. But upon meeting one's enemies?[10]

Majakovskij went on to add that he could not write better than Belyj and that he had nothing with which he could oppose "the aesthetics of the past". Majakovskij saw the necessity of "serious training". He realized that he could not write poetry: "Attempts were pathetic" (I, 18).

In 1911, Majakovskij enrolled in the Institute of Fine Arts. There he met David Burljuk, who discovered the poet in him, encouraged him to pursue poetry as a career, read French and German poets to him, and for some time supported him financially. As for the birth of Russian Futurism, Majakovskij wrote in his autobiography:

David had the anger of a master who had outpaced his contemporaries, and I had the fervor of a socialist who was aware of the inevitable destruction of the old. Russian Futurism was born (I, 19).

To be sure, Majakovskij made this statement in retrospect, but it does contain a grain of truth. Burljuk's notions of art as a quest for novelty, of a rejection of the art of the past, and of bringing art and poetry to the streets and squares were very likely the major factors which attracted Majakovskij to Futurism.

In 1913, after giving numerous poetry lectures and readings in Moscow and St. Petersburg, Majakovskij, Burljuk, and Kamenskij toured Russia to propagate Futurism, to describe and explain the new poetic principles, to insult, ridicule, amuse and to inculcate new tastes. This tour of seventeen cities, prompted in large part by the 'boycott' of the Futurist

[10] Majakovskij, I, 17-18.

press,[11] produced scandals and seriously alarmed the police. More importantly, perhaps, the tour made Futurism a sensation.[12] The phenomenal success of this tour was due primarily to the biting wit and the thundering voice of Majakovskij, who finally found his vocation.

2. MAJAKOVSKIJ'S PREREVOLUTIONARY ESTHETICS AND POETRY

Majakovskij cannot be considered a linguistic and poetic theoretician of the type of Belyj. Majakovskij simply lacked the erudition for this. He was, however, profoundly concerned with problems of poetic craft and language. His esthetic views clearly reflect his concern, but they are not always very helpful as a guide to his poetic practice. He was a vigorous supporter of the principles of the 1912 manifesto, that is, that the enterprise of poetry is verbal organization, not an interpretation, reflection or objective knowledge of reality. He expressed the view that "the word is the end of poetry", and paraphrased the views of his fellow Futurists. He supported Xlebnikov's and Kručënyx's neologistic and phonemic experiments, and considered them factors in the "burgeoning of poetry" (I, 276). Majakovskij seems to have expressed these views primarily to preserve the appearance of Futurist solidarity.

Majakovskij also expounded other views, some of which only seemingly contradicted the 1912 Futurist manifesto. For example, in 1913 he noted that "The history of art, if it is only capable of becoming a science, will be a social science" (I, 282). In fact, Majakovskij's very first article documents his attempts to formulate an 'industrial' esthetics and to make the city the point of reference for Futurist poetry. For Majakovskij, the rapid growth of technology – which impressed, if not terrified him – and its capacity to satisfy the material wants of man, demanded a new and dynamic language that would reflect the character of the modern, machine age. For this reason, he, like many others, considered the art and the language of the past ill-suited to the demands of a new social situation.

Majakovskij saw in the industrial age "elements of beauty": airplanes, express trains, brick buildings, factory chimneys, elevators, moving machines, soot, smoke and electric lights.[13] Unlike the Italian Futurists,

[11] For an excellent discussion of this tour, see N. Xardžiev, "Turne kubo-futuristov 1913-1914", in *Majakovskij: Materialy i issledovanija*, V. Percov and N. Serebrjannyj, eds. (Moscow, 1940), 401-415.
[12] See Vasilij Kamenskij, *Junost' Majakovskogo* (Tbilisi, 1931), 53.
[13] Quoted in Katanjan, 56.

however, he did not believe that poetry should glorify those elements. Like the Russian Symbolists, Majakovskij saw beauty in the evil and ugliness of the city and machine age, and sought to describe the phenomena and experiences of city life by deliberate distortion of the real: "...art is not a copy of nature; its task is to distort nature so that it is fixed in a different consciousness" (I, 279).

In sum, then, Majakovskij's esthetics have roots in Symbolism (and Cubism), and are fairly consistent.

Majakovskij's prerevolutionary poetry is essentially marked by social and metaphysical rebellion, by a strong passion for martyrdom and suffering and transforming the universe; its orientation is apocalyptic. Majakovskij sees his poetic mission as that of a martyr or savior of humanity who must suffer to overcome his spiritual estrangement from humanity ("Vladimir Majakovskij: A Tragedy", 1913) and to redeem it from the terrors of "things" and the "Hell-City", which is frequently depicted as a grotesque prison from which there is no escape ("Cloud in Pants", 1915). Suffering therefore not only provides consolation in the face of estrangement and injustice, but is also a means of ennoblement and self-fulfillment ("Vladimir Majakovskij: A Tragedy").[14]

The theme of the suffering poet is a basic feature of Majakovskij's prerevolutionary poetry, which has strong roots in Symbolist poetry, Dostoevskij's novels,[15] the New Testament, and in the philosophy of Nikolaj Fëdorov (1828-1903).[16] Not unlike Ivan Karamazov, Majakovskij accepts the notion of God, but rejects his universe because of his deep humanitarian feelings, from which his rebellion basically stems. He identifies himself, however, with the 'historical' Jesus because Majakovskij's own situation is analogous to that of Jesus: both are seeking to change the morality of their age, both are protesting the quality of social life, both have great compassion and love for suffering humanity, and both are prepared to suffer and sacrifice themselves for universal

[14] "His [Majakovskij's] modernism consists...in the absolute sense of estrangement his work as a whole conveys, the loneliness, the pain swathed in hyperbolic noise" (Sidney Monas, "Poets and Literary Men of Russia", *Massachusetts Review*, V-VI [Spring, 1964], 582).

[15] See L. Brik, "Predloženie issledovateljam", *Voprosy literatury*, No. 9 (1966), 203-208. Pasternak comments on Majakovskij's prerevolutionary poetry: "It is definitely a continuation of Dostoevskij. Or rather it is lyric poetry written by one of his younger rebellious characters" (Quoted in V. Kožinov, "Dostoevskij ili geroi Dostoevskogo?", *Voprosy literatury*, No. 9 [1966], 208).

[16] Notably, Fëdorov "made a great impression on V. Solov'ëv Dostoevsky, and Tolstoy" (N. Lossky, History of Russian Philosophy [New York, 1951], 75).

redemption and immortality for all ("War and the Universe", 1915-1916).

In Majakovskij's prerevolutionary poetry, World War I plays a major role. He sees it as the destruction of the universe, which is for him the prelude to the Kingdom of Man on earth, the new Universal City. The Kingdom of Man is the very antipode of the grotesquely depicted "Hell-City". In "War and the Universe", Majakovskij views the universe in biblical terms, as the "time of tribulation", and draws on the philosophy of Fëdorov to express his vision of the Kingdom of Man and to glorify man. If one can speak of a culminating or mature theme in Majakovskij's prerevolutionary poetry, it is apocalyptic or revolutionary humanism. This was very likely his profound longing as "Comrade Konstantin". He becomes, as a Futurist poet, the architect of the Kingdom of Man on earth. The following discussion augments the above views of Majakovskij's prerevolutionary poetry with illustrations.

Majakovskij's early works were sketches of the city which evolved from the urban poetry of Blok and Belyj. Majakovskij portrays the characteristics of the city and the natural elements which act upon them. Like the Russian Symbolists, he views the city as a source of corruption, pain, suffering and violence:

Veter koljučij
trube
vyryvaet
dymčatoj šersti klok.
Lysyj fonar'
sladostrastno snimaet
s ulicy
černyj čulok. (I, 39)

The biting wind
tears a
piece of smoke-colored wool
off the smoke stack.
A bald street lamp
voluptuously strips
the black stocking
of the street.

Adišče goroda okna razbili
na kroxotnye, sosuščie svetami adki.
Ryžie d'javoly, vzdymalis' avtomobili,
nad samym uxom vzryvaja gudki. (I, 55)

The windows of the enormous hell-city were broken
into miniature hells sucked by their lights.

Red-haired devils, the automobiles rose up,
exploding their horns right in my ear.

Ulica provalilas', kak nos sifilitka... (I, 62)

The street caved in, like the nose of a syphilitic...

To determine his poetic mission, Majakovskij wrote his first major work in 1913: *Vladimir Majakovskij: A Tragedy*. He also produced and directed it for the stage. It was written under the influence of Nikolaj Evreinov, whose novel theory was that:

Every play could be the drama or comedy of a single personage, a central hero, the crowd of other personages...must be only shown from a single point of view, that of the hero...one could thus produce externally all the variations of the hero's state of soul, extract them and project them in the form of characters...[17]

Majakovskij himself is consequently the only true character of the play because he is its prime mover, and all other characters echo his ideas. Most of these characters are terrible victims of city life: "a feminine friend" who attends the poet but does not speak; "an old man several thousand years old with dried-up black cats; a man without an eye and ear, a man without a head; a man with a long face; a man with two kisses; an ordinary young man; a woman with a small tear; one with an ordinary tear; another with a large tear; and finally, boys, girls, etc" (I, 153).

Majakovskij sees himself in the first act as a Savior who has come to feed the victims of the city:

Vam li ponjat',
počemu ja,
spokojnyj,
nasmešek grozoju
dušu na bljude nesu
k obedu iduščix let. (I, 153)

How can you understand,
why I,
calm,
like a thunderstorm of jeers
bear my soul on a platter
to the feast of coming years.

17 Quoted in Lawrence Stahlberger, *The Symbolic System of Majakovskij* (The Hague, 1964), 26.

Then Majakovskij, like Christ, calls on the victims to be comforted:

Pridite vse ko mne,
kto rval molčanie
kto vyl
ottogo, čto petli poldnej tugi... (I, 154)

Come to me all
who have broken silence
who have wailed
because the nooses of noondays are tight...

As Majakovskij speaks of "kindling a world festival", he is interrupted by the Ancient Man, who observes in him "a tormented cry crucified on the cross of laughter". He then tells Majakovskij of the "great grief" which has gripped the city, of "soulless things" which threaten to obliterate the inhabitants, and of God, who, "gone mad, looks at the wailing of the human horde". When things and the city begin their revolt ("and everywhere the chimneys danced on the rooftops", "even the side streets have rolled up their sleeves for a fight"), the Man with Cats and the Man with a Long Face discuss the question of man's spiritual liberation from, or enslavement by, material things:

Vešči nado rubit'!
Nedarom v ix laskax providel vraga ja!

We must smash things!
Not for nothing have I foreseen the Enemy in their caresses!

To which the Man with the Long Face replies:

A možet byt', vešči nado ljubit'?
Možet byt', u veščej duša drugaja?

But perhaps we should love things?
Perhaps they have a different soul?

This provides Majakovskij with the opportunity to relate that his search for a "soul" has been futile; for when he found it, it was the personification of banality:

Vpročem,
raz našël eë –
dušu.
Vyšla
v golubom kapote,
govorit:
"Sadites'!

Ja davno vas ždala.
Ne xotite li stakančik čaju?" (I, 159)

However,
I found her once –
that soul.
She came out
in a blue house-coat
and said:
"Sit down!
I've been expecting you so long.
Won't you have a cup of tea?"

After a revolt of things takes place in the city, Majakovskij is proclaimed prince in another city. He is prepared to receive people who will worship him and present their gifts – tears, symbolic of their suffering. After receiving three women who present their tears, and after listening to the story by the Man with Kisses, in which the poet's mission to become a scapegoat is implied, Majakovskij is overwhelmed by the enormity of his task and says:

Gospoda!
Poslušajte, –
ja ne mogu!
Vam xorošo,
a mne s bolju-to kak. (I, 159)

Gentlemen!
Listen!
I just can't bear it!
You're fine,
but I have all this pain.

When Majakovskij is told that he "alone can sing songs", that is, that he alone can alleviate people's sufferings and bring them "to his beautiful God", Majakovskij takes up their burdens and begins his journey. He thus abandons his throne and renounces his title of "prince" so as to overcome his isolation from humanity. His new mission of assuming its sufferings is an act of affirming his solidarity with humanity:

Ja
s nošej moej
idu,
spotykajus',
polzu
dal'še
na sever,

tuda,
gde v tiskax beskonečnoj toski
pal'cami voln
večno
grud' rvët
okean-izuver.
Ja dobredu –
ustalyi,
v poslednem bredu
brošu vašu slezu
tëmnomu bogu groz
u istoka zverinyx ver. (I, 170-171)

I
with my burden
go,
staggering,
I crawl
further
to the north,
where
in the grip of eternal longing,
with the fingers of waves
the mad ocean eternally
tears its breasts.
I'll get there limping,
wearied,
in my last delirium
will fling your tear
to the dark god of the storms,
at the source of animal faiths.

In 1915 Majakovskij wrote the "Cloud in Pants". The original title of the work was *The Thirteenth Apostle*, but it was changed on the demand of the Censor. Although Majakovskij added a new theme of unrequited love to his poetry,[18] it is still related to the metaphysical theme under discussion. Unrequited love not only produced despair in Majakovskij, but intensified his rebellion. He continues to identify himself with Christ, however, and sees himself as a martyr:

Èto vzvelo na Golgofy auditorij
Petrograda, Moskvy, Odessy, Kieva
i ne bylo ni odnogo,

[18] For an excellent treatment of this theme, see Helen Muchnic, *From Gorky to Pasternak* (New York, 1961), 206-214, and Edward J. Brown, *Russian Literature Since the Revolution* (New York, 1963), 45-51.

kotoryj
ne kryčal by:
"Raspni,
raspni ego!"
No mne –
ljudi,
i te, čto obideli –
vy mne vsego dorože i bliže. (I, 184-185)

This led to the Golgotha of auditoriums
of Petrograd, Moscow, Odessa, Kiev
where there wasn't one
who
would not shout:
"Crucify,
crucify him!"
But to me –
you people,
even those who reviled me –
you are dearer and more precious than anything.

Majakovskij then crucifies himself to consummate his act of redeeming humanity. He thus becomes, in terms of Fëdorov's philosophy, the "Son of Man":[19]

ja – gde bol', vezde;
na každoj kaple slezovoj teči
raspjal sebja na kreste.
Uže ničego prostit' nel'zja.
Ja vyžeg duši, gde nežnosti rastili. (I, 185)

I am where pain is – everywhere;
on every drop of the flow of tears
I have nailed myself to the cross.
It's too late to forgive.
I've seared souls where tenderness was bred.

[19] "To attain the measure of the stature of Christ means to become in fact a son of man, for Christ called Himself the Son of Man" (Nicholas Fyodorov, "The Question of Brotherhood or Relatedness, and of the Reasons for the Unbrotherly Dis-related, or Unpeaceful State of the World, and of the Means for the Restoration of Relatedness", in *Russian Philosophy*, eds. J. Edie et al. [Chicago, 1965], III, 26). According to Vjačeslav Zavališin, *Early Soviet Writers* (New York, 1958), 84-85, "the artist Vasilij Čekrygin, author of the 'Resurrection of the Dead' series of paintings, had introduced Majakovskij to the philosophy of Fyodorov's *The Common Cause...*" Čekrygin was Majakovskij's fellow student at the School of Painting, Architecture, and Sculpture. See L. Žegin, "Vospominanija o Majakovskom", in *V. Majakovskij v vospominanijax sovremennikov*, 99-101.

Now that "It's too late to forgive", Majakovskij considers the Coming of Christ anachronistic, for he himself has redeemed humanity by his own crucifixion:

> I kogda,
> prixod ego
> mjatežom oglašja,
> vyidete k spasitelju –
> vam ja
> dušu vytašču,
> rastopču,
> čtob bol'šaja! –
> i okrovavlennuju dam, kak znamja. (I, 185)
>
> And when,
> you announce his coming
> with a revolt,
> you go to the Savior –
> I will
> tear out my soul
> and trample it
> so that it be large enough
> to give you bloody as a banner.

After the outbreak of World War I, Majakovskij wrote that he "accepted it enthusiastically" (I, 22). He apparently felt that it would fulfill his dreams of a new social order. He entertained the notion that the War would effect "the realization of one's true personality", which would in turn mark "the dawn of the birth of the new man" (I, 330). He soon changed his views, however, and wrote that "war is disgusting", and that "to speak of war, one should see it" (I, 22).

World War I and Majakovskij's view of "the new man" are the major themes of "War and the Universe". In this work, the world for Majakovskij is bent on self-destruction. He pictures the war as a battle between "sixteen gladiators" in a coliseum, and "all Europe burning like a chandelier". He sees battlefields as a "forest" in which dead silence reigns and only "ravens and nights hover above in black robes, like a monastic procession". Guns "pounce on the cadaverous cities and villages" and "gorge everything like brazen ugly faces". The earth is drenched in blood and begins to yield it:

> Odinakova –
> kamen',
> boloto,
> xalupa li,
> čelovеč'ej krovišcej vymočili ves' ego,

Vezde
šagi
odinakovo xljupali,
mesja dymjaščeesja mira mesivo.
V Rostove
rabočij
v prazdničnyj otdyx
zaxotel
vody dlja samovara vyžat', –
i otšatnulsja:
vo vsex vodoprovodax
sočilas' ta že ryžaja žiža. (I, 225)

Everywhere the same:
stone,
swamp
and hovel
are soaked in human blood world-wide,
Everywhere
footsteps
splashing
kneading the smoking mass of the world.
In Rostov,
a worker
on a holiday
wanted some water for his samovar,
but recoiled:
In all the waterpipes
the same red slime oozed out.

In "War and the Universe", Majakovskij adds a new dimension to the Dostoevskian theme of martyrdom and suffering. In this work, Majakovskij sees his mission as the "only messenger of future truths on earth". This message appears to be that man's spiritual redemption on earth consists in assuming the guilt and the suffering for the war. Since universal suffering is the path to salvation and the Kingdom of Man on earth, there can be no question of who is guilty:

Ubity –
i vsë ravno mne, –
ja ili on ix
ubil. (I, 229)

The slaughtered ones –
it makes no difference to me
whether I or he
has killed them.

Before universal resurrection can be realized, however, one final act remains for Majakovskij: he must become the sacrificial lamb so as to "erase by blood the name of 'murderer' which has stigmatized man". Majakovskij then asks, "for the sake of Christ", forgiveness for all the sins of men since "the sun gave its first rays". This act of self-execution will redeem the whole of history of its sins:

Vselennaja rascvetët eščë,
radostna,
nova.
Čtob ne bylo bessmyslennoj lži na nej,
kajus':
ja odin vinovat
v rastuščem xruste lomaemyx žiznej! (I, 230-231)

The universe will come to bloom yet,
joyfully,
freshly.
So that there be no absurd lie behind it,
I repent:
I alone bear the guilt
for the growing crackle of lives being broken.

Majakovskij is now prepared to come to a new metaphysic of man, who will be free of torment and assume qualities of God:

Vyteku srublennyj,
i nikto ne budet –
nekomu budet čeloveka mučit'.
Ljudi rodjatsja,
nastojaščie ljudi,
boga samogo miloserdnej i lučše. (I, 233)

I'll run out chopped off,
and no one will –
there will be no one to torment man.
Men will come into being,
real men,
more merciful and better than God Himself.

With "man more merciful and better than God Himself", Majakovskij suggests that men can be architects of their own universe – that man can realize the Kingdom of Man on earth. This is precisely the burden of Fëdorov's philosophy of the "common task:" the task of Christianity is not passively to contemplate the Kingdom of God, but to create it here on earth by mastering scientifically and technically the "blind, death-dealing forces" of nature.[20] Two major aims of this mastery are to resurrect man's ancestors and to overcome human discord. Thus, when Majakovskij read Fëdorov's *Philosophy of the Common Task*, he derived the notion of universal resurrection from it and seemingly felt a strong kinship with Fëdorov, who, like Majakovskij, "was excruciatingly tormented...by a sense of human isolation and the absence of brotherly relations".[21]

In Part V of "War and the Universe", Majakovskij resurrects and recreates the city-universe. The "earth opens its black lips" and yields its dead. The buried human bones arise and take on human flesh, and, together with the dead of the sea, return "healthy and whole" to their families. Nature adds to the resurrection and festival of life as there is "more sun on the little finger of a tiny girl than ever in the whole world". Men's eyes assume such proportions that they are able to scan the universe as their heads "reach the height of mountains". Each country, "like priests who march out with the sacrament in remembrance of the drama of expiation", presents its gifts to Man. In this Kingdom of Man, pruned of paralyzing fetishes, myths, mystery, injustice, and suffering, there is only "glory, glory, glory to all". Love and hate are finally reconciled as Majakovskij, "more merciful...than God Himself", liberates the damned from Hell. If the supreme question of ethical consciousness has heretofore been, "Cain, where is thy brother Abel?", in the Kingdom of Man it will be for Majakovskij, "Abel, where is thy brother Cain?"[22]

Zemlja,
otkuda ljubov' takaja nam?
Predstav' –
tam
pod derevom
videli
s Kainom

[20] Fyodorov, 26.

[21] Vasily Zenkovsky, *A History of Russian Philosophy*, trans. G. Kline (New York, 1953), II, 594-595. Georg Florovskij, *Puti russkogo bogoslovija* (Paris, 1937), 322-330, considers Fëdorov's philosophy one of "humanistic activism", "social construction", and "not in the least Christian".

[22] See Nicholas Berdyaev, *The Destiny of Man*, trans. N. Duddington (London, 1954), 276-277. Berdjaev adds: "N. Fedorov expressed a bold and startling idea of raising all the dead. But his idea must be carried further and deeper. Not only must all the dead be saved from death and raised to life again, but all must be saved and liberated from hell. This is the last and final demand of ethics." This is precisely what Majakovskij has done in "War and the Universe".

igrajuščego v šaški xrista.[23]

Earth,
where do we find such love?
Just imagine –
there
under the tree
Christ was seen
playing checkers with Cain.

Thus Man becomes for Majakovskij the New Gospel of Humanity, who in the future will reign supreme and who will create the true realm of freedom and happiness on earth. With this profound hope, Majakovskij concludes:

I on,
svobodnyj,
oru o kom ja,
čelovek –
pridët on,
ver'te mne,
ver'te. (I, 242)

And he,
the free man
about whom I shout –
he'll come,
believe me,
believe.

Finally, in 1917, Majakovskij saw in the Bolshevik revolution the glorious consummation of all his apocalyptic expectations. One has no serious difficulty in understanding, in the light of his life and poetry, Majakovskij's immediate and unflinching acceptance of the revolution: "To accept or not to accept? For me (as for other Moscow futurists) there was no such question. *It is my revolution*... Worked and did all that was needed" (I, 25). For Majakovskij, there could be no pause for reflection or hesitation or restraint when the new City of Man awaited its creators and when the revolution demanded a thundering voice for its celebration. His "Open

23 Majakovskij, I, 241. "A vision of the future is inescapable from the most essential pages of Majakovskij...For Majakovskij, the future is a dialectical synthesis. This removal of all contradictions finds its expression in the playful image of Christ at checkers with Cain, in the myth of a universe permeated by love, and in the proposition: 'The commune is a place where bureaucrats will vanish and there will be poetry and song'!" See Roman Jakobson, "The Generation that Squandered its Poets (excerpts)", in *Yale French Studies: Literature and Revolution*, No. 39 (1967), 120.

Letter to the Workers" is a significant document for the light that it sheds on his passion for acceptance and service, and on his mythopoeic notion of the revolution. It also defines the new role of Futurism in the post-revolutionary era:

Comrades.

The dual fire of war and revolution has devastated both our souls and our cities. The sumptuous palaces of yesterday remain like scorched skeletons. The sacked cities await new builders. The ugly [korjavyj] roots of slavery have been extirpated from our souls by the whirlwind of the revolution. The souls of the people await a great mending.

I turn to you, who have accepted the legacy of Russia, to you, who (I believe) will become the masters of the whole universe tomorrow, with a question: What songs and music will pour from your windows? To what Bibles will you open your hearts?

I look with amazement as Aida and Traviata ring from the stages of the captured theatres with all the Spaniards and the counts, as in the poetry you have accepted those very roses of the grand greenhouses, and how your eyes dazzle before the portraits which depict the magnificence of the past.

Or, when the elements raised by the revolution abate, will you appear on holidays before your district soviets with chains on your vests and ceremoniously play croquet?

Know that for our necks, necks of Goliathan labor, there are no fitting sizes in the collar wardrobe of the bourgeoisie.

Only the eruption of a Revolution of the Spirit will strip [*očistit*] us of the rags of the old art.

May reason protect you from committing physical violence to the remains of the art of antiquity. Give them back to the schools and the universities for the study of geography, the daily way of life [*byt*], and history, but repel indignantly anyone who presents you these fossils instead of the bread of living beauty.

A revolution of content – socialism-anarchism – is unthinkable without a revolution of form – futurism.

Avidly tear to pieces the healthy young coarse art which we offer.

No one knows what huge suns will illumine the life of the future. Perhaps artists will transform the gray dust of the cities into a hundred-colored rainbow. Perhaps the thunderous music of volcanoes transformed into flutes will resound incessantly from the mountain ridges; perhaps we will compel the waves of the ocean to run their fingers over the network of strings which extend from Europe to America. For us one thing is clear: we have inaugurated the first country in the modern history of arts.[24]

[24] Majakovskij, XII, 8-9. In 1918, Andrej Belyj saw the city as "rows of enormous skeletons", the doorways of which recalled mouths which bare their teeth. He added that this is "death", and "we must renounce it and create the city of life – 'The New City,' 'The City of the Sun'" (Andrej Belyj, *Na perevale: Krizis žizni* [Petersburg, 1918] 84). In that same year Belyj saw the Bolshevik revolution as the resurrection of Christ.

3. SOME ASPECTS OF MAJAKOVSKIJ'S POETRY

For Majakovskij, the poetic process is a struggle against tradition, conventions, order and conformity; and he passionately drives to liberate himself from them so as to achieve maximum individual expression. Majakovskij strives in his poetry to deliberately shock and unnerve his reader, to evoke his indignation, to focus his attention on various lexical and morphological phenomena which conjure up his perception of poetic reality. As an inveterate avant-gardist, Majakovskij makes a conscious effort to violate tradition, and in that process he unconsciously creates a new 'tradition'. In this destructive act, there are new and infinite creative possibilities. For the avant-gardist, there is a certain logic – however perverse – in Bakunin's notion that the "passion for destruction is a creative passion". This is undoubtedly the banner of avant-gardism, but it does not mean that tradition plays no role in the poetic process: the assimilation of tradition is a prelude to 'innovation'. Many of the formal aspects of Majakovskij's poetry are largely direct and indirect products of this 'struggle' against tradition (and of other factors). When seen from this perspective, the formal aspects of Majakovskij's poetry become increasingly meaningful.

One of the most striking features of Majakovskij's poetry is his impressionistic depiction of the city, which has its origins in painting and in "decadent sensibility".[25] The modern city, with its vice and corruption, is a source of fascination for Majakovskij. His city, like Baudelaire's, Brjusov's, and Blok's, "is closely associated with vice and evil and an all-pervading feeling of profound solitude...is merely the scene of the poet's hopeless grief, his personal abyss..."[26] Majakovskij often sees the city as a source of intense pain and suffering. For example:

> Ulica muku molča pěrla.
> Krik torčkom stojal iz glotki.
> Toporščilis', zastrjavšie poperěk gorla,
> puxlye taksi i kostljavye prolětki.
> Grud' ispešexodili.
> Čaxotki plošče. (I, 182)
>
> The street silently pushed torment along.
> A shout stood erect in the gullet.

[25] George Gibian, ed., "The Grotesque in Russian and Western Literature", in *Yearbook of Comparative and General Literature*, XIII (1964), 57.

[26] Georgette Donchin, *The Influence of French Symbolism on Russian Poetry* (The Hague, 1958), 162.

The plumpish taxis and bony cabs,
Which bristled, stuck in the throat.
My chest has been trampled in,
Flatter than consumption.

One of the aims of depicting the city in evil and hyperbolic terms is to evoke horror or disgust. Polonskij observes that Majakovskij "wanted to demonstrate at once to people the most terrible thing in the world".[27] In Majakovskij's poetry, the city is compared to hell:

Kak traktir, mne strašen vaš strašnyj sud!
Menja odnogo skvoz' gorjaščie zdanija
prostitutki, kak svjatynju, na rukax ponesut
i pokažut bogu v svoë opravdanie. (I, 62)

I'm terrified by your terrible Judgement as I am terrified by a saloon!
Prostitutes will carry only me, through
the flaming buildings, like a sacred thing,
and show me to God as their redemption.

The city is often compared to the Cities of the Plain:

v buduarax ženščiny
– fabriki bez dyma i trub –
millionami vydelyvali pocelui, –
vsjakie,
bol'šie,
malen'kie, –
mjasistymi ryčagami slepajuščix gub. (I, 169)

In the boudoirs women
– smokeless and stackless factories –
were producing kisses by millions –
of all kinds,
large ones,
small ones –
with the fleshy levers of smacking lips.

Majakovskij transforms the village into a modern Sodom:

Tixie!
Nedolgo požili.
Srazu
železo rel's vsočilo po žile
v zagar dereven' gorodov zarazu.
Gde peli pticy – tarelok ljazgi.
Gde bor byl – ploščad' stodomym sodomom.

[27] Vjačeslav Polonskij, *O Majakovskom* (Moscow, 1931), 13.

Šestiètaznymi favnami rinulis' v pljaski
publičnyj dom za publyčnym domom. (I, 216-217)

The quiet ones!
They didn't live for long.
All at once
the iron of the rails soaked up the infection of the cities
along the veins, into the sunny villages.
Where the birds sang, now is the clatter of dishes.
Where the forest was, now is a hundred-house Sodom.
Public house after public house,
like a six-storied fauns, rushed into a dance.

The city is Sodom, in which:

Ljudi
ili valjalis',
kak upivšijsja Noj,
ili groxatali mordoj mnogoxamoj!
Nažrutsja,
a posle,
v nočnoj slepote,
vyvaljas' mjasami v puxe i vate,
spolzutsja drug na druge potet',
goroda sodragaja skripom krovatej. (I, 216)

People
either sprawled out
like drunken Noah,
or howled like [a beast] with a multitude of boor-snouts.
They gorge themselves,
and later,
in the blindness of night
wallow like flesh in down and cotton,
crawl up on each other to sweat,
shaking the cities with the creaking of their beds.

Another striking aspect of Majakovskij's poetry is his neologisms, which are used to create new shades of meaning, to achieve greater expression, and to attract attention morphologically. Most of Majakovskij's neologisms are metonymic,[28] and are created analogically from productive word forms. His neologisms were shaped by the search for novelty which was characteristic of the age, by his struggle against philistinism and corruption,[29] and by the need to depict the city in terrible terms.

[28] See the thorough study of Majakovskij's neologisms by Assya Humesky, *Majakovskij and His Neologisms* (New York, 1964).
[29] G. Vinokur, *Majakovskij – novator jazyka* (Moscow, 1943), 24.

As noted, Majakovskij was not primarily a linguistic or poetic theoretician. He did, however, theorize. His article *How to Write Poetry* (1926) offers insights into the nature of his poetry and language. Majakovskij wrote:

> One must always have in view the audience to which this poetry is directed... One must take, depending on the audience, an intonation that is cogent, or pleading, one which commands or questions. The majority of my works are based on conversational intonation. (XII, 113)

Majakovskij's poetry is designed to be declaimed in an auditorium, or in the streets. It is declaimed – indeed, shouted – for the ear, and not written primarily for the eye. His language is slangy, familiar, oratorical, emotional and often vulgar. It is replete with exclamations and questions, as though he were conversing with an audience. For example:

Poslušajte!
Ved', esli zvězdy zažigajut –
značit – eto komu-nibud' nužno?
Značit – kto-to xočet, čtoby oni byli?
Značit – kto-to nazyvaet èti plevočki žemčužinoj? (I, 60)

Now listen!
Surely if the stars are lighted
does it mean that anyone needs them?
Does it mean that someone wants them?
Does it mean that someone calls these spitlets a pearl?

Ej, vy!
Nebo!
Snimite šljapu!
Ja idu! (I, 196)

Hey, you!
Sky!
Off with our hat!
Here I come!

Majakovskij often introduces 'direct conversation' into his poetry, as in this extended metaphor:

Allo!
Kto govorit?
Mama?
Mama!
Vaš syn prekrasno bolen!
Mama!
U nego požar serdca.

Skažite sëstram Ljude i Ole, –
emu nekuda det'sja. (I, 179-180)

Hullo!
Who's speaking?
Mama?
Mama!
Your son is wonderfully ill!
Mama!
His heart's on fire.
Tell Liuda and Olia
he can't get out.

Ja živu na Bol'šoj Presne
36. 24.
Mesto spokojnen'koe.
Tixon'koe.
Nu? (I, 72)

I live on Great Presna
36. 24.
It's quite a peaceful little place.
Very quiet.
Well?

As will be noted, the very nature of Majakovskij's language largely precludes syllabo-tonic meters because they cannot contain the features peculiar to it. Jakobson observes that the "rhythmical inertia of syllabo-tonic poetry imposed an artificial phraseology and intonation on poetic language. Russian poetry of the 19th century did not take into account the reduction of unstressed vowels in the literary language. Unstressed syllables in conversational speech disappeared, were muffled; they were taken into account in poetry, were artificially emphasized, and became sharp and clear. This also affected rhyme..."[30] What is more, in syllabo-tonic poetry, ictuses may have equal value, and there is a regularity of unstressed syllables between stresses. In Majakovskij's mature poetry, the principle of equal syllables does not operate, but the accentual principle. This does not mean that syllabo-tonic meters did not find expression in his poetry. The resolution of this apparent contradiction is that Majakovskij yoked the two systems.

To organize the rhythmic-syntactic and intonational features and the phraseological orientation of his declamatory language, Majakovskij

[30] Roman Jakobson, *O češkom stixe, preimuščestvenno v sopostavlenii s russkim* (Prague, 1923), 101.

created an unusual metrical system. His early works, however, especially those describing the urban setting, were written primarily in syllabo-tonic meters. Gradually, Majakovskij varied, like other poets (e.g. Gumilëv), traditional versification canons largely by dropping unstressed syllables, and evolved a system uniquely his own.

By 1914, according to Trenin, Majakovskij "finally developed and consolidated his system of tonic or accentual verse, in which the isosyllabism of the lines is removed... and the intonational movement of the verse is shaped solely by the repetition of word stresses, allowing substantial variations in both the number of unstressed syllables and also in the number of stresses in separate lines".[31]

The number of stresses per line and the quality or strength of the stress vary in Majakovskij's tonic verse. He can thus vary the unstressed syllables from zero to eight or nine. Žirmunskij cites the following example in which the stresses per line vary from two to four and the number of unstressed syllables between stresses varies from zero to six:

> Prišli, / rasselis' v zemnyx dolinax
> gosti / v strašnom narjade.
> Mračno poigryvajut na šejax dlinnyx
> ožerel'ja jader.
> Zoloto slavjan. / Čërnye mad'jar – usy.
> Negrov neprogljadnye pjatna.
> Vsex zemnyx širot jarusy
> vytolpila s golovy do pjat – ona.[32]

To be sure, Majakovskij's intonational tonic verse must be seen from the perspective of his conversationally oriented diction, in which, as Jakobson has pointed out, certain unstressed syllables are weak or disappear, and unstressed vowels and words are reduced. Vinokur adds that in Majakovskij's speech "the formal links are weakened at the expense of the semantic ones, and each separate word is capable of being a complete and independent syntactic whole, free of the syntactic dependence with respect to words which are hierarchically higher. In other words, it is that type of speech in which there is no distinction between a word and a sentence."[33]

Because there are varying degrees of stress and intonational patterns

[31] V. Trenin, *V masterskoj stixa Majakovskogo* (Moscow, 1937), 66. For a discussion of 'regulated' *dol'niki* in Majakovskij's poetry, see Viktor Žirmunskij, "Stixosloženie Majakovskogo", *Russkaja literatura*, No. 4 (1964), 11.

[32] As cited in Žirmunskij, 12.

[33] Vinokur, 92.

in his poetry, Majakovskij structures his verse lines on semantic-syntactic units, which can contain one word or groups of words that have independent stress. In a verse line, a group of words are yoked by one strong stress – to which weaker stresses are subordinate – which is usually on the last word of the syntactic unit. Ščerba observes:

A sentence can be broken up into segments which are characterized by strengthening of the stress on the last word and which express *in the given context* a single, even if complex, concept.[34]

What makes Majakovskij's intonational verse distinctive is that it can yoke "under one strong stress...much broader accent groups of various meters, not only words, but in many instances whole phrase groups – a circumstance that gives the structure of his poetry a *principally new quality*".[35] Thus a word or groups of words in Majakovskij's verse lines are independent semantic-syntactic units, whose "independent stress... becomes the only indispensible criterion".[36] In the following example, Majakovskij singles out words so as to give proper intonational emphasis to the semantic-syntactic units in the verse line. Each line is an independent utterance:

Allo!
Kto govorit?
Mama?
Mama!
Vaš syn prekrasno bolen!
Mama!
U nego požar serdca.
Skažite sëstram Ljude i Ole, –
emu nekuda det'sja. (I, 179-180)

In the following example,

Zemlja,
otkuda ljubov' takaja nam?
Predstav' –
tam
pod derevom
videli s Kainom
igrajuščego v šaški Xrista. (I, 241)

"otkuda" takes medium stress, "ljubov'" weak stress, and "takaja nam"

[34] Quoted in V. Vinogradov, "Ponjatie sintagmy v sintaksise russkogo jazyka", in *Voprosy sintaksisa sovremennogo russkogo jazyka*, ed. V. Vinogradov (Moscow, 1950), 210.
[35] Žirmunskij, 12.
[36] Jakobson, 103.

strong stress on "takaja". In "videli s Kainom", there is weak and strong stress respectively, and in the last line, "igrajuščego" takes weak stress, "v šaški" medium stress, and "Xrista" strong stress.[37]

Although Majakovskij fragments his poetry for purposes of stress and intonation, what is the ultimate criterion for interpreting stress in his verse line? Artobolevskij writes:

One should bear in mind that in the course of one of Majakovskij's poems, lines with varying stresses can alternate in no fixed pattern. Therefore one should not 'stretch' the number and arrangement of stresses to any scheme. Further, one may pronounce the same line with a greater or lesser number of stresses. One should be guided only by the free rhythm of speech, determined by the thought of the speaker.[38]

Majakovskij's innovations in rhyme stem largely from his innovation in tonic verse. Rhyme organizes and cements his poetry, and *partly* serves as its semantic vehicle. Majakovskij was aware of the role of rhyme in his poetry:

...without rhyme (understanding rhyme broadly), poetry will crumble. Rhyme brings us back to the preceding line, compels us to remember it, forces all the lines which form a single idea to be held together...I always put the most distinctive word at the end of the line and find a rhyme for it at all costs. (XII, 105-106)

Majakovskij went on to say that the traditional notion of rhyme, in which there is harmony of the last words in two lines and in which the stressed vowel and the posttonic sounds are approximate, was only one of the methods of rhyme, yet "the simplest and the crudest" (XII, 105). He then pointed out various methods of rhyme with which he experimented in his early works. "Utro" ("Morning", 1912) marks his first experiment in rhyming the end of a line with the beginning of the next:

Ugrjumnyj dožd' skosil glaza.
I za
rešëtkoj
čëtkoj
železnoj mysli provodov –
perina.
I na
neë
vstajuščix zvëzd
legko operlis' nogi.

37 See other examples in Žirmunskij, 17-18, and in Jakobson, 103. Jakobson was the first to note the role of "dynamic stress" in Majakovskij's poetry.
38 Quoted in Žirmunskij, 17.

No gi –
bel' fonarej... (I, 34)

In "Iz ulicy v ulicu" ("From Street to Street", 1913) Majakovskij rhymes the beginning of lines:

U –
lica.
Lica
u
dogov
godov
rez –
če.
Če –
rez... (I, 38)

Majakovskij failed to point out his more ingenious methods of rhyming lines with which he experimented in *War and the Universe*. In the following example, the compound rhyme extends to the second line and rhymes with the final word of another line:

Morščiny okopov legli na čelo!
T-s-s-s-s-s-s... –
...
NAČALOS'. (I, 219)

The initial and final two words of one line with the final word of another line:

Poslednij na štyk nasažen.
Naši otxodjat *na Kovno*,
na sažen'
čelovеč'ego mjasa *našinkovano*. (I, 228)

The end of one line rhymes with the end of another and the beginning of another:

Teper' i mne *zapad!*
Budu idti i idti tam,
poka ne oplačut tvoj *glaza*
pod rubrikoj...[39]

The majority of rhymes in Majakovskij's early works are exact rhymes. As he seeks, however, to create the technical framework that will provide him with greater intonational range, Majakovskij begins to introduce

[39] As cited in N. Xardžiev, "Zametki o Majakovskom", in *Literaturnoe nasledstvo: Novoe o Majakovskom*, LXV (Moscow, 1958), 411.

compound rhymes and assonances which ultimately become characteristic of his intonationally oriented poetry.

In Majakovskij's mature rhyme, the identity of stressed vowels, as in classical rhyme, is preserved. Unlike classical rhyme, however, there is identity in rhyme between the pre-stress supporting consonant and identity or approximation between pre-stress vowels and consonants. For example:

lži za nej – žiznej (I, 231)

prostore ja – Astorija (I, 128)

prelest' – aprel' est (I, 193)

očeredi – noč' rjadi (I, 199)

bredu moju – pridumaju (I, 208)

osenjalo – arsenalov (I, 218)

While classical rhymes contained an equal number of syllables, Majakovskij introduced heterosyllabic rhymes, in which the first of the final two post-stress vowels is 'muffled' as in live conversational language, since it is the weakest vowel:

tol'ko – stolika (I, 103-104)

vremeni – remni (I, 184)

naglo – nagolo (I, 219)

pjatna – pjat ona (I, 221)

donositsja – pobedonosca (I, 226)

oxalo – zagloxla (I, 227)

In masculine rhymes, Majakovskij drops the post-stress consonant of the closed syllable:

nel'zja – lizat' (I, 230)

tebe – Tibet (I, 238)

mogu – vokrug (I, 247)

konce – koncert (I, 199)

aviator – Travjata (I, 203)

Majakovskij at times uses voiced-voiceless consonantal pairs as supporting pre-stress consonants: p – b, š – ž, k – g, t – d:

gorbatye – karpaty (I, 235)
šajki – lužajke (I, 241)
šara – žara (I, 251)
golgofe – kofe (I, 246)
skoro – gorod (I, 110)
dannika – botanikov (I, 251)
tel ona – sdelano (I, 229)
vladel'ca – tel'ca (I, 254)

One observes a tendency in Majakovskij's prerevolutionary poetry to use voiced-voiceless consonantal pairs in the first postonic consonant:

naprasno vam – prazdnovat' (I, 247)

As for the 'stress' features of his compound rhymes, Majakovskij will give additional, stronger emphasis to a final syllable of a word (in the unbroken rhyme). For example, in the rhyme "takaja nam – Kainom" the "om" in "Kainom" will receive emphasis. The rhythm, the "position of the word in a phrase", and the "intonation of the phrase", seem to dictate this emphasis.

The above discussion seems to point to the conclusion that Majakovskij is not an unimpressive poetic craftsman. His innovations in rhyme and tonic verse are worthy of special note.[40] One might consider that Majakovskij's notion of bringing poetry to the streets perhaps played a certain role in shaping his poetic practice. In Folejewski's view, "Mayakovsky's assertions that form is equally, or more, an expression of revolutionary spirit as content, must be taken into account in every assessment of Mayakovsky's concept of futurism. Form must not lag behind the changing rhythm of life."[41]

Finally, one must also remember that Majakovskij's poetic technique is part of an artistic age which consciously sought to create new poetic methods and devices. Although he attempted to reject the 'past', as it were, his poetic system and its formal aspects stemmed largely from his assimilation and exploitation of the potentialities of 'traditional' rhymes and meters.

40 According to Valerij Brjusov, "O rifme", *Pečat' i revoljucija*, No. 1 (1924), 117, the new rhyme was "prepared by the symbolists, but completely developed only by the futurists. This is the great achievement of our futurism in the realm of poetic technique." See also T. Gric, "Rifma Majakovskogo", *Literaturnyj kritik*, No. 3 (1939), 155-164.

41 Zbigniew Folejewski, "Mayakovsky and Futurism", *Comparative Literature Studies* (Special Advance Issue, 1963), 73.

III

DAVID BURLJUK

1. BURLJUK AND THE ORGANIZATION OF FUTURISM

David Burljuk was born in 1882 in Xar'kov. His father was an agronomist and an estate manager.[1] The mother, on the other hand, was artistically inclined and had a university education. Burljuk's mother passed on to her children her enthusiasm for art; the family had its own studio.[2]

The young David Burljuk was tutored until 1894, when he went to the gymnasium. Because his father moved from estate to estate, Burljuk attended various schools until 1898. His major interest was language: Greek, German, and French. The next year, Burljuk enrolled in the Kazan' Art School. In 1900, when his father moved again, Burljuk continued his studies at the Odessa Art School. He also wrote poetry and several articles for the Xerson newspaper *Jug (South)*.

In 1902, after failing to qualify for the St. Petersburg Academy of Fine Arts, Burljuk went to Munich to study art. In 1904, he studied in Paris. When he returned to Russia in 1905, he was influenced by the recent art trends abroad: Primitivism, Impressionism, Fauvism, and later, Cubism and Expressionism.

In 1907, a wealthy patron invited Burljuk to exhibit his paintings in Moscow. While Burljuk was unsuccessful in selling his paintings, he met Mixail Larionov and Natalja Gončarova, two leading Russian artists who were primarily responsible for introducing French Impressionism into Russia and who attempted to synthesize them with native traditions. In that same year, with Larionov and Gonočarova, Burljuk organized an art exhibition in Moscow with the financial aid of his father. This exhibition was unsuccessful; it did, however, serve as a model for other

[1] See David and Marussy Burljuk, "Hilea: 1907-1913", *Color and Rhyme*, No. 57 (1965), 5A.

[2] For a portrait of the Burljuk family, see Benedikt Livšic, *Polutoraglazyj strelec* (Leningrad, 1933), 33-34.

exhibitions.[3]

Burljuk organized another art exhibition with Nikolaj Kul'bin and Aleksandr Benois in 1908. This exhibition, Burljuk noted, "was greeted with very sharp criticism", and was also unsuccessful. He recalled:

Dr. Kulbin gave over the first hall to the fifty canvases of one totally blind painter, who had executed them with the help of his wife. His pictures were very foggy spots, but Kulbin proclaimed all of them "great art" and their creator a genius and a prophet. However, this enormous exhibition was opened too late, as by late May people had already left for the "dachas", the south, or Europe.

Burljuk added:

Also in the spring of 1909 in Moscow, Rjabušinsky again opened a large exhibition of French painters, among them Matisse, Marc, Rouault, Mangin and other French neoimpressionists, who were not yet known in Russia.[4]

Due to the lack of a positive response to the new avant-garde art trends, Burljuk modified his style, and began to paint in a style less identified with the French schools, and with a growing interest in incorporating national folk-art traditions.[5]

In 1909, Burljuk formed a circle of artists whom he had met at exhibitions: Elena Guro, her husband M. Matjušin, and Vasilij Kamenskij. When Xlebnikov joined the circle, Burljuk decided to publish a collection of poetry as a reaction against Symbolism. This, too, resulted in failure.

In 1911, Burljuk returned to the Odessa Art School and received a diploma. There he met Vasilij Kandinskij, who invited Burljuk to exhibit his paintings at *Der Blaue Reiter* exhibition in Munich. This exhibition was a reaction against Cubism. Since Burljuk painted well in many styles, adaptation to the esthetic requirements of the exhibition hardly made demands on him. In fact, one of his early paintings – "Horses and Coachman" – reflected the style of the work of one of the organizers of the exhibition, Franz Marc. That Burljuk was able to paint well in many styles paradoxically limited his success as an artist: he failed to develop

[3] For Larionov's influence on early Futurist poetry, see Camilla Gray, *The Great Experiment: Russian Art 1863-1922* (New York, 1962), 94.

[4] David and Marussy Burljuk, "Mayakovsky", *Color and Rhyme*, No. 31 (1956), 20. By introducing Western avant-garde art into Russia, the Russian artists were implicitly demonstrating their dependence on the West and revealing to the art critics the roots of their own art. By imitating foreign models, the Russian artists were considered to be repudiating their own native art. This supplied the art critics with ammunition in the assault on Western avant-garde art trends, and they accused the Russian artists of blindly imitating Western originals. See Livšic, 65-66.

[5] Gray, 97.

his own style.

In September, 1911, Burljuk met Majakovskij at the Moscow Academy of Art. He soon discovered Majakovskij's poetic talent, undoubtedly contributed to the shaping of his poetry, and supported him financially. Together they gave lectures on poetry and exhibited their paintings. A year later, after he made another of many unsuccessful attempts to create an alliance of avant-garde artists and poets, Burljuk organized a group of poets who came to be known as Cubo-Futurists.

Some of the Russian Futurists clearly acknowledged that the organization and success of Futurism were due primarily to Burljuk's erudition, eloquence, financial support, initiative, shrewdness and persistence.[6] Kamenskij remarked that Burljuk was able to discover and enlist talented students, artists and poets, and inspired them with his knowledge of art.[7]

The Futurists, however, seem to be silent on Burljuk's aim in organizing Futurism. In his memoirs, Burljuk almost deliberately avoids making any concrete statement about his 'aims' in organizing Futurism or about Futurism itself. His articles on Futurism are full of irrelevancies and almost meaningless generalities. For example:

Futurism as an art movement in Russia is closely connected with the history of that country. Later on it will be examined as one of the greatest currents of the aspect of future life. Futurism was born in February 1910 in Petersburg in a gray room with its windows facing a court-yard on Stone Island Prospect in the vicinity of the River Karpouka Bridge.[8]

One might wait for this "later on", but it never comes. Burljuk noted elsewhere, apparently alluding to Xlebnikov and Majakovskij: "In Czarist Russian atmosphere, futurism had much social significance. It had two main streams; one which attempted to explore the past, the other which dreamed of the future."[9] In the early 1940's, Burljuk was somewhat close to the mark; he saw the 'basis' of Futurism in this way:

All styles, all epochs, the good things of the whole world. Not the narrowing but the broadening of the program, protest against the formal Art for Art's sake, for Art is for all, for the mob, for the street. Art for the circus, and circus for Art.[10]

[6] V. Percov, *Naš sovremennik* (Moscow, 1940), 29, and Vasilij Kamenskij, *Put' èntuziasta* (Moscow, 1931), 116.

[7] Kamenskij, 167.

[8] David and Marussy Burljuk, "Hilea: 1907-1913", 34.

[9] Quoted in Michael Gold, *David Burljuk: Artist-Scholar, Father of Russian Futurism* (New York, 1944), 6.

[10] Quoted in Katherine Dreier, *David Burljuk* (New York, 1944), 94.

Is there any explanation for Burljuk's 'silence' on Futurism in his memoirs? It may very well be that for him there were poets of opposing tendencies within Futurism, and he therefore found it difficult to speak of it in 'positive' terms.

2. THE ESTHETICS AND POETRY OF BURLJUK

Burljuk cannot be considered a coherent theoretician of Russian Futurism. His theoretical views on poetry are not in accord with his poetic practice, and are derivative and diverse as his paintings.[11] They also appear to be at times contradictory.

Burljuk supported the cardinal principle of the 1912 Futurist manifesto: poetry is autotelic and a self-contained activity. In his article in the manifesto, Burljuk wrote: "Yesterday we had no art, today we do have art. Yesterday it was only a means, today it has become an aim."[12] In saying this, Burljuk was undoubtedly alluding to the Russian Symbolists, who had subjected poetry to metaphysical purposes. The Futurists, according to Burljuk, had restored to poetry its true purpose: verbal organization. A year later, Burljuk wrote that "what you are saying about content, spirituality, ideology...is the highest crime against art".[13] This remark recalls Brjusov, who also decried utilitarian art, and whom Burljuk admired and considered his poetic "mentor".[14] In 1914, Burljuk again wrote that the word is "only a verbal mass", and of value to the poet insofar as it had no meaning.[15] Yet in the same article, Burljuk noted:

> Is the creation of words possible, and to what extent? Where is one to find the criterion for the beauty of the new word? Should the creation of the word stem from the root or by chance?
>
> In answering theoretically the first question, I will say that it is possible *ad infinitum.* In practice, to be sure, it is a little different: the word is connected with the life of myth, and only myth is the creator of the living word. In connec-

[11] Livšic, 94, notes that "for Burljuk...futurism, like cubism, was only a manner, a style, a *method* of work and by no means a strictly rational *[produmannyj]* system of artistic views".

[12] Quoted in A. Metčenko, "Rannij Majakovskij", in *V. Majakovskij*, ed. A. Dymšic (Moscow, 1940), 14.

[13] Quoted in Metčenko, 13-14.

[14] See David and Marussy Burljuk, "Mayakovsky", 11.

[15] David and Nikolaj Burljuk, "Poètičeskie načala", in *Pervyj žurnal russkix futuristov*, No. 1-2 (Moscow, 1914), 84.

tion with this, the second answer becomes clear: the criterion for the beauty of the word is myth.[16]

This seems to echo Vjačeslav Ivanov's notion of myth as a symbolic system from which poetry derives its structure.

Burljuk's views on art are of major importance for an understanding of the theoretical and practical relationship between Cubism and Russian Futurism. Like Majakovskij, Burljuk observed at the Jack of Diamonds exhibition in 1912 that "art is a distortion of reality, and not its copy"; and he saw the foundation of contemporary painting on three principles: "disharmony, dissymmetry and disconstruction".[17] During the Futurist tour of Russia in 1913-1914, Burljuk's talk to one audience accurately reflects his attempts to synthesize avant-garde art trends, and to elucidate the esthetic principles of Cubism which were met with hostility at his and other art exhibitions. Burljuk speaks of Cubism without ever mentioning it:

Now, at this time, today, at this moment, before you, contemporaries, your apostles are speaking, your poet-futurists, who are praising the culture of the city, the dynamics of the world, the mass movement, the inventions, discoveries, the radio, the cinema, airplanes, automobiles, machines, electricity, express trains – in a word, all the new that contemporary life offers. And we think that you should demand of art a bold reflection of reality. And when we offer you not Raphael, but a dynamic construction of highly colorful lines, shifts and the breaking down of planes, experiments in constructivism, the introduction of new materials into a work, when we put up for show the whole laboratory of our searchings, you state that the futurist paintings are not very intelligible. I should say so! After Aivazavskij and Repin, to see on canvas a running man with twelve legs – is this not absurd.

(Voices:)

"Absurd! Right!"

"I have only two legs."

(Burljuk:)

You have two legs if you sit and count them. (laughter) If you run, however, then any spectator will see that the flashing combinations leave the impression of twelve legs. There is no absurdity here. Art is not a sausage factory. An artist is not a dealer in sausages! (applause) The right of an artist is the right of an inventor, a thinker, a master of his craft. But the right of the spectator is to look at the works of the new art with the new vision of a contemporary.

(Voices: "Right!")

Burljuk did not resist the opportunity to heap scorn on the 'realistic'

[16] David and Nikolaj Burljuk, 83.

[17] Quoted in Livšic, 85.

movements in art, or on the critics who attacked the avant-garde art exhibitions:

Stop living with your glasses on the back of your heads and stop admiring the colored photographs of Messrs "Exhibitionists" and various "Worlds of Art" – these provincial aesthetes and haughty contemplators of "pretty" women who have been commemorated on canvases in church-golden frames. Enough of banal aestheticism! It's time to look ahead from a contemporary perspective and not with external eyes alone, but also with the eyes of intellect, reason, calculation. It's time to see in painting geometry and planes, material and texture, dynamics and construction. It's time to learn to understand how the art of futurism is constructed. It's time to spit on the ignorant, dull-witted newspaper critics – these sharpy agent provocateurs, who are turning out lines of arrogant ignorance, who are purposely stacking the deck so as to clutter and choke your minds with all sorts of rubbish. Damn the persecuters and butchers of futurism! (Thunderous applause) Down with the parasites![18]

There can be little doubt that talks of this kind made Futurism a sensation among the art-conscious in Russia.

In sum, then, one may safely assert that Burljuk largely gave Futurism its ideological orientation: to bring art and poetry to the streets and thus yoke art and life, to reject the art and poetry of the past, to see art and poetry as an unending quest for novelty and the creation of new forms.

Just as Burljuk painted in many styles, he also wrote poetry in many styles. Gollerbax points out that, "in comparing various poems by Burljuk (at times dated the same year), one gets the impression that these are works by different authors, completely opposed to each other in world views, temperament, style".[19] Burljuk's early poetry strongly reflects the Symbolist themes of the occult, escape, mystic, eroticism and desire for death. For example:

....
Davno prinjal čestnuju sximu
I do konca kanony treb
Postigši smert' s vostorgom primu
Kak vranom prinesënnyj xleb
Vokrug vzneslisja ostro skaly
Veršiny ix venčany l'dom
V večernyj čas xranjat opaly
Kogda už tëmen skudnyj dom
Ja poljubil svjatye knigi
V nix žizn' moja nemaja cel'
................................[20]

18 Quoted in Vasilij Kamenskij, *Žizn' s Majakovskim* (Moscow, 1940), 18-20.
19 E. Gollerbax, *Poèzija Davida Burljuka* (New York, 1931), 15.
20 See *Sadok sudej*, No. 1 (Moscow, 1910), 83.

....
Long ago I embraced the honest monastic habit
And completely the canons of religious rites
Having perceived death I'll accept with rapture
The bread as brought by the raven
All around cliffs rose sharply
Their peaks crowned with ice
In the evening opals keep watch
When the wretched home is already dark
I have grown fond of holy books
In them life is my mute aim
....

This passage seems to reflect two major Symbolist notions. First, that life is possible only in 'religious' withdrawl. Second, that death is preferable to life, as an escape from the banality of life and a way of discovering the unknown.

Burljuk's major poetic 'device' is to create 'shock' metaphors, to juxtapose disparate phenomena and to use epithets to contradict the traditional notion of poetry. These aspects of his poetry, to be sure, are in the Symbolist tradition, of which Burljuk's poetry is a direct continuation.

If Burljuk has any significance for Futurist poetry, however, it seems to lie in his poetic contributions to early Futurist publications and in his influence on the early poetry of Majakovskij. In Burljuk's poetry of 1913-1914, the poetic themes of Baudelaire and Rimbaud appear to predominate: an obsession and fascination with the ugly and macabre, the 'strangeness of beauty', and meditation on death. For example, in one poem in the Futurist publication *A Slap in the Face of Public Taste*, Burljuk transforms the city into a Baudelairean *cimetière:*

Nemaja noč', ljudej ne slyšno,
V prostranstvax carstvie zimy.
Zdes' v'juga nametaet pyšno
Grobnicy belye sred' t'my.
Gde fonari, gde s ljazgom šumnym
Zmeej skol'znuli poezda,
Tvoj vzgljad kazalsja kamnem lunnym,
Nočej pogasšaja zvezda.
Kak gluboko pod čërnym snegom
Prekrasnyj trup poxorenën...
Promčis', promčis' že šumnym begom,
V par uvijas' so vsex storon...[21]

[21] Quoted in I. Postupal'skij, *Literaturnyj trud D. Burljuka* (New York, 1930), 6.

The mute night, no sound of people,
the reign of winter in open spaces.
Here the snow storm forms sumptuously
White sepulchres in the middle of darkness.
Where with their street-lamps and with noisy clangor
Trains slipped by like serpents,
Your look seemed a moonstone,
The extinguished star of nights,
How deeply beneath the black snow
A beautiful corpse is buried...
Fly past, fly past, then, in noisy flight,
Engulfing yourself in steam from all sides...

The poetry of the Futurists had deep roots in Symbolism. Futurist poetry, however, served to parody Symbolist poetry as a way of renewing perception and redirecting poetry to new forms. Trenin and Xardžiev note that the "path to the creation of a new form, as always in poetry, was through parody, reinterpretation and shifting of former constructive elements".[22]

In their seeming efforts to *épater le bourgeois*, to shock and disorient readers and critics, the Futurists drew on the themes of Baudelaire, Rimbaud, Mallarmé and Corbière, which were introduced into Russia by the Symbolists, especially Brjusov. Interestingly, Brjusov noted in his review of Futurist poetry in 1913 that Rimbaud was the "first futurist".[23]

Burljuk took an active part in these efforts. For example:

Puskaj sud'ba liš' gor'kaja izdevka,
Duša – kabak, a nebo – rvan',
POÈZIJA – ISTREPENNAJA DEVKA,
a krasota koščunstvennaja drjan'.[24]

Let fate be only a bitter taunt,
The soul – a pub, and the sky – puke,
POETRY IS A WORN OUT TART,
and beauty – blasphemous rubbish.

As noted, Burljuk's poetry influenced the early poetry of Majakovskij. In his autobiography, Majakovskij commented on the role that Burljuk played in shaping his poetry:

I think of David with constant love. A remarkable friend. My real teacher. Burljuk made a poet of me. He read me French and German [poets]. Gave me

[22] V. Trenin and N. Xardžiev, "Poètika rannego Majakovskogo", *Literaturnyj kritik*, No. 4 (1935), 181.
[23] Quoted in Trenin and Xardžiev, 180.
[24] *Pervyj žurnal russkix futuristov*, 37.

books to read. He would walk around and talk endlessly. He never let me out of his sight. He gave me fifty kopeks daily so that I would not starve while writing.[25]

Majakovskij went on to mention one of Burljuk's poems, which served as a model for his early poems. Burljuk's "Port":

Zaraženy čerty i steny
igloju lomanyx ognej,
Tak bryzgi lunnoj edkoj peny
Marajut rёbra korablej
...Kakie strannye ulybki,
Rukopožat'ja fonarej,
Akvarjumov bleščut rybki,
Setej svobodny rybarej.[26]

The lines and walls are infected
By the needle of broken lights,
Thus the sprays of caustic lunar foam
Dirty the ribs of ships.
...What strange smiles,
The handshakes of the street lamps,
The small fish of aquarium shine
Free of the nets of fishermen.

Majakovskij's "Sailing":

Prostynju vod pod brjuxom krylij
porval na volny belyj zub
Byl voj truby kak zapax lilij
Ljubov' kričavšix medju trub
I vzvizg siren zabyl u vxodov
Nedoumen'e fonarej
V ušax ogloxšix paroxodov
goreli ser'gi jakorej.[27]

The bed-sheets of water beneath the belly of the wings
were broken into waves by a white tooth
There was the howl of smoke-stacks like the smell of lilies
The love of smoke-stacks which shouted like copper
And the screech of sirens forgot at the entrances
The perplexity of the street lamps
In the ears of deafened steamboats
the earrings of anchors shone.

25 Vladimir Majakovskij, *Polnoe sobranie sočinenij*, I (Moscow, 1955-1961), 20.
26 As cited in Trenin and Xardžiev, 184.
27 As cited in Trenin and Xardžiev, 183. Majakovskij later renamed this poem "Port", and made changes in the first six lines. See Majakovskij, I, 36.

There can be little doubt that Majakovskij's work is thematically, metaphorically, and metrically under the strong influence of Burljuk's poem. Both works personify urban phenomena, juxtapose disparate phenomena, and use 'extended' metaphors. Notably, 'extended' metaphors are a major feature of Majakovskij's poetry, and apparently developed from his imitation of Symbolist poetry. The lines "There was the howl of smoke-stacks like the smell of lilies" is a typical Symbolist metaphor plus analogy. The lines "The handshakes of street lamps" in Burljuk's poem and "The perplexity of street lamps" in Majakovskij's poem are the most striking points of comparison. Metrically, both works are written in iambic tetrameter, and have identical rhyme scheme. One might add that Majakovskij's work is a kind of prelude to the grotesque descriptions of the city which characterize his early poetry.

3. CONCLUSION

Until World War I, Burljuk toured Russia with Majakovskij and Kamenskij. With the advent of the War, Spasskij notes that "Burljuk reckoned that the War was unfavorable to his art; that against the background of the War, the noisy performances of the futurists would appear out of place."[28] What is more, open protest against the War was proscribed, and the Futurists were opposed to it. As the Futurist tour ended, so did the close working relationship between Burljuk and Majakovskij, and Majakovskij apparently could no longer rely on Burljuk for financial support: "In thinking of what I would eat, I began to write for the *New Satirikon*."[29] In 1915, Majakovskij also became friendly with Maksim Gor'kij, and formed a new 'partnership' with Osip and Lilja Brik and Viktor Šklovskij. This partnership gave Russian Futurism new life and led to the formation of Russian Formalism. Osip Brik now began to publish Majakovskij's poetry and pay him handsomely for it. Burljuk recalls with some irony and bitterness:

> ...Majakovskij happily made the historical acquaintance of Lila and Osip Brik. They had money. In December 1915 they published the magazine "Vzjal," and in September 1915 his new friends published his great poem, "Cloud in Trousers"...*But now Majakovskij was paid 50 cents for every line he wrote, by Osip Brik.*[30]

28 Sergej Spasskij, *Majakovskij i ego sputniki* (Leningrad, 1940), 82.
29 Majakovskij, I, 23.
30 David and Marussy Burljuk, "Hilea: 1907-1913", 16 (italics – Burljuk's). See also Majakovskij, I, 24.

In 1917, Burljuk saw the Bolshevik revolution as a creative palingenesis. Reunited by the revolution, Burljuk and Majakovskij published a newspaper – *Gazeta futuristov* (*The Newspaper of the Futurists*, March 15, 1918)[31] – in which they desired the democratization of the arts by bringing art from the galleries, palaces, salons, libraries and theatres to the streets: "Let the streets be a holiday of art for all...'All art is for all the people'."[32] On the day of the publication of the newspaper, Burljuk hung his pictures on a street with the help of a large crowd.[33] In the newspaper, Burljuk observed that "Art is all and always mindless fancy" (*bezumnaja prixot'*), and called upon rival art groups to compete individually "for winning the hearts which have been destined for beauty".[34]

In April 1918, for some unknown reason, Burljuk "fled from Moscow to the Baškirian Steppes on the left bank of the Volga".[35] When the civil war came to that region in September 1918, Burljuk and his family boarded a freight train to Siberia.[36] In Vladivostok, Burljuk joined the future *Lef* Futurists Aseev, Čužak, Tret'jakov and Neznamov, and wrote articles for their journal *Tvorčestvo (Art)*. In one issue of the journal, Burljuk remarked that, "on the streets – for a new life, [new] words, [new] themes – the futurists prove to be the best prepared".[37] Burljuk also gave lectures on art and exhibited his paintings. In 1920, when the White army gained control of Siberian territories, Burljuk apparently was unable to escape to Soviet Russia. Fearing White reprisal for his pro-Bolshevik activities, Burljuk escaped to Japan and continued his activities there.[38] Two years later, he settled in New York.

During the 1920's Burljuk maintained a high interest in the fate of Russian Futurism. In the late 1920's, when Futurism was under savage attack as a remnant of petty bourgeois decadence, Burljuk could not remain silent in New York. He now saw himself as the "Father of Russian Proletarian Futurism", and called himself "the first true Bolshevik in literature" because he was the first to speak of a "class literature" in his

31 This was the only issue of the newspaper.
32 Quoted in V. Katanjan, *Majakovskij: Literaturnoe Xronika*, 4th ed. (Moscow, 1961), 96.
33 Kamenskij, 267.
34 Quoted in L. Švecova, "*Lef i Novyj Lef*", in *Očerki istorij russkoj sovetskoj žurnalistiki 1917-1932*, ed. A. Dement'ev (Moscow, 1966), 312.
35 David and Marussy Burljuk, "Hilea: 1907-1913", 1.
36 "Hilea: 1907-1913", 2.
37 Quoted in A. Xailov, "Periferijnye žurnaly", in *Očerki istorij...*, 476.
38 Spasskij, 132.

art lectures before the revolution.[39] Burljuk could not understand how Futurism was a "bourgeois eructation" when it was the first to give "a slap in the face of bourgeois art".[40] He vigorously defended the Futurists as revolutionaries in art and therefore as forerunners of the Bolshevik revolution. He agreed with the Futurists that the preponderance of Puškin's and Tolstoj's works had created a wrongheaded notion of their historical significance for, and relevance to, the art of the revolutionary era. For Burljuk, their works only stifled "*the quest for novelty*" in literature.[41] When Majakovskij took his own life in 1930, the central pillar of Futurism collapsed, and there was now nothing left for Burljuk to defend.

Finally, until his death on Long Island in January 1967, Burljuk remained an artist of diverse styles and travelled to many countries to exhibit his paintings. Two of his great passions in life were to bring art to the streets and to achieve fame. The former was a kind of faith, perhaps a utopian vision that was characteristic of his age; the latter ruthlessly eluded him. The sad irony of Burljuk's life is that he organized an avant-garde movement of the first magnitude while he himself failed to achieve significant recognition.

39 David Burljuk, *Ѐntelexizm* (New York, 1929), 11.
40 *Ѐntelexizm*, 6.
41 *Ѐntelexizm*, 11 (italics – V.B.).

IV

ALEKSEJ KRUČËNYX

1. KRUČËNYX'S PATH TO FUTURISM

Aleksej Kručënyx was born to a peasant family in Xerson Province in 1886. Upon completion of his early education, he decided to take up painting. It is clear from his unpublished memoirs that Kručënyx felt, as all painters do, that he could best express his 'inner world' in painting. Not only painting, but the atmosphere of the Bohemian life of the painter appealed to him:

In the Odessa Art School, I fell into the world of Bohemia. There was no need for me to become used to this world: I literally lived in it already for hundreds of years. My friends in school were long-haired and poor who considered themselves geniuses. Everyone, however, worked savagely and really loved art. They were in hunger and needed everything, but believed in the future and scorned everyone who did not understand their extraordinary works...[1]

While still an art student, Kručënyx, like Majakovskij, worked for the Bolshevik party in Odessa as a distributor of illegal literature. In 1905 he was arrested and sentenced to prison for this activity. Upon his release he returned to his art studies. A year later he received a teaching diploma in graphic arts. Kručënyx, however, considered teaching necessary only in "moments of difficult living", and his real ambition was to make caricatures and lithograph portraits.[2]

Before coming to Moscow in 1907, Kručënyx "painted and published lithograph portraits of Karl Marx, Engels, Plexanov, Bebel [the German socialist] and other leaders of revolution".[3] In Moscow, he continued this work and also began to draw for humor magazines, in which he caricatured his professors.[4] In 1910 he published an album on his own

[1] Quoted in N. Xardžiev, "Majakovskij i živopis'", in *Majakovskij: Materialy i issledovanija*, V. Percov and N. Serebrjannyj, eds. (Moscow, 1940), 348.
[2] Aleksej Kručënyx, *15 let russkogo futurizma* (Moscow, 1928), 57.
[3] Kručënyx, 58.
[4] Xardžiev, 348.

entitled "All Xerson in Caricatures, Cartoons and Portraits". The aim was to give affront – a kind of revenge on the people whom he disliked or resented.[5]

In September, 1911, David Burljuk introduced Kručënyx to Majakovskij. Earlier, Kručënyx had collaborated with the Burljuk brothers "in propagandizing Cubism in art in the southern press".[6] Kručënyx soon became a member of Burljuk's group, and eagerly took part in debates on art with Burljuk and Majakovskij.

At one debate in the beginning of 1912, Burljuk introduced Kručënyx to Xlebnikov. At another meeting with Xlebnikov, Kručënyx showed him his first poem. Xlebnikov spontaneously began to add his own lines to the poem.[7] In the summer of 1912, the poem was published jointly as "Igra v adu" ("A Game in Hell"), which to one critic at least was the "acme of Russian Baudelairism" and "an amassment of ugliness, horrors and absurdities":[8]

V očkax sideli zdes' kosye,
Xvostom podmyškoj ščekoča,
Xromye, lysye, rjabye,
Kto bez brovej, kto bez pleča.
Rogatoe, dvunogoe
Vraščaet zrački
I rylo s trevogoju
Ščiplet pučki.
....
Ved'mina pëstraja kak žaba
Sidit na žarenyx nogax,
U rta prijatnaja uxaba
Smešala s zlost'ju detskij "ax!"[9]

They sat here, cross-eyed and wearing spectacles,
Tickling themselves with a tail armpit,
Lame, bald, pock-marked
Some without eyebrows, some without a shoulder.
A horned, two-legged one
Rolls his eyes
And his snout eagerly
Nibbles on the tufts of hair.
....

[5] See Kručënyx, 58.
[6] *Ibid.*
[7] See N. Xardžiev, "Kommentarij", in Velimir Xlebnikov, *Neizdannye proizvedenija* (Moscow, 1940), 438.
[8] V. Družin, "Velimir Xlebnikov", *Zvezda*, No. 3 (1930), 226-227.

A witch, motley like a toad
Sits on burned legs,
On the mouth a pleasant thief
Mixed a child's "oh!" with maliciousness.

By contradicting the traditional view of poetry, Kručënyx (and Xlebnikov) were perhaps merely testing their ability to shock and disorient.

The joint publication of "Igra v adu" subsequently led to a close friendship and working relationship between Kručënyx and Xlebnikov. Kručënyx came to regard Xlebnikov as his teacher, and frequently sent him his works for review and approval.[10] Kručënyx undoubtedly listened with fascination to Xlebnikov's utopian projects, one of which was the creation of a universal language. Both shared an intense yearning for a primitive way of life, including an idea of primitive language. Kručënyx became interested in Xlebnikov's notion of trans-sense language and apparently derived his own notion of trans-sense language from Xlebnikov's. Kručënyx seems to have grafted the principle of artistic distortion onto language by equating the stroke on the canvas with sounds or phonemes, both of which were to him free from 'reality', and which apparently liberated him from it. For Xlebnikov, trans-sense was to be a systematic universal language of words whose initial phoneme was their semantic guide. For Kručënyx, trans-sense was basically to consist of arbitrary and logically meaningless but suggestive phonemic sequences which would express emotions and perhaps associative chains. Kručënyx seems to have seen in these phonemic sequences and associative chains a new way of perceiving the world.[11]

For Kručënyx, trans-sense gave one the freedom "to crumble words according to a definite phonetic (or other) task".[12] He saw trans-sense flourishing in poetry and prose (especially in the nineteen twenties), and saw new possibilities for it in the development of the theatre because it was the only language that could keep pace with the film. He was determined to see trans-sense as a leading mode of expression. Indeed, he even considered it "the first step to a world language", and "the art of the

[9] Quoted in Družin, 227. There were a number of versions of this work. See Xardžiev, "Kommentarij", 438-441. For an analysis of this work, see Vladimir Markov, *The Longer Poems of Velimir Khlebnikov* (Berkeley, 1962), 83-86. There is a 'plan' of the work in Velimir Xlebnikov, *Sobranie proizvedenij*, II (Leningrad, 1929-1933), 308-310.
[10] See Xlebnikov's letters to Kručënyx in Xlebnikov, *Sobranie proizvedenij*, V, 297-308.
[11] Markov, 77, notes that Xlebnikov paid "little respect to this [Kručënyx's] anarchistic concept".
[12] Aleksej Kručënyx, *Fonetika teatra* (Moscow, 1923), 9.

future".[13]

Armed with this theory of trans-sense, Kručënyx clearly saw his role in Futurism. He later wrote concerning this period:

> ...sensing the imminent doom of painting and its replacement by something else, which later took the form of photomontage, I broke my brushes in advance, threw away my palette and washed my hands so that I could take up the pen and work for the glory of, and destruction by, futurism...[14]

Kručënyx's remarks are direct and to the point. He saw in Futurism a new and more effective means of reacting against bourgeois society and of nihilistically assaulting traditional tastes and conventions. That Puškin, Lermontov, Tolstoj and Dostoevskij and other important writers were to be attacked as well seems to have aroused a perverse delight in Kručënyx. Was there a better opportunity to gain notoriety and to shock? In terms of his previous 'shock work', this was hardly a formidable adjustment for him to make, as will now be demonstrated.

2. KRUČËNYX: THEORY AND PRACTICE OF TRANS-SENSE 1913-1928

For Kručënyx, the bane of Russian literature of the nineteenth and twentieth centuries was its deep involvement with insoluble problems of human existence. He believed that Russian writers were almost obsessed with describing and analyzing human passions and feelings, with psychological probing and with solving the "enigmas of the spirit". Kručënyx dedicated this poem to the "fathers" of Russian literature as a means of solving all their "fateful" problems:

poskoree pokončit'
nedostojnyj vodevil' –
o konečno
ètim nikogo ne udiviš'

žizn' glupaja šutka i skazka
starye ljudi tverdili
nam ne nužno ukazki
i my ne razbiraemsja v ètoj gnili[15]

let's quickly put an end
to this *worthless comic act*

[13] Kručënyx, *Fonetika teatra*, 12.
[14] Kručënyx, *15 let...*, 58.
[15] Aleksej Kručënyx and Velimir Xlebnikov, *Slovo kak takovoe* (Moscow, 1913), 11.

of course
you won't surprise anyone with this

life is a stupid joke and a fairy tale
our elders repeatedly said...
we don't need instructions
and we don't understand this rot

Russian literature, Kručënyx continued, because of its concerns with "fateful" questions, was consequently "spiritualistic and cachectic", "a society for salvation", and a pathetic and hopeless captive of meaning, philosophy, and psychology.[16] This obsession with meaning, reason, psychology and philosophy placed serious limitations on poetic imagination, invention, verbal play and spontaneous intuition. Kručënyx suggested that the "emptier" the poetic imagination, the more creative and fruitful the poetic result: the penetration of the mysteries beyond the rational world. Lermontov he felt to be the first to introduce the themes of despair and loneliness which the Symbolists continued in their poetry. After a century of this ideological captivity, Kručënyx, echoing Brjusov, demanded the liberation of Russian literature and a return to the true aims of poetic creation. While the Symbolists spoke at times of freeing the word from meaning, Kručënyx rejected the idea of any 'sense' or 'meaning' as necessary to a work of art:

Before us no art of the word ever existed...Clear and decisive proof of this fact is that until now the word has been in fetters and is subordinate to meaning. Until now they have maintained that 'meaning governs the word, and not the contrary.' We have pointed out this error and have provided a free language, trans-sense and universal. Through meaning, former artists approached the word. We, however, approach it through immediate comprehension...The word is broader than its meaning. Each letter, each sound has its relevance...Why not repudiate meaning and write with word-ideas that are freely created?...We do not need intermediaries – symbols, meaning...[17]

If the ideology of Russian literature was bad, its verbal organization was equally bad. He noted that the sound organization of Puškin's "Evgenij Onegin" consisted of the endings *eni – ani* and *s – s – s*. He gave the

[16] See Aleksej Kručënyx, *Čort i rečetvorcy* (Moscow, 1913), I, and V. Zakrževskij, *Rycari bezumija: Futuristy* (Kiev, 1914), 118.

[17] Aleksej Kručënyx, "Novye puti slova", in Troe (Moscow, 1913), 23-33. Brjusov once noted: "Art is the comprehension of the world by other than rational means... The history of the new art is above all the history of its liberation... Art is at last free. Now it is consciously giving itself to its higher and only calling: to be the cognition of the world beyond rational forms, beyond thinking by causality" (Quoted in V. Gofman, "Jazyk simvolistov", in *Literaturnoe nasledstvo*, XXVII-XXVIII [Moscow, 1937], 57).

following examples to illustrate:

> v toske bezumnyx sožal*enij*
> k eja nogam Evg*enij*
> ona vzdoxnula i molčit
> i na *One*gina gljadit
> bez udivlenija bez *g*n*e*v*a*...
> ego bol'noj ugasšij vzor
> mo*lja*ščij vid *ne*moj ukor –
> ej v*nja*tno vsë.
>
> Onegin dobryj moj prijatel'
> rodil*sja* na bregax Nevy
> gde možet byt' rodi*lis'* i vy
> ili *blis*tali moj čitatel'...
> *S sv*oej suprugoju dorodnoj
> priexal tolstyj Pu*stja*kov...
> Skotininy, četa sedaja,
> s det'mi vsex vozrastov, sčitaja...[18]

Kručënyx added that poets avoided verb rhymes because they were too simple, and instead used *el*... *te*... *sja*... *tsja*... Puškin, Kručënyx continued, by using rhyme "inwardly", expanded the range for *sja* and *tsja*. Kručënyx concluded that Puškin's "Evgenij Onegin" could be summed up in two lines: *eni – voni, si – e – tsja*.[19]

In Lermontov's poetry, Kručënyx found the sound organization no different. In his poetry, the voiceless phonemes "p" and "t" were frequent, which sounded like *pa-pa-pa, pi-pi-pi, ti-ti-ti* in the lines "Po nebu polunoči angel letel, I tixuju pesnju on pel..."[20] Kručenyx found this "pallid", "unsatisfying", unsuited to his age, and only cause for indigestion to a healthy person.[21]

For other writers, Kručënyx went on, language had to be "clear, pure, honest, sonorous, pleasant (tender) to the ear, expressive, vivid, graphic, juicy".[22] These requirements, however, were not for a poetry of dissonance, but for weak and effeminate poetry, for poets who seek the "eternal feminine, the beautiful". Quite conceivably, Kručënyx was ridiculing the Russian Symbolists, especially Blok. Kručënyx noted that "the skirt had

[18] Quoted in Kručënyx, "Tajnye poroki akademikov", in his *Apokalipsis v russkoj literature* (Moscow, 1923), 19. This article was first published as a pamphlet in 1914.
[19] Kručënyx, "Tajnye poroki akademikov", 32.
[20] Kručënyx and Xlebnikov, *Slovo kak takovoe*, 8.
[21] *Slovo kak takovoe*, 9.
[22] *Slovo kak takovoe*, 10.

become mystical" as a result.[23]

According to Kručënyx, poets had lost sight of the irrational character of artistic creation because they approached it through denotative meaning.[24] As he saw it, the justification for approaching the word through its sound texture could be made in this way:

> Thought and language do not keep pace with the experience of the inspired person; therefore the artist is free to express himself not only in common language (of concepts), but also in a personal language (the artist is an individual) and in a language which has no definite meaning, in (an uncongealed) trans-sense [language]. A common language is binding; a free one allows one to express himself more fully.[25]

By rejecting conventional reality through linguistic deformation, Kručënyx sought, "like Adam", to recreate language by renaming things. For him this was a way of achieving a new perception of the universe. He found, for example, that the word *lilija* (lily) was "ugly" because it was "spoiled" and "violated", and perhaps because it was a loan word. In order to restore "original purity" to this word, Kručënyx identified it with vowels and called it *euy*.[26]

One of his early poems consisted solely of vowels, which he called a "universal language":

o e a

i e e i

a e e e[27]

Kručënyx believed that trans-sense language was demanded by the confused character of contemporary life and served as an antidote to the paralysis of common language. These reasons also justified for Kručënyx the destruction of syntax and grammar: "We have realized that to depict the dizzy life of today and even more of the on-rushing future, we must combine words anew; and the more chaos we introduce into the structure of sentences, the better."[28]

As an example which best expressed the poet's dissonance and which

[23] *Ibid.*

[24] Kručënyx, "Novye puti slova", 24. "The trans-rational *[zaumnoe]*", Kručënyx also noted, "is given to us just as immediately as the rational *[umnoe]*."

[25] Aleksej Kručënyx, "Deklaracija slova kak takovogo", in his *Apokalipsis v russkoj literature*, 43.

[26] *Ibid.*

[27] "Deklaracija slova...", 44.

[28] Kručënyx, "Novye puti slova", 29.

expressed "more Russian nationality than all of Puškin's poetry",[29] Kručënyx gave an example which seems to reflect not only the destruction of syntax and grammar, but trans-sense language based on pure sound associations and new 'words' free of meaning:

dyr bul ščyl
ubeščur
skum
vy so bu
r l èz 30

Many believed that Kručënyx had uttered, especially concerning Puškin, a cardinal blasphemy; and with the destruction of conventional reality in his 'poem', Kručënyx had certainly achieved his objective. For he became "the most militant and popular" of the Futurists,[31] and the object of excoriation by the critics of Russian Futurism during the pre-revolutionary years.

At the beginning of the literary revival after the Bolshevik revolution, however, Kručënyx seems to have realized that, in order for his theory of trans-sense to be useful to poets and writers, he had to expand its range. Arbitrary and meaningless sounds could serve no 'constructive' purpose. Yet Kručënyx feared that, if he eviscerated or diluted his theory, he would transgress the 1912 Futurist manifesto. He thus compromised.

This compromise was reflected in his manifesto of 1921, "Deklaracija zaumnogo jazyka" ("Declaration of Trans-sense Language"). Kručënyx repeated his earlier justification for the artist's need for trans-sense,[32] and assigned it first priority. He then proceeded to describe the conditions under which it was to apply. He viewed trans-sense as the primordial form of poetry, and noted its almost magical ability to give rise to ur-sound and ur-images, which were to him "precisely indefinable". Kručënyx suggested that writers resort to trans-sense when they wished to

[29] Kručënyx and Xlebnikov, *Slovo kak takovoe*, 9.

[30] *Ibid.* Interestingly, Kručënyx wrote to Xlebnikov concerning this poem. Xlebnikov remarked in his reply that the poem "soothes precisely the most uncontrolled *[rasxodivšijsja]* passions" (Xlebnikov, *Neizdannye proizvedenija*, 367).

[31] N. Stepanov, "Tvorčestvo Velimira Xlebnikova", in Xlebnikov, *Sobranie proizvedenij*, I. 37.

[32] See Kručënyx, "Deklaracija slova...". From 1916-1921, Kručënyx was in the Caucasus, where he created scandals and waged polemics with Vjačeslav Ivanov and Sergej Gorodeckij. He formed an organization called "The Company of 41 Degrees", which claimed trans-sense as the "obligatory form of embodying art". The aim of the organization was "to use all the great discoveries of the members of the organization and to put the world on a new axis". See Aleksej Kručënyx, *Zaumniki* (Moscow, 1922), 21.

express vague imagery and to hint at things rather than name them directly; when invented names of fictional heroes, localities, and cities were necessary; when in moments of religious ecstasy, outrage, anger, jealousy and hatred; when baby talk, pet names and nicknames were necessary. Kručënyx rightly pointed out that this verbal play was peculiar to many writers. As to why this verbal play needed emphasis, Kručënyx did not say. He considered it, however, a form of trans-sense, which "aroused and gave freedom of creative fantasy".[33] Finally, Kručënyx concluded by proposing three basic forms of verbal art: "rational", "random", and "trans-sense". To be sure, the last was for Kručënyx the "most concise" and the "most universal art", and therefore pregnant with possibilities of becoming a universal poetic language.[34]

These theoretical views were largely reflected in Kručënyx's poetic practice of the nineteen-twenties. Many of his works were written in almost pure trans-sense, often with an indication of their emotional orientation.[35] Other works hardly contained trans-sense, and were highly suggestive. For example:

Golodnja... Golodnjak...
Glod... Gludun... Golodijca...
Glyd... ryk
MYR SDYX...
GLOD i MOR.
Noč'... Nuč'... tyč'... tuč...
Xod drog... grob... glux...
Zvuk pal... krik!
Blesk! NOŽ KR-R!
Teč'... krov'... tix...
ZOL GLOD!
MOR HAGL!
NOZ GORD!
MIR PAD!...[36]

This 'poem' seems to concern a famine, its consequences, and a man's apparent refusal to become a cannibal because of it. The first two lines contain words that are variations of the "glod" and "golod" – 'hunger' – and suggest many kinds of hunger. Line three suggests the 'gnawing' and the 'roar' of pain that follows hunger. In line four, the ultimate result

33 Aleksej Kručënyx, "Deklaracija zaumnogo jazyka", in his *Apokalipsis v rosskoj literature*, 45.
34 Kručënyx, "Deklaracija zaumnogo jazyka", 46.
35 See Kručënyx, *Zaumniki*.
36 Aleksej Kručënyx, *Golodnjak* (Moscow, 1922).

of that pain seems to be that the 'world is croaking' from hunger. Cannibalization apparently ensues. Once again hunger and pestilence is emphasized in line five. Line six suggests a dark, oppressive, and endless night full of mental suffering. In the next line, there is the 'procession of wagons' ("xod drog") which bring the dead to the burial grounds ("grob") and then silence ("glux"). "Zvuk pal" is the fall of a sound and then a 'cry' of astonishment. "Blesk" indicates the 'flash' of a knife, with "KR-R" suggesting the penetration of the knife into the man's body. The flow of blood follows and then death ("tix"). Kručënyx concludes by saying, it seems, that the "famine is angry" and the "pestilence is outraged" because they have been cheated of death. The 'knife' emerges victoriously. Peace, however, has come at last ("mir pad"). One might add that Kručënyx may have witnessed such an event during the famine which raged during the years of the civil war in Russia.

It is interesting to note the 'harsh' sound orientation of the poem. The repetition of one syllable sounds in the second half of the poem seems to suggest rapid, incessant, and irresistible 'pounding' which Kručënyx perhaps identifies with death.

In the following example, Kručënyx rather ingeniously breaks up a word (*orava* 'crowd') for sound effect. He uses the word to create the metaphor of a 'crowd' of geese which converge on a dying man. He thus breaks up the word so that it will harmonize with the sounds of geese:

On tak ispugalsja čto vovse ne pisknul!
A za puxlym nasledstvom
Za pačkoj pudovoj
Skvoz' rešëtki i ščeli
V dver' nadvigalas' pojuščix rodstvennikov
O-ra-a-va
ga, ga-ga-ga!...[37]

He was so frightened that he did not even squeak!
And for the plump inheritance
For the pood bundle
Through the screens and cracks
The singing relatives came through the door
Howling
Ha-aou-ga!

The nineteen-twenties were undoubtedly Kručënyx's most 'productive' years with his theory of trans-sense. The struggle against ideological

[37] Kručënyx, *Zaumniki*, 2.

art was relentless. "We are living in barbarous times", Kručënyx noted, when "the deed" *(delo)* is placed above "the word".[38] The vulgarizing campaign to "dislodge" Puškin and to shock continued also:

> Esli b'ëššja i zlaja rifma nikak nikak ne vyxodit –
> Pojdi i spljun' drugu na rozovyj žilet!
> Zatancujut v gorle tvoëm brilljantinovye kolody
> (brilliantovye kolodcy)
> I posypjatsja zubotyčiny sozvučij
>
> kak s Olimpa
> velosiped
> draz
> raz
> mizug
> z-z-z
>
> vybit liceist!...[39]

> If you are racking your brain and the malicious rhyme just won't come –
> Go and spit on your friend's pink vest!
> Brilliantine chains will start dancing in your throat
> (diamond wells)
> And teeth-smashing harmonies will scatter all around
>
> as from Olympus
> a bicycle
> draz
> raz
> mizug
> z-z-z
>
> a Lycéeist will be dislodged!...

Kručënyx believed that he was and could continue to be influential by providing detailed guidelines for writers. He gave illustrations of what certain phonemic combinations would suggest. He began to assign "texture" *(faktura)* to phonemes, especially to the phoneme "z", which was apparently his favorite. He noted that "z" was suitable for conveying the idea of swift movement, discontent, screeching, clanging, sliding, cold, fury, envy, nervous irritation and excitement. He gave the following 'poetic' example in which he created neologisms from the morpheme *zud* 'to itch, nag':

> U menja izumrudno nepriličen každyj kusok
> ....

[38] Aleksej Kručënyx, *Sdvigologija russkogo jazyka* (Moscow, 1923), 31.
[39] Kručënyx, *Sdvigologija*..., 40-41.

Ja – tormoz, poezdu rvuščij zub,
Zudač zemli!...
Žil – byl zuden'
Žena – ego zudynja
I deti – zudenyši.[40]

Every bite of mine is "emeraldly" unseemly
....
I am the brake which pulls out the train's tooth,
The nagger of the earth!
There was once a nagger
His wife was a naggeress
And the children naggerets.

Kručënyx was also a vigorous propagandist for *Lef*, Futurism, and for the propaganda poetry of the Futurists, which he believed had to meet two conditions: first, that it be "very popular, generally understandable in meaning, language and form"; second, that it be "very artistic and original".[41]

Kručënyx even boldly asserted the existence of a "definite" and "united" trans-sense school of poetry, to which Xlebnikov, Aseev, Kamenskij and others belonged.[42] To be sure, the existence of such a school was a rank fiction, and Kručënyx was perhaps merely trying to recapture the notoriety of his prerevolutionary years. There was, however, some truth as to what united these poets: all had used trans-sense in their poetry to a certain degree. Many others had done so – and others would continue to do so.

This is precisely what Kručënyx observed in the development of Soviet literature. For him the verbal play and experimentation of the period were not so much the legacy of Symbolism, Acmeism, and Futurism and the efforts of writers to create new modes of expression. Soviet literature was rather developing "under the badge" of trans-sense. Kručënyx saw the use of neologisms, transcriptions of foreign languages – Chinese, Japanese, and provincial dialects – into Russian and sound descriptions of phenomena as manifestations of trans-sense. When Sejfullina, Vsevolod Ivanov, Babel' and Leonov used them in their work, Kručënyx saw them as a genuine affirmation of the expressive value of his trans-sense theory. He noted that when Sejfullina used the lines

40 Aleksej Kručënyx, *Faktura slova* (Moscow, 1923), 3.
41 Aleksej Kručënyx, *Lef-agitki Aseeva, Majakovskogo, Tret'jakova* (Moscow, 1925), 3-4.
42 Kručënyx, *Zaumniki*, 12.

Aj dyn-bindy dyndy-bindy
Aj dyn-bindy dyndy-bindy

in a song, this was for Kručënyx her use of trans-sense, an example of "heightened phonetics, guessing through sound, or a manifestation by sound of our subconsciousness".[43] When Sejfullina used *ixa* instead of *ix* in *ixa mat'* (their mother) and when she described a shot as *bax-bax* – these, too, he claimed as expressions of trans-sense. To be sure, *ixa* is not a manifestation of trans-sense, but analogical to *ixnij* and in common usage. Similarly with *bax-bax*, which is onomatopoeic and also in common usage.

As Kručënyx wrote on, his idea of what trans-sense really was became less clear, and he began to doubt the authenticity of Sejfullina's trans-sense, after having attributed it to her: "...she does not create trans-sense language, but only now and then picks up a concrete, and mainly an undeveloped word with which she freshens her story."[44] However embryonic Sejfullina's trans-sense was, it was, according to Kručënyx, her salvation and guide "to the right track".[45] As for the other writers, Kručënyx apparently considered any 'deformation' of the Russian language in their works as a manifestation of trans-sense. Now that all 'deformation' was a form of trans-sense for Kručënyx, he finally observed that no definition of it was really needed, and cited instead his 1921 "Declaration of Trans-Sense Language". Kručënyx's apparent confusion perhaps stemmed from the realization that 'trans-sense' is characteristic of creative and experimental periods of literature, and its efficacy is gauged by its ability to *extend*, not transcend, meaning. Moreover, poetry is often a process of interaction between 'trans-sense' and 'sense'.

By extending his definition of trans-sense to an extreme degree, Kručënyx thereby made it so broad as to be characteristic of almost any poetry or verbal play, effectively robbing the term of any discrete meaning.

3. THE CRITICS OF KRUČËNYX'S TRANS-SENSE

Kručënyx's notion of trans-sense and the problem of the relationship between sounds and meaning in poetry brought forth considerable and interesting discussion from eminent critics and writers. In his sym-

43 Aleksej Kručënyx, *Novoe v pisatel'skoj texnike*, (Moscow, 1926), 14.
44 Kručënyx, *Novoe v pisatel'skoj texnike*, 15.
45 *Novoe v pisatel'skoj texnike*, 17.

pathetic study of early Futurism, Zakrževskij called Kručënyx "an extreme anarchist in art" whose "aim in the Futurist battle was to reject not only meaning, but also any hint of it".[46] Despite his clearly extreme judgement, Zakrževskij saw the usefulness of Kručënyx's struggle against meaning in a time of "mildewed 'literariness'" and as a reaction against Symbolism.[47] Similarly, for Èjxenbaum, "the Futurists' experiments in 'trans-sense' assumed major significance as a reaction [*demonstracija*] against symbolism, which was not determined to go beyond 'instrumentation,' which formed an accompaniment to meaning, and therefore vulgarized the role of sounds in poetic language".[48]

Tret'jakov and Šklovskij saw Kručënyx's trans-sense as an attempt to explore new avenues in sound. Tret'jakov compared Kručënyx impressionistically to a word foundry which forges bright, piercing, and resilient words by melting verbal scraps and rust, and by chemical analysis.[49] Šklovskij noted that trans-sense assumed many literary and non-literary manifestations, which are psychologically and biologically motivated. In certain instances, pure sound could express emotions and 'communicate' more effectively than common language.[50] In general, Šklovskij pointed out as examples the sounds "o" and "u", which to him were universal expressions of "gloom" and "sullenness".[51] Significantly, he remarked that only religious sectarians used trans-sense in "its pure form" partly because they "identify trans-sense with glossolalia – with that gift of speaking in tongues..."[52] As noted, Kručënyx entertained similar notions concerning the use of trans-sense.

When Šklovskij raised the question of trans-sense as language and the question of meaning in trans-sense and in poetry in general, he had come to the core of the problem. He put the problem thus:

If we add, as a demand for the word as such, that it must serve to designate understanding, that it must be generally meaningful, then of course 'trans-sense language' as something of an externally relative language falls by the wayside. But it does not fall alone: the facts that we have adduced force one to wonder whether words always have meaning in trans-sense and in simple poetic speech, or whether this is only a view that is wrongheaded and a result of our careless observation.[53]

46 Zakrževskij, 12, 119.
47 Zakrževskij, 134.
48 Boris Èjxenbaum, *Literatura, teorija, kritika, polemika* (Leningrad, 1927), 122.
49 Sergej Tret'jakov, "Buka russkoj literatury", in *Živ Kručënyx* (Moscow, 1925), 17.
50 Viktor Šklovskij, "O poèzij i zaumnom jazyke", in *Poètika* (Petrograd, 1919), 14.
51 Šklovskij, 15.
52 Šklovskij, 22-23.
53 Šklovskij, 25.

Šklovskij cautiously gave no direct answer to this interesting problem. He pointed out, however, that even if one rejects trans-sense in non-poetic language, it still remains a solid poetic fact. He strongly suggested that poetry is "created" and "apprehended" not by meaning alone.[54]

If Šklovskij had no direct answer, Žirmunskij certainly did. He observed that "the sounds of poetic language always have 'meaning,' although this meaning is not always reducible to 'understanding' [*ponjatie*]".[55] The meaning (in the broad sense) of a poem, Žirmunskij continued, is closely related to the sound orientation of the poetic word. Therefore meaningless sounds for Žirmunskij did not exist in poetic language. To the extent that they were related to meaningful words, sounds assumed meaning. As for Kručënyx's *dyr bul ščyl – ubeščur*, Žirmunskij did not consider them words. At best, they are able to create "a vague and common sound or emotional relationship with real words".[56]

As for the question of trans-sense as a 'language', Vinokur categorically denied the possibility as such. The very notion of trans-sense language was for him a contradiction in terms. Vinokur maintained that language by definition had to be communicative and meaningful. What is more, trans-sense sounds were not peculiar to language: they were devoid of "significative content", grammatically incomprehensible, and "torn from their articulatory context".[57] He admitted that trans-sense as "combinations of pure sensory data...can be the object of our perception and also capable of producing an aesthetic effect". If, however, an "actually aesthetic experience" was the question, one that transcended "simple amusement and 'pleasant feeling'", then trans-sense could not be included.[58]

What, then, was trans-sense for Vinokur? From the viewpoint of "linguistic *practice*", it was not the expression of "human personality". It was rather "the product of a purely bestial and animal art".[59] He did not deny the value of trans-sense as a poetic device, verbal play or experimentation. In fact, Vinokur saw the positive uses of trans-sense in "the creation of a new system of elements of social designation [*naimenovanie*] [e.g. classification, or naming of new products etc]. From this

54 *Ibid.*

55 Viktor Žirmunskij, "Vokrug 'Poètiki' Opojaza", in his *Voprosy teorij literatury* (The Hague, 1962), 343.

56 Žirmunskij, 343.

57 G. Vinokur, "Rečevaja praktika futuristov", in his *Kul'tura jazyka* (Moscow, 1929), 314.

58 Vinokur, 315.

59 *Ibid.*

viewpoint, trans-sense art takes on a completely special and significant meaning."[60] It could take on this meaning, on the condition that trans-sense be "provided with corresponding historical instructions and commentaries".[61] Vinokur strongly doubted, however, if trans-sense could meet this condition since it had only "*potential* meaning". He added: "In order to write trans-sense poetry with these 'productive' aims, Kručënyx must in advance create his own new *history*."[62]

A not wholly unsympathetic critic of Kručënyx's trans-sense was Trotsky. He remarked that Kručënyx's assertion concerning the 'nationality' of *dyr bul ščyl* was "something midway between philologic poetics, and insolence of bad manners".[63] Whether Kručënyx was correct Trotsky could not say since *dyr bul ščyl* was "not a poetic extract from a Futurist work – so there is really nothing for one to compare".[64] He likened trans-sense sounds to "verbal musical scales and exercises" which were best suited for music students. One simply had to wait for the day when a poet who used these scales and exercises would better Puškin. Trotsky also remarked that language develops conservatively and in terms of strict necessity. While Kručënyx's – and Xlebnikov's – experiments were of interest and could contribute to the development of both common and poetic language, they were peripheral to poetry.[65]

Kručënyx's rather unsympathetic critics were Čukovskij and Gorlov. For Čukovskij, trans-sense had always been, to some degree, an intrinsic feature of poetry; and poets had always made a cult of trans-sense, the autotelic word. He saw the use of trans-sense in Futurist poetry as an attempt to broaden the range of the autotelic word so as to make it "the material of art".[66] If this were possible, Čukovskij remarked, he would be the first to welcome it. Čukovskij went on to say that while he approved of the use of trans-sense in poetry, he found it discouraging that "a whole generation of poets had given themselves up to it, by rejecting, therefore, all the higher forms of cultured human speech".[67] If these

[60] G. Vinokur, "Futuristy – stroiteli jazyka", *Lef*, No. 1 (1923), 212.
[61] Vinokur, "Rečevaja praktika...", 317.
[62] *Ibid.* For another linguistic point of view, see I. A. Baudouin de Courtenay, "K teorij 'Slova kak takovogo' i 'Bukvy kak takovoj'", in his *Izbrannye trudy po obščemu jazykoznaniju*, II (Moscow, 1963), 243-246.
[63] Leon Trotsky, *Literature and Revolution* (New York, 1957), 132.
[64] Trotsky, 133.
[65] *Ibid.* See also V. Arvatov, "Rečetvorčestvo: Po povodu zaumnoj poèzii", *Lef*, No. 2 (1923), 79-91.
[66] Kornej Čukovskij, *Futuristy* (Peterburg, 1922), 43.
[67] Čukovskij, 45-46.

poets took delight in emotional belching, then it only reflected the poverty of the mental and spiritual life of the age. For this mode of "expression was characteristic of wild shamans, idiots, imbeciles, maniacs, eunuchs, runners [*begun*], jumpers..."[68]

The burden of Čukovskij's critique of trans-sense was similar to Vinokur's. Trans-sense was not a 'language,' but a "pre-language, pre-cultural, pre-historical... when there was no discourse, conversation, but only cries and screams..."[69] The strange irony of the situation was, according to Čukovskij, that, in their passion for the future, the Futurists had "selected for their future poetry the most ancient of the very ancient languages". By rejecting culture and attempting to liberate themselves from a thousand years of history, Futurism was clearly "anti-futurism".[70]

For Gorlov, it was quite natural that there was a conscious effort to rename things and to create new and abbreviated words in a new and revolutionary age. This principle had equal justification for poetry.[71] Kručënyx's trans-sense, however, insofar as it related to this creative effort, was anachronistic because it was destructive. As for its application to poetry, Gorlov pointed out that it was effective only against the background of meaning, as "a semantic echo reflected in other words".[72] The aim of trans-sense, as Gorlov saw it, was to amplify "semantic language", not destroy it. In these terms, for Gorlov trans-sense was "semantic".[73] He agreed that an unfamiliar word or name of a thing could evoke "a strong and deep emotion. This happens, however, only when we ourselves substitute a vivid and clear semantic content for a sound image that is not clear to us... In the majority of cases, a semantic image is drawn to a given sound combination by way of association..."[74]

Gorlov did not even consider Kručënyx a Futurist, since Futurism had already passed the stage of anarchic revolt. "He is a destroyer in art. And this means that he is no longer a futurist... Futurism is dynamic... A. Kručënyx is static. He has not moved one iota since 1913."[75] Kručënyx indeed wanted to build, Gorlov remarked, "but in such a way so as first to raze the old to the ground".[76] Kručënyx was unaware that "the

68 Čukovskij, 46.
69 *Ibid.*
70 Čukovskij, 50.
71 N. Gorlov, *Revoljucija i futurizm* (Moscow, 1923), 31.
72 Gorlov, 34.
73 *Ibid.*
74 Gorlov, 32.
75 Gorlov, 31.
76 Gorlov, 32.

revolution is not killing the old language, but is reconstructing, purifying and renewing it".[77] And his attempts to convince the readers that his trans-sense was far more expressive than common language only convinced them of the contrary.[78]

4. CONCLUSION

From the preceding discussion, it is quite apparent that Russian Futurism had in Kručënyx a radical, a vulgarizer, an irreverent votary and a prolific propagandist of non-ideological art. One may recall that this was precisely the heart of the 1912 Futurist manifesto. It may very well be that it was written largely by Kručënyx.

Kručënyx certainly played the role of a watchdog against ideological art. In 1914, one critic remarked that Kručënyx was the "*enfant terrible*" and the "jingoist" of Futurism whom every literary group needs. He also questioned whether his poetry redeemed his "mischief".[79] The Futurists, too, were aware of Kručënyx's role. In his comment of Kručënyx's critics in 1914, Livšic observed that "to focus attention on Kručënyx as the central figure of Russian 'cubo-futurism' means above all to evoke surprise and laughter in a number of 'cubo-futurists' themselves".[80] In 1925, at a conference of proletarian writers, Majakovskij stated that he would be an "idiot" if he said, "'Comrades, copy Aleksej Kručënyx with his *dyr bul ščyl*'."[81] Significantly, in 1928 Kručënyx himself piously observed that the "fundamental principles of futurism, as proclaimed in the 'Slap in the Face' and in a number of subsequent declarations in 1913-1916 have remained unchanged".[82]

Apart from his role as a Futurist, however, Kručënyx rejected 'rational' language because for him it represented a confused, alien, artificial and oppressive material world. The rejection of the latter was implicit in the former. Pasternak suggested that Kručënyx knew of no other way of taking revenge on the material world.[83] He thus plunged into the unintelligible – into the world of irrational sounds as a way of soothing his

77 *Ibid.*
78 *Ibid.*
79 See *Pervyj žurnal russkix futuristov*, No. 1-2 (Moscow, 1914), 124.
80 B. Livšic, "Dubina na golove russkoj kritiki", in *Pervyj žurnal russkix futuristov*, 102.
81 Vladimir Majakovskij, *Polnoe sobranie sočinenij*, XII (Moscow, 1955-1961), 270.
82 Kručënyx, *15 let*..., 8.
83 Boris Pasternak, "Kručënyx", in *Živ Kručënyx*, 1.

apparently disaffected mind, partly as a mystical quest, and partly as a febrile effort to establish contact with some 'other reality'. Kručënyx never realized that this was in the main a major hallmark of Symbolism. As Žirmunskij observed:

As a literary method, Symbolism is only the consequence of the new attitude toward life, for which realistic description of reality by means of enumerating insignificant facts and details has lost all meaning, insofar as beyond these insignificant facts the depths of the depths have come to light. Hence the urge to communicate what is inexpressible in human language, through a synthesis of mood, by words, beyond which the infinite is divined.[84]

[84] Viktor Žirmunskij, *Nemeckij romantizm i sovremennaja mistika* (Peterburg, 1914), 195.

V

VASILIJ KAMENSKIJ

1. KAMENSKIJ AND THE FORMATION OF RUSSIAN FUTURISM

Vasilij Kamenskij was born in 1884 on a steamboat on the Kama River. His mother painted and his father was a goldfield inspector in the Urals. At the age of four, Kamenskij became an orphan; his aunt and uncle took him to Perm, where most of his childhood was spent on the banks and wharfs of the Kama River, which inspired in Kamenskij a profound zest for life, adventure, freedom and a desire to "explore unknown lands".[1] His childhood ambition was to become a poet, and he avidly read Puškin, Lermontov, and Nekrasov. One of Kamenskij's first poems concerns the Kama River:

Vesna otkryla Kamu,
A ja otkryl okno.
Začem, začem mne sirotoju
Ostat'sja suždeno?
Paroxodiki, voz'mite menja,
Uvezite v neizvestnye kraja.[2]

Spring opened up the Kama,
And I extended my horizons.
Why, O why am I fated
To remain an orphan?
Boats, take me,
Take me away to unknown lands.

In 1903, Kamenskij became interested in the theatre. He went to Moscow to take part in an actor's company which toured Russia. In 1905, he played a leading role in a general strike in Lower Tagila and gave political lectures and poetry readings to workers.[3] When the strike was

1 Vasilij Kamenskij, *Put' èntuziasta* (Moscow, 1931), 9.
2 Kamenskij, 22.
3 Kamenskij, 63.

suppressed, Kamenskij was arrested and placed in solitary confinement. He later fled to Constantinople and Teheran, where he also gave poetry readings.

In 1907, Kamenskij came to St. Petersburg to study agronomy and painting; the latter, as already noted, was rapidly becoming the dominant art form. A year later he published his poetry in the newly created journal *Vesna (Spring)*, and shortly after became its editor. Through this journal Kamenskij met Xlebnikov and published one of his works.[4] During this time Kamenskij also exhibited his impressionistic paintings at avant-garde exhibitions. In 1909, Kamenskij met David Burljuk, who introduced Kamenskij to his newly formed poetic circle. Kamenskij observes that he and Burljuk decided to organize a poetic movement and a united front of avant-garde artists.[5] After their art exhibition was unsuccessful, Burljuk and Kamenskij decided to publish the poetry of their circle, which came to be known as *Sadok sudej (A Trap for Judges)*. At this juncture Kamenskij introduced Xlebnikov to Burljuk and his circle and suggested that the neologistic orientation of Xlebnikov's poetry form the theoretical basis of their movement. Kamenskij must now be assigned a critical role in the formation of Russian Futurism.

When *Sadok sudej* failed to bring any recognition to the Burljuk circle, the restless and peripatetic Kamenskij turned to aviation and went to Italy, France, and Germany to fly there. In 1911, he survived a plane crash by falling into a swamp. He then took up farming and began to write his "Sten'ka Razin", who was Kamenskij's idol and childhood hero.

In 1913, Kamenskij joined Burljuk and Majakovskij so as to tour Russia and give lectures and poetry readings: Kamenskij comments on one of the notions about which he spoke during the tour:

> I developed the idea that we were the first poets in the world who were not bound by publishing poetry for the book stores, but that we were bringing our new art to the masses, streets, squares, stages. We desired to democratize our art and thus beautify life, to make it joyful, to create inspiration for it...[6]

The notion of bringing art and poetry to the streets and squares – which Kamenskij shared with Burljuk and Majakovskij – and the notion of 'revolt' in poetry and verbal play, 'revolt' against traditions, museum art, and the stagnation of society almost undoubtedly attracted Kamenskij

4 Kamenskij relates in his memoirs that Xlebnikov "literally jumped with joy when I brought him [Xlebnikov] the journal with the publication of his 'Sinner's Temptation'". See Kamenskij, 96.

5 Kamenskij, 103-104.

6 Kamenskij, 171.

to Futurism. In Kamenskij's poetic theory and practice this will be transparent.

2. KAMENSKIJ'S POETRY: THEORY AND PRACTICE

Kamenskij's poetic theory and practice are very much in accord with the fundamental premises of Russian Futurism as defined, for example, by a Futurist critic in 1916: "Contemporary poets [i.e., Futurists] have a different approach to the word. The form of the word, the yoking of letters, their shape, sound are more important than any possible meaning... Hence not a new symbol, but a new organization of the word – word creation."[7] Interestingly, in that same year Kamenskij's observations on the word were strikingly similar: "Contemporary poetry, the poetry of our time is clearly divided into two currents. The poets of the first current use the word only as a means, as a vehicle for expressing their poetic conceptions. The poets of the other, left current have advanced this watchword: down with the word-means, long live the self-contained, self-valued word."[8] After postulating the 'musical' orientation of the autotelic word, Kamenskij asserted the poet's right to his own, unique understanding and vision of 'poetic beauty' so as to discover new poetic paths.[9]

The revolt against meaning in poetry often led to anarchic verbal play. In this regard, Kručënyx has a strong rival in Kamenskij. Gusman notes that "Perhaps no one has felt the sound as an aim in itself, as a unique joy as Vasilij Kamenskij."[10] For example:

Zgara-amba
Zgara-amba
Zgara amba
Amb.
        Amb-zgara-amba
        Amb-zgara-amba
        Amb-zgara-amba
        Amb.
Šar-šor-šur-šir.
Čin-drax-tam-dzzz.[11]

[7] Celjunati, "Liriki", in *Moskovskie mastera. Žurnal iskusstv* (Moscow, 1916), 79.
[8] N. Stepanov, "Vasilij Kamenskij", in *Vasilij Kamenskij, Stixotvorenija i poèmy* (Moscow-Leningrad, 1966), 19.
[9] Stepanov, 19-20.
[10] B. Gusman, "Vasilij Kamenskij", in his *Sto poètov* (Moscow, 1923), 120.
[11] Vasilij Kamenskij, *Stixotovorenija i poèmy*, 121. Efrejmin notes that "Kamenskij is one of the apostles and masters of word creation as the basic principle of cubo-

Kamenskij's poetic theory also includes bizarre attempts to assign concepts and characteristics to Russian phonomes, a feature which he shares with Lomonosov,[12] Belyj, Bal'mont, Xlebnikov and Kručënyx. It may very well be that Xlebnikov influenced this aspect of Kamenskij's theory. For Kamenskij, sounds were concrete symbols of universal concepts and endowed with a 'destiny', 'existence', and 'character' of their own. He believed that the phoneme "ju" expressed feminality, movement, and excitement.[13]

Like Majakovskij's, Kamenskij's verbal play also extended to the 'breaking down' of words:

Izlučistaja
Lučistaja
Čistaja
Istaja
Staja
Taja
Aja
Ja.[14]

Broadly speaking, Kamenskij's poetry lacks the apocalyptic and urban orientation of that of the Russian Symbolists and Majakovskij. It rather breathes a deep joy of life and love of, and communion with, nature in all its manifestations. In 1922, Čukovskij observed that Kamenskij was "the gayest of contemporary poets; everywhere there are carousels, bells, carnival...His feeling toward life is not unlike that of a bird."[15] Such a mood was present in Kamenskij's poetry in 1909:

Žit' čudesno! Podumaj:
Utrom rano s pesnjami
Tebja razbudjat pticy –
O ne žalej nedovidennogo sna –
I vytaščat vzgljanut'
Na rozovoe, solnečnoe utro.[16]

futurism". See L. Efrejmin, "Tvorčeskij put' Vasilija Kamenskogo", in V. Kamenskij, *Izbrannye stixi* (Moscow-Leningrad, 1934), 7. See also A. Lunačarskij, "V. V. Kamenskij: K 25-letiju literaturnoj dejatel'nosti", in his *Sobranie sočinenij v vos'mi tomax*, II (Moscow, 1964), 539.

12 See Dmitry Chizhevsky, *History of Russian Literature from the Eleventh Century to the End of the Baroque* (The Hague, 1962), 420.

13 See Vasilij Kamenskij, *Ego-moja biografija velikogo futurista* (Moscow, 1918), 123-124. See also *Kamenskij*, *Put' èntuziasta*, 193-195, for other theoretical notions.

14 *Futuristy: Rykajuščij parnass* (Moscow, 1914), 46.

15 K. Čukovskij, *Futuristy* (Petrograd, 1922), 35, 37.

16 Kamenskij, *Stixotvorenija i poèmy*, 52.

Life is wonderful! Think a bit:
Early in the morning the birds
Awake you with songs –
O don't regret the unfinished dream –
And they'll pull you out to look
At the rosy, sunny morning.

One also senses a certain 'cosmism' and primitivism – a feature which Kamenskij shares with Xlebnikov – in his poetry.[17] Like Majakovskij, Kamenskij is also a lyrical – and dramatic – poet. His poetry is conversationally oriented and meant to be declaimed, or sung, or both; and many of his poems are written as though they were musical compositions.[18] Efrejmin considers Kamenskij "one of the creators of Russian auditory [*sluxovoj*] poetry".[19]

The notion of a mass peasant revolt is central to Kamenskij's major works, especially his *The Heart of the People is Sten'ka Razin* (1918);[20] this notion of revolt yokes his poetry to Russian Futurism.[21] Kamenskij wrote the work between 1912-1918, and recited excerpts at many poetry readings in his tour of Russia. Like Xlebnikov and the Russian Symbolists, Kamenskij turned to folklore and history to interpret the *present*, to resurrect the past as the present, or to create, as Brjusov put it, "new myths".[22] This orientation towards "historical figures and events took on", as Men'šutin and Sinjavskij rightly note, "not so much an independent significance as they served as a means of expressing thoughts and feelings directly linked with contemporary life".[23] Kamenskij himself observed in his memoirs that his dream was to build a bridge between Razin and contemporary life.[24]

Here a brief historical account of Razin's revolt will be useful. In 1670, Razin, a Don Cossack, led a revolt in the Lower Don region in the name

17 E. Beskin, in "O poètičeskom tvorčestve V. V. Kamenskogo", *Literaturnaja gazeta*, March 29, 1933, took Kamenskij to task for the "cosmism" in his poetic interpretation "of the social tasks and perspectives of the Revolution, long rejected by Soviet poetry".
18 Lunačarskij, 539.
19 Efrejmin, 7.
20 Kamenskij also wrote a novel *Sten'ka Razin* (1916). His other major poetic works include *Emel'jan Pugačëv* (1931) and *Ivan Bolotnikov* (1934).
21 Vladimir Markov points out that the 'theme of revolt' is a basic feature of Russian Futurist poetry (*The Longer Poems of Velimir Xlebnikov* [Berkeley, 1962], 61). Notably, Stepan Razin also was of particular fascination for Xlebnikov. See his *Razin* (1920), and *Razin's Boats* (1922).
22 Valerij Brjusov, "Smysl sovremennoj poèzij", in his *Izbrannye sočinenija v dvux tomax*, II (Moscow, 1955), 327.
23 A. Men'šutin and A. Sinjavskij, *Poèzija pervyx let revoljucij* (Moscow, 1964), 197.
24 Kamenskij, *Put' èntuziasta*, 208.

of freedom for discontented peasants and serfs. Escape or revolt was the only possible reaction of peasants and serfs against serfdom. Razin's revolt drew strength from non-Russians: the Tatars, Chuvaš, Mari, Mordva and others. Significantly, the revolt was not against the Russian Tsar, but against his 'favorites' and 'traitors' – the landowners, who were killed and whose land was plundered during the revolt. Thus, the revolt assumed the character of a class war. In 1671, the revolt was crushed and Razin was executed. He thereafter embodied the hopes and aspirations of the weak, poor and oppressed who believed that Razin was destined to return to liberate them.[25]

The folklore on Razin is, to be sure, not without interest. Puškin considered Razin "the only poetic figure in Russian history".[26] In Russian folklore, Razin has a solid tradition and is one of the richest cycles of an historical hero which penetrated almost every region of Russia. Lozanova points out that "In prerevolutionary folklore, perhaps there is not a single historical and epic hero about whom so many songs, stories, legends and tales have been created. This is the most convincing proof of the extent to which Razin exists in the minds of the masses."[27]

The folklore on Razin is also relevant for an understanding of the Russian revolutionary mentality during the beginning of the twentieth century. The memory of Razin was apparently evoked by the 1905 Russian revolution, and then slowly and firmly gripped the Russian imagination.[28] The Bolshevik revolution did nothing to stifle this folklore, which, in fact, took on added significance because of it.[29] After a folklore

25 For a detailed account of Razin's revolt, see for example "Krest'janskaja vojna pod predvoditel'stvom S. T. Razina", in *Očerki istorij SSSR: period feodalizma XVII v.*, A. Novsel'skij and N. Ustjugov, eds. (Moscow, 1955), 277-308.

26 Aleksandr S. Puškin, *Polnoe sobranie sočinenij v desjati tomax* (Moscow, 1966), X, 108.

27 A. Lozanova, "Krest'janskie vosstanija XVII-XVIII vv., v ustno–poètičeskom tvorčestve", in *Pesni i skazanija o Razine i Pugačeve* (Moscow-Leningrad, 1928), LV.

28 Notably, during the 1890's Razin finds expression in Russian literature. See *Russkaja literatura konca XIX – načala XX v. Devjanostye gody*, B. Bjalik, ed. (Moscow, 1968), 164, 187, 234.

29 Men'šutin and Sinjavskij note that during the Bolshevik revolution "scores of authors of the most different persuasion" wrote about Razin to express the "raging people's element" (177). A very recent study of the reaction of the provinces to the revolution observes that in the Urals pro-Bolshevik "combat squads...began to operate independently, committing anarchistic excesses more evocative of the *Pugačovščina* than of a Marxist revolution" (John Keep, "October in the Provinces", in *Revolutionary Russia*, Richard Pipes, ed. [Cambridge, 1968], 197). It was perhaps more evocative of *Razinščina*. As for the prevalent view of Lenin in the provinces during the revolution, Keep remarks that "Lenin appeared more as an image than as an individual" (221).

expedition in the Lower Volga region in 1920 and 1922, Sokolov observed that the "legends compiled in our region about him alone [i.e. Razin] could make up a whole book".[30] Even in 1926, Piksanov remarked that the "power of Razin over the Russian consciousness in our time has been revealed as never before".[31]

Kamenskij's work on Razin, one of his best and quite popular during the revolutionary years,[32] belongs to the anarchistic and utopian prophecy of the time. Kamenskij sees the 1917 Revolution as an elemental and national revolt against the nobility. The revolt, in which for Kamenskij everyone becomes Razin himself, is made in the name of Mother Russia – which is symbolized by the Volga River – its peasantry and poor and extends to the Asian peoples, who are called upon to join. The revolt is a call for a wild celebration of 'total freedom' *(volja)*:

Za narod – za sermjažnyj da bednyj
Da za Rus' udaluju svoju –
Ja o tom, čto izžito – izvedeno
So slezami o vole poju.
Dlja menja volja vol'naja slašče
I p'janee ljubvi i vina –
Liš' by žizn' molodeckaja čašče
Byla družboj edinoj sil'na.[33]

For the people – for peasant and poor
And for my daring Russia –
I sing with tears of total freedom
Of what has been overcome – destroyed.
For me boundless freedom is sweeter
And more intoxicating than love and wine –
If only a valiant life more often be
Powerful as common friendship.

Soon, however, the notion of 'total freedom' yields to a Symbolist and Futurist vision of 'brotherly life' and a new world of harmony and human solidarity.

Budet den' – i otkroet vorota
Každyi – dlja vol'nyx gostej
Čtoby v žizni ljubaja zabota
Byla ravnoj dlja ravnyx zatej

[30] See Lozanova, "Predanija i rasskazy o Stepane Razine", in *Pesni i skazanija...*, 73-74.
[31] N. Piksanov, "Social'no-političeskie sud'by pesen o Stepane Razine", *Xudožestvennyj fol'klor*, No. 1 (1926), 57.
[32] See for example, Men'šutin and Sinjavskij, 179.
[33] Kamenskij, *Stixotvorenija i poèmy*, 460-461.

Budet den' – i zakružatsja kružno
V xorovodax naveki druz'ja –
I spletuxja vse ruki zadružno
Bednjaki – i kupcy – i knjaz'ja.
Budet den' – vse v sem'ju soberutsja
Pod edinym zavetnym oknom
I togda èti pesni prol'jutsja
V serdce každogo krepkim vinom.
Budet den'.[34]

The day will come, and everyone
Will open the gates for free guests
So that in life every care
Be equal for equal undertakings
The day will come – and friends will begin
To whirl in dances forever
The poor, and the merchants and the princes.
The day will come – all will gather as a family
Under a united cherished window
And then these songs will pour forth
Into the hearts of each like heady wine.
The day will come.

3. CONCLUSION

After the end of the Futurist tour in 1914, Kamenskij wrote poetry for journals and became involved in literary, theatrical, and artistic circles. He also maintained close ties with the Futurists and was a frequent visitor at the Briks', which Kamenskij aptly termed the new "headquarters" of Russian Futurism.[35] To be sure, he also toured Russia once again to declaim and sing his poetry, to lecture on the "creative joys of life" and on the Futurists, whom he believed were creating a new art and who were dedicated to a "new beauty of life".[36]

In March, 1917, Kamenskij organized in Moscow the "First Republican Evening of the Arts", which Burljuk, Majakovskij, Tatlin and Malevič and others attended. Kamenskij observes that "Everyone spoke of the need to bring their craft to the streets, to give art to the mass workers, for these democratic tasks were always part of the Futurist program."[37]

[34] *Stixotvorenija i poèmy*, 469.
[35] Kamenskij, *Put' èntuziasta*, 231.
[36] See Stepanov, 15-16.
[37] Kamenskij, *Put' èntuziasta*, 247.

With the advent of the Bolshevik revolution, Kamenskij saw it as an expression of "social justice" and as a force that would transform Russia into a festival of creative freedom and activity.[38] Like Majakovskij and Burljuk, Kamenskij also issued his 'decree' to poets and artists:

Poety!
Berite kisty, nu,
I afiši – listy so stixami,
Po ulicam s lestnicej
Raskleivajte žizni istinu, –

...
Xudožniki!
Velikie Burljuki,
Pribivajte k domam karnaval'no
Jarčajsie svoj kartiny,
Taščite s plakatami tjuki,
Raspisyvajte steny genjal'no,
I ploščadi, i vyveski, i vitriny.[39]

Poets!
Take your brushes, now,
And posters – sheets of poetry,
Paste the truth of life
Along the streets with a ladder –

...
Artists!
Great Burljuks,
Put on your brightest painting
On homes like a carnival,
Carry your bales with placards,
Paint the walls brilliantly,
And the squares, signboards, and store windows.

During the revolutionary years, Kamenskij organized with Majakovskij and Burljuk the "Café of Poets", celebrated the Revolution in numerous poetry readings and wrote for Futurist publications. He also served as a cultural worker for the Southern Bolshevik Army, perhaps out of an inherent need to travel. In the nineteen-twenties, Kamenskij did not play a very active role in Futurism. Although he published some of his 'trans-sense' poetry in *Lef* and vigorously supported the Futurists, Kamenskij devoted most of his time to writing plays and novels as the

[38] See Kamenskij, *Èto i est' biografija* (Tiflis, 1927), 5 and *Put' èntuziasta*, 265.
[39] Kamenskij, *Stixotvorenija i poèmy*, 111.

fierce and often unedifying polemics raged between literary factions. His two autobiographies – *This Also is a Biography* (1929), and *The Career of an Enthusiast* (1931) – should be viewed as his contributions to the Futurist-Formalist 'literature of fact'. In 1931, a year after the dissolution of Futurism, Kamenskij remarked in an apparent attempt to defend the Futurists in the face of their defeat:

It is true that as 'members of various rank' we were never proletarian poets, and although we had no great understanding of the ideology of scientific Marxism, we always acted in the interests of the revolutionary proletariat, beginning with 1905.

In this admission there is no stretching of the point or evasion, for all our activity was open and many works speak in our behalf.[40]

Kamenskij would not compromise on one of the cardinal Futurist principles:

I will not argue that perhaps some of the Futurists – including myself above all – were greatly inspired by an enthusiasm for 'form', even if overdone. This 'laboratory,' however, is indispensible for craftmanship so as to compel the WORD to serve a true purpose – to exalt content.[41]

Finally, Kamenskij's poetry is part of the Symbolist and Futurist revolt against urban society and industrialism. To understand this revolt, one must seek its mainsprings in the artist's alienation and disaffection from a society which created uncertainty as to his audience, means of support, function and role. In this regard, Kamenskij's supreme efforts to bring his poetry to the streets cannot be ignored.

40 Kamenskij, *Put' èntuziasta*, 253.
41 *Put' èntuziasta*, 195.

VI

EARLY RUSSIAN FUTURISM IN PERSPECTIVE

Early Russian Futurism was a most complex literary and historical phenomenon. If one attempts to see it as a 'unified movement', one is faced with the absurdity of accepting Majakovskij and Burljuk as practitioners of 'trans-sense language' and Xlebnikov and Kručënyx and Kamenskij as poets of the city. This is not to say, however, that there were no unifying elements within Futurism. One critic was close to the mark in noting in 1914 that "a slap in the face of public taste" united the Futurists.[1] Livšic pointed out in his memoirs that Futurism "was a stream of heterogenous and diversely oriented minds whose characteristic was above all *the unity of negative goals*".[2] These negative goals appear to have been the revolt against the language of the Symbolists, literary tradition and society.

The Futurists' revolt against tradition was partly polemical and programmatic. Their antagonism towards Puškin and Dostoevskij was an effort to define themselves, their own aims, to chart their own poetic quest. This antagonism towards tradition was not confined to extremist movements, as Poggioli observes, "it belongs also to the more moderate moderns..."[3] As for the Futurists' 'nihilistic' revolt against society, Poggioli remarks that "its true significance is a revolt of the modern artist against the spiritual and social ambience in which he is destined to be born and to grow and to die".[4]

This aspect of revolt, along with experimentalism, links Russian

[1] See *Pervyj žurnal russkix futuristov*, No. 1-2 (Moscow, 1914), 126.

[2] Benedikt Livšic, *Polutoraglazyj strelec* (Leningrad, 1933), 282.

[3] Renato Poggioli, *The Theory of the Avant-Garde* (Cambridge, 1968), 53. Even Brjusov, despite all his protestations against ideological art, observed in a review of new poetic currents in 1913 that "in the protest of the futurists there is also a 'truth,' inasmuch as they are revolting against that 'common realm' to which our poetry has begun to give way for the last few years" ("Novye tečenija v russkoj poèzij", *Russkaja mysl'*, No. 3 [1913], 133).

[4] Poggioli, 64.

Futurism to the phenomenon of 'modernism'. Like their Western counterparts – Yeats, Pound, Eliot, Breton, Eluard, Aragon – the Russian Futurists used poetry as a weapon against the moral and spiritual disintegration of society, against its barrenness and religious void which were products of industrialism. Poetry and art became a kind of temple in which these poets rediscovered and recreated the values of the past which they believed would reappear in the future, and which they opposed to a chaotic reality. Moreover, they believed that their poetic visions of universal harmony and the re-creation of the past would inspire their creation in actuality.

When one discusses the strong anarchic strain of the Futurists, one can see that it stemmed from their literary and social revolt and from a compassion for human suffering (Majakovskij and Xlebnikov). Political anarchy seems to have added fuel to their drive for 'liberation'. Čukovskij noted that early Russian Futurism was an expression of anarchic revolt against culture, esthetic canons, urbanism, industrialism and its transformation of human life.[5] These are some of the basic features of the modern avant-garde artist:

> ...the avant-garde artist means to react not so much against society itself as against the civilization created by the society. To him the mass culture looms as a pseudo-culture, against whose specious values he directs his revolt. Faithful to a qualitative system of values, the modern artist, faced with the quantitative values of modern society, feels both left out and rebellious. This state of mind has practical social consequences, but above all it arouses in the modern artist, a particular anguish: a consciousness that artists of other times and civilizations never felt so rejected or isolated, even if they were infinitely less free. From this feeling of isolation emerge dreams of revolution or reaction, of past and future utopias, and other equally impossible visions of new orders to come or old ones revived.[6]

As noted, Majakovskij and Xlebnikov were certainly not without their "impossible visions of new orders to come or old ones revived". This notion, however, was both the legacy and the injunction of the Russian Symbolists, especially of Belyj and Ivanov.[7] The poet was called upon

[5] Kornej Čukovskij, "Futuristy", in his *Lica i maski* (St. Peterburg, 1914), 134-135.
[6] Renato Poggioli, "The Artist in the Modern World", in his *The Spirit of the Letter: Essays in European Literature* (Cambridge, 1965), 324-325.
[7] "Out of art will come a new life – and the salvation of mankind" (A. Belyi, "Venok ili venec", *Apollon*, No. 11 [1910], 3). See also Vjačeslav Ivanov, "Mysli o simvolizme", in his *Borozdy i meži* (Moscow, 1916), 160-162. Some Symbolists, however, saw in poetry a means of personal salvation. For example, Gippius: "Until we find a common God, or at least understand that we are all aspiring to Him, to Him alone, until then our prayers and our poetry, living for each of us, will not be intelligible or necessary to anyone" (Quoted in Georgij Plexanov, *Literatura i èstetika*, II [Moscow, 1958], 487).

to change or transform the world, to discover or create the meaning of history,[8] to provide a moral vision of the future that would be the very antithesis of the banal and abominable reality in which he lived and which he often distorted in his poetry.

For this reason, the ideological similarities between Majakovskij and Xlebnikov, despite the basic differences in their poetic orientation, are so striking. They both lived in an age in which it was quite difficult not to be a Symbolist. Like the Russian Symbolists, both saw themselves not merely as poets, but as prophets and saviors of humanity.[9] Like the Russian Symbolists, both were obsessed with one grandiose mythopoeic vision of universal harmony and solidarity, which assumed the character of a religious hope or belief. With Xlebnikov, this harmony was possible only in the natural harmony of prehistory. With Majakovskij, it was possible only in future Universal City of Man in which secular humanism would reign supreme. Moreover, both Majakovskij and Xlebnikov reacted against the despair of the literature and poetry of their age. Both reacted against the violence and destruction of their time from moral motivation. As earthly exiles, both revolted against their society in their art because of their social disaffection and material instability.[10] Art almost came to be a way of defining the limits of rebellion. Their struggle against history and time developed from their impatience with, and rejection of, reality as they experienced it; hence, too, their passion for unity with the universe.

Because of this ideological affinity with Symbolism, world view obviously could not have played a role in Futurism's reaction against Symbolism. Ivanov-Razumnik observed that "the transformation of the world about which symbolism spoke was also proclaimed by futurism".[11] On the contrary, literary devices, emphasis on new poetic forms, and more significantly perhaps, a fundamental reorientation of *language* were the dominant factors. The literary devices, as already noted, were ap-

[8] In a lecture at Cornell University on April 8, 1968, Alexander Schmeman, Dean of St. Vladimir's Orthodox Seminary, pointed out that the obsession with the 'meaning' and 'finality' of history is one of the major features of Russian religious thought.

[9] Like Xlebnikov, Majakovskij also ventured a prediction of a revolution: "...in the thorny crown of revolutions, the year 1916 is drawing near." See Vladimir Majakovskij, *Polnoe sobranie sočinenij*, I (Moscow, 1955-1961), 185.

[10] Kornej Čukovskij, in "Majakovskij", in his *Sobranie proizvedenij*, II (Moscow, 1965), 352-353, relates that in the prerevolutionary years Majakovskij "was in extreme need", "hardly ate daily", and a "peg" was the only piece of "furniture" in his room. With Xlebnikov, the situation was no different.

[11] R. Ivanov-Razumnik, *Vladimir Majakovskij* (Berlin, 1922), 23.

parently inspired by Cubism whose principles the Futurists grafted onto poetry. The notion of the self-contained word in particular was derived from Cubism. Poetry, like Cubism, was seen as a distortion of reality, as a state of flux, as a deliberate mixture or 'shift' of meters and linguistic styles. In this connection, Tynjanov's remark, although more directed to literary evolution, seems to be relevant: "Strictly speaking, every deformation, every 'mistake', every 'irregularity' of normative poetics is potentially a new constructive principle...like the means of the semantic shift of the Futurists."[12] Šklovskij saw the function of poetry as the reestablishment of the palpability of reality, the freshening of perception which was to be achieved by distortion, by 'impeded form' *(zatrudnennaja forma)*, and by 'making-it-strange' *(ostranenie)*. Šklovskij observed that words and objects, when they fail to arouse perception, are 'resurrected' by new literary devices. Šklovskij saw the 'shift' and esthetic deformation as the central factors in the renewal of perception of reality. This for him was the cardinal function of poetry.[13] For Žirmunskij, these devices were teleologically motivated by the Futurists' desire to "reject a boring and exhausted literary tradition".[14] Concerning language, Èjxenbaum noted that the Russian Symbolists had divorced poetic language from "living language", from "living intonations", and from oral delivery *(proiznesenie)*.[15] It was thus natural, he continued, that poets wanted to "direct their efforts to restore the word, to orient poetry towards living language by subjecting poetry to a dynamic, motor principle".[16] Èjxenbaum went on to explain that the "interest of the Futurists in the meaningless word, in 'trans-sense language' resulted from their desire to sense anew namely the oral semantic element of the word – not the word as a symbolic sound, but the word as a direct articulation which has real meaning".[17] Thus the key to the literary problem of evolving a new poetic style and forms consisted in language – primarily the language of the street. One recalls that Majakovskij, Burljuk, and Kamenskij wanted to bring poetry and art to the streets. "The loud oratorical word", Èjxenbaum remarked, "had to replace the soft, intimately lyrical language."[18]

12 Jurij Tynjanov, "O literaturnom fakte", *Lef*, No. 2 (1924), 109.
13 See Livšic, 201.
14 Viktor Žirmunskij, rev. of Roman Jakobson, *Novejšaja russkaja poèzija* (Prague, 1921), *Načala*, No. 2 (1919), 215.
15 Boris Èjxenbaum, *Anna Axmatova. Opyt analiza* (Peterburg, 1923), 64.
16 Èjxenbaum, 64.
17 *Ibid.*
18 Èjxenbaum, 65.

Finally Brjusov rightly saw the significance of Russian Futurism in its emphasis on language as "the material of poetry...that this material can and should be cultivated by poets in accordance with the aims of creative art".[19] This emphasis on, and experimentation with, language in poetry gave rise almost directly to Russian Formalism, which was closely associated with Futurism until 1930.[20] Perhaps of equal significance were Majakovskij's, Burljuk's, and Kamenskij's efforts to confront the problem of the divorce between artist and society, between art and life, between the language of poetry and the language of the street. This is quite clearly evident in their notion that art and poetry be brought to the streets and auditoriums. This appears to be in Markov's view "in the symbolist tradition of merging Life and Art".[21] The Futurists, as noted, were largely social exiles whose isolation and poverty nourished the urge to rebellion and martyrdom (Majakovskij), to solipsism (Kručënyx), and to the creation of utopian projects (Xlebnikov). Evgen'ev-Maksimov observed that it would be a serious mistake to assume that the Futurists' rebellion was limited to language and esthetics. He considered the Futurists as "representatives of that layer of urban intellectuals who had no materially secure place in the bourgeois world and were alien to its productive system".[22] In his observations on prerevolutionary Futurism, the Futurist poet Aseev remarked that, "by bringing literature out of the study rooms and garrets onto the streets", the Futurists tried to find "a new consumer" instead of working for "an impersonal market".[23]

This notion of integrating the artist into society, of "merging Life and Art", of finding "a new consumer", had its theoretical and practical premises – however utopian or vague – in the prerevolutionary years. Immediately after the Bolshevik revolution, this notion emerged with sudden and dramatic urgency and assumed several forms throughout the 1920's. The Futurists and Formalists advanced it at first with a sense of grave crisis – a major feature of their mentality – and later with the aim of solving literary problems which they believe were raised by the revolutionary era.

[19] Valerij Brjusov, "Včera, segodnja i zavtra russkoj poèzij", *Pečat' i Revoljucija*, No. 7 (1922), 65.
[20] See Victor Erlich, *Russian Formalism: History-Doctrine*, 2nd, rev. ed. (The Hague, 1965), 42-50.
[21] Vladimir Markov, *The Longer Poems of Velimir Xlebnikov* (Berkeley, 1962), 62.
[22] V. Evgen'ev-Maksimov, *Očerki istorij novejšej russkoj literatury* (Moscow-Leningrad, 1927), 211.
[23] Nikolaj Aseev, "Majakovskij", in *Almanax s Majakovskim* (Moscow, 1934), 20.

One of the central aims of the Futurists (and Formalists) was to realize that notion of integrating the artist into society – to make him an active and leading participant in the events of his time. The historical denouement of that notion will now come under discussion.

VII

FUTURISM IN THE POSTREVOLUTIONARY PERIOD

1. THE FUTURISTS AND THE ARTISTIC AVANT-GARDE

Despite the political turbulence that raged between 1917-1921, the revolutionary years were artistically active and creative. In 1920, Avram Èfros, an avant-garde leader, correctly noted that a great experiment had been made in the autonomy of art, resulting in a "reform of artistic education – plastic, musical, dramatic – and a rapid development of artistic institutions in all spheres of art throughout the whole country".[1] One of the largest and most significant art exhibitions took place during this period of turmoil, when three hundred fifty nine artists exhibited their works in the Palace of Arts in Petrograd.[2] In 1920, Vasilij Kandinskij appealed to all artists of the world to come to Russia for the First World Congress of Arts in order to discuss the forms and problems of past and future art.[3] In 1930, Jakov Tugendxol'd looked back on the revolutionary years with intense yearning and characterized them as one of creative ferment and fervor, when young artists emerged from the underground and took to the streets to unleash their artistic energies.[4] Tugendxol'd added that artists frequently met then to discuss and reappraise fundamental artistic problems and values and to debate the relevance of 'tradition' to their age; many artists saw art as a means of "creating a new environment, a new living atmosphere, a new formation of the whole of life". Art, they passionately believed, would transform "the very face of life"

[1] Avram Èfros, "My i zapad", *Xudožestvennaja žizn'*, No. 2 (1920), 1.

[2] See *Obzor dejatel'nosti izobrazitel'nyx iskusstv* (Petrograd, 1920), 88.

[3] Vasilij Kandinskij, "O Velikoj Utopij", *Xudozestvennaja žizn'*, No. 3 (1920), 2-4. The article's title is significant.

[4] Jakov Tugendxol'd, *Iskusstvo oktjabr'skoj èpoxi* (Leningrad, 1930), 16. In one of the very few addresses to artists during the revolutionary years, the Bolshevik regime encouraged this activity and remarked that once artists merged with the masses, they "would never return to their loneliness" ("K xudožnikam i artistam", *Pravda*, April 16, 1920).

and project society "into the future, into the Kingdom of the Commune".[5] These utopian notions and apocalyptic expectations, which the Revolution inspired, dominated the minds of many Russians. At the peak of the revolutionary upheaval in 1919, Anatolij Lunačarskij remarked optimistically: "Our land is being turned into a paradise, and is being made under the dictatorship of human genius. I am certain that the heights that will be achieved in the field of art under socialism will exceed all that has been created on this earth up to this time."[6] The avant-garde artists who headed the Section of Fine Arts shared this optimism: "The Board is completely convinced that in the coming two-to-three years Europe will witness the extraordinary flowering of Russian artistic life. The proletariat will destroy all the obstacles, will smash all the chains that bind free artistic activity; and that is why the government is concerned with the free development of proletarian culture, as never before in history has any other government been concerned with a similar endeavor."[7] It is against this background that one must view the avant-garde's efforts to consummate an unprecedented artistic revolution.

Three months after the Bolsheviks seized power, Lunačarskij, the newly appointed Commissar of Education *(Narkompros)*, called upon the Union of Artists to join in the regime's efforts to organize and sustain the artistic life of the country. He assured it that the new regime would pursue a policy of strict neutrality towards all art groups and would favor their free development, even with financial support. The Union of Artists, composed of heterogeneous art groups but headed primarily by artists and bureaucrats oriented towards "official", "realistic", and "academic" art, largely opposed the Bolshevik regime, and did not expect it to triumph or survive for long. Several months of negotiations for a *modus vivendi* between Lunačarskij and the Union's leaders proved fruitless. By June 1918, however, the Union of Artists was willing to collaborate with Lunačarskij on the condition that a 'select' group control the Section of Fine Arts under the new regime with the guarantee of complete autonomy. Lunačarskij found this unacceptable. He believed that the "renowned old leaders" would perpetuate the cumbersome bureaucracy of the Union of Artists which he wanted to eliminate as a "remnant of Czarist institu-

[5] Tugendxol'd, 16.

[6] Quoted in Howard Holter, "A. V. Lunačarskij and the Formulation of a Policy Towards the Arts in the RSFSR 1921-1927", Unpublished Doctoral Dissertation, University of Wisconsin, 1967, 30.

[7] "Otčet o dejatel'nosti Otdela izobrazitel'nyx iskusstv", *Vestnik narodnogo prosveščenija sojuza severnoj oblasti*, No. 6-8 (1918), 87.

tions". He also feared that they would 'sabotage' the regime's art policy and alienate and discriminate against a small group of avant-garde artists who supported the Bolshevik regime and who were hostile to the Union of Artists.[8] Two alternatives thus faced Lunačarskij: to turn to avant-garde artists against the will of the leaders (and many members) of the Union of Artists, or to face the prospect of artistic paralysis of the country which could only arouse further resistance to the Bolshevik regime. The first alternative would also arouse resistance to the regime! He decided to do the former.

The avant-garde, which included the Russian Cubo-Futurists, consisted of artists and critics who were largely oriented towards West-European art movements – primarily Cubism and Impressionism – and emphasized the centrality of formal experimentation in art. The key figures were: David Šterenburg, Nikolaj Punin, Natan Al'tman, Aleksandr Rodčenko, Kazimir Malevič, Marc Chagall, Vladimir Tatlin, Vasilij Kandinskij, Vladimir Majakovskij, Osip Brik and Viktor Šklovskij. In June 1918, they accepted Lunačarskij's offer to run the *Narkompros*' Section of Fine Arts, with the task of "constructing and organizing all art schools and the entire art life of the country".[9] The avant-garde and the Cubo-Futurists saw a political alliance with the new regime as a necessary prelude to the realization of their esthetic aims; at least they appeared to equate collaboration with their control of the Section. They believed that their anti-bourgeois orientation during the pre-revolutionary period constituted valid credentials for interpreting the shape and direction of revolutionary art. Vjačeslav Polonskij rightly pointed out that the avant-garde's contempt for literary and artistic idols and their passion for formal innovation made them natural allies of the new regime. As the most oppressed literary and art group of pre-revolutionary society, the avant-garde had nothing to lose by joining the new regime and linked their own fate with it.[10]

There were other reasons for Lunačarskij's acceptance of the avant-garde. He undoubtedly sympathized with their struggle for artistic recognition during the pre-revolutionary era. He admired their art and

[8] "Iz literaturnogo nasledstva A. V. Lunačarskogo", *Novyj mir*, No. 9 (1966), 236-239. See also Osip Brik, "Majakovskij – redaktor i organizator", *Literaturnyj kritik*, No. 4 (1936), 114-116, and Nikolaj Punin, "V dni krasnogo oktjabrja", *Žizn' iskusstva*, No. 816, November 18, 1921.

[9] "Otčet o dejatel'nosti izobrazitel'nyx iskusstv", 82.

[10] Vjačeslav Polonskij, *Očerki literaturnogo dviženija revoljucionnoj èpoxi* (Moscow-Leningrad, 1929), 25.

considered it an important factor in the development of 'proletarian' art. Their views on artistic reform coincided with his own. Boris Kušner, a Cubo-Futurist, had written a manifesto in 1917 on behalf of the avant-garde. He pointed out the need to guarantee the right to exist of all art movements, to create the most favorable conditions so that fresh and creative forces would be brought into the art world and to make all works of art available to all people.[11] What is more, Lunačarskij considered the avant-garde more reliable politically. For him, they possessed the daring and vitality to carry out necessary reforms. As he later recalled: "Even relatively left-wing artists would have been frightened at the time by the need to struggle with the almost age-old foundations of artistic life. In this connection, a great deal of fervor, faith and, perhaps, youthful zeal were necessary. That is why I vigorously supported the youth who gathered around Comrade Šterenburg..."[12]

The avant-garde and the Cubo-Futurists thus became commissars of art; as Trotsky put, they "reigned almost unchallenged" in the Section of Fine Arts.[13] They were profoundly aware of the unique historical character of their political power, their experiments and views: "It is quite possible that in our views we will be at times quite daring and hence prone to mistakes", Šterenburg remarked. "Well, what of it! We live and work in such an epoch where even mistakes have profound significance."[14] In October 1918, The Section outlined its plans for the artistic organization of the country. Its principle aim was to create the conditions and opportunities for the growth of a "great artistic culture". To achieve this aim, the Section promised the free development of all movements. It planned to buy all different types of art works for showing in Russian and West-European museums.[15] Art schools were to be built to attract

[11] Boris Kušner, *Demokratizacija iskusstva* (Petrograd, 1917), 7. In effect, Kušner's views became the policy of the Section.

[12] "Iz literaturnogo nasledstva A. V. Lunačarskogo", 238. Lunačarskij observes that he chose Šterenberg to lead the Section because he was a personal friend, a supporter of the regime, the most suitable candidate, an outstanding artist, and quite knowledgeable about West-European art life.

[13] Leon Trotsky, *Literature and Revolution* (Ann Arbor, 1960), 111.

[14] David Šterenburg, "Ot redakcij", *Izobrazitel'noe iskusstvo*, No. 1 (1918), 6.

[15] One of these exhibits in 1918, designed to "show the state of contemporary Russian art", was open to all who wished to participate. Interestingly, the regime cautiously noted that it would not bear any responsibility for the works at the exhibit. See "Vseobščaja xudožestvennaja vystavka", *Plamja*, No. 22 (1918), 360-361. For some reviews of art exhibits, see A. Sidorov, "Xudozestvennye vystavki", *Tvorčestvo. Žurnal literatury, iskusstva i nauki*, No. 2-4 (1920), 34-35, and D. Mel'nikov, "Po povodu 'levoj' živopisi na 19-i gosudarstvennoj vystavke", *Ibid*, No. 7-10 (1920), 42-44.

"fresh proletarian forces" into the art life of the country.[16] Public debates and lectures on art were also planned. The Section wanted to introduce courses on art history into public education. Esthetic principles were to be introduced into industrial production. The Section dreamed of the physical transformation of the country: "Considering that our cities must be esthetically beautiful, the Board is taking a number of measures to come to the aid of urban construction, to develop it systematically and to deliver it from the chaos in which it now finds itself. Everyone knows that our homes look like boxes or graves... The Board is thus striving to create an artistically constructive apparatus which will take up the task of rebuilding our cities, to transform the squares and markets, to change the form of streets etc."[17]

To be sure, the Section was also concerned with countering the enormous resistance to its exercise of power. It believed that lectures and debates on the principles of avant-garde art would create a climate of tolerance and thus erode resistance to its authority. In a series of lectures to art instructors, Punin, one of the most learned art critics of the time, gave a broad survey of the major trends in West European art and identified the Russian avant-garde with them. He defined the avant-garde artist as a creatively spontaneous and inventive individual who has no teachers in the past, who violates all artistic canons and rules in an effort to "enrich humanity with new artistic principles" and to create "paths to new artistic possibilities". As Punin saw it, the major aim of artistic activity was to transform the world through new forms of beauty. What distinguished the avant-garde artist from 'old artists' was the lack of any philosophical or moral content in his art. Formal experimentation was the content of avant-garde art. In concluding his lectures, Punin remarked: "I think that after we part, within the limits of this course, you will leave here less prejudiced against young artists than before."[18]

The avant-garde's most trenchant theoretician, Osip Brik, observed in a lecture that an evaluation of the phenomena of contemporary artistic life had to be made in terms of the Bolshevik Revolution, and

[16] The pedagogical principles of the art schools were formulated in *Vestnik narodnogo prosveščenija sojuza severnoj oblasti*, No. 4-5 (1919), 21-28.

[17] David Šterenburg, "Raskrepoščenie iskusstva", *Vestnik žizni*, No. 3-4 (1919), 108.

[18] Nikolaj Punin, *Pervyj cikl lekcij, čitannyx na kratkosročnyx kursax dlja učitelej risovanija* (Petrograd, 1920), 7, 11, 33, 35, 51, 83. For an art debate in which Punin participated, see "Disput ob iskusstve", *Žizn' iskusstva*, May 16, 1919. For Punin's lecture on Picasso, see "Lekcija o Picasso", *Ibid*, October 17, 1919. Malevič began lecturing before the Section was organized; his lectures were published in the May and June issues of the newspaper *Anarxija*, 1918.

not in terms of the petty struggles of various art movements. He added that he did not believe in the "internal autonomy of art". He noted that every social movement entailed the revaluation of the whole of the past. Brik described the aim of socialist-artistic culture as the quest for new forms of artistic perception and new methods of cooperative work. His audience offered no sharp opposition to his basic premises, but the discussion that followed was lively and mainly concerned objections against the avant-garde as functionaries of the state and against the 'destructive tendencies' of their art.[19]

In their eagerness to assert the validity of their artistic principles, the avant-garde could not, however, resist attacking the art of the past. They called 'academic' art of the prerevolutionary period stifling, unoriginal and monotonous. Majakovskij, the 'poet of the Revolution', echoed this mood poetically:

> Enough of the petty truths!
> Erase the past from your hearts!
> The streets are our paint-brushes,
> The squares are our palettes![20]

The avant-garde believed that the orientation of pre-revolutionary art towards feeble and mindless imitation of old artistic forms and blind adherence to the artistic canons of realism merely produced stagnation and decay and stifled individual creativity. Young artists were thereby deprived of the opportunity to select their own sources of inspiration and instruction.[21] Art academies also precluded the growth and development and competition of art movements. Academic art, bureaucratized, isolated from the cultural mainstream of the country, could not shape life because it was so passive and contemplative.[22]

Perhaps the most radical assault on pre-revolutionary artistic life came from Osip Brik. He believed that the artist was robbed of his spontaneous

[19] See "Xronika Xudožestvennoj žizni", *Vestnik žizni*, No. 6-7 (1919), 83. A recent study of the organization of the arts during the revolutionary years asserts that the avant-garde were fascist and dictatorial (S. Fitzpatrick, *The Commissariat of Enlightenment: Soviet Organization of Education and the Arts under Lunačarskij* [London, 1970], 121, 156-157).

[20] Vladimir Majakovskij, *Polnoe sobranie sočinenij* (Moscow-Leningrad, 1958), 83.

[21] At a conference of young artists in May 1918, it was resolved that art schools should be free and that each student should be free to select his own art instructor. At this conference, Lunačarskij remarked that he intended "to liberate the young from the noxious influence of the old institutions which had outlived their time". See "Rezoljucija konferencii učaščixsja iskusstvu", *Anarxija*, May 12, 1918.

[22] See for example, "Xudožestvennoe vospitanie i kul'tura", *Iskusstvo*, No. 8 (1918), 5, and "Iskusstvo v trudovoj škole", *Xudožestvennaja žizn'*, No. 12 (1919), 24.

activity because his work was reduced to an object of leisure and idle amusement. Alienated from life, the artist sought to "realize his creative freedom not in life, but in dreams".[23] Because the artist could not actively and meaningfully take part in the creation of "real life", his art became a distortion of reality.

For Brik, almost every human product is capable of being expressed artistically. The artist must not distort life and nature by trying to compete with them. As a craftsman and producer, the artists shapes and directs life; and his fundamental aim is to create real, material things. Brik defined his function: "These artists know how to make pictures, decorations, to paint ceilings and wall, to make sketches, placards, signs, monuments and many other things. Such artists are needed in the commune. They do completely determined, socially useful work; they do real work which requires special competence, special knowledge."[24]

Brik's views gave rise to an almost utopian, revolutionary art policy of the Section of Fine Arts. The Section proceeded from the assumption that during the Renaissance, when artistic workshops prevailed, art was an integral feature of the daily existence of all. The subsequent isolation of the masses from art produced "the anomalous situation in which a small group of people became monopolists of art".[25] To vanquish the isolation of the masses from art, to socialize it and to make it once again a pervasive feature of daily life, the Section set up workshops, art schools, exhibitions and lectures near industrial plants and factories so as to discover and develop the creative capacities of workers. This was done in collaboration with factory and workshop committees. The Section also realized the delicate problem of formulating esthetic principles in relation to machine production. In the artistic education of workers, primary attention was devoted to the relationship between form and material or between art forms and productive processes. Brik explained the worker's role:

We want every worker who gives a definite form and color to an object to understand why precisely this color and this form are necessary. We want the

[23] Osip Brik, "Iskusstvo i kommuna", *Izobrazitel'noe iskusstvo*, No. 1 (1918), 25. Cf. Karl Marx who maintained: "In a communist society, there are no painters but only men who paint as one of the forms of their activity" (*K. Marx i F. Engels ob iskusstve v dvux tomax*, I [Moscow, 1967], 230).

[24] Brik, "Iskusstvo i kommuna", 25.

[25] "Xudožestvennoe vospitanie i kul'tura", 5. The comment seems to echo Marx, who once noted that the division of labor had led to "the exclusive concentration of artistic talent in certain individuals and its consequent suppression in the broad masses" (*Marx i Engels...*, I, 230).

worker to cease to be a mechanical executor of some plan that is alien to him. He must consciously and actively participate in the artistic process of creating things. Then there will be no need for a special group of artists-decorators. Artistry will blend into the very creation of things.[26]

The question naturally arises: what did the Section's policy lead to in terms of establishing industrial workshops and training workers? Approximately two years after the Revolution, the Section had created eight regional workshops with an enrollment of three hundred fifty students, one district workshop with eight students, and seven workshops in Petrograd with a large number of students. Seven more workshops were being organized by 1919. One reporter noted that the study of artistic production attracted "enormous interest" in the district provinces of Smolensk and Duxovšinskij.[27]

The ultimate aim of this education was not economic, but esthetic: to produce various articles expressive of artistic forms that would penetrate and transform life. The Section carefully pointed out that, by meeting the requirements of artistic form, "these articles must serve as models so as to convey an understanding of the object to the masses, to develop the artistic tastes of the multitudes and to renew the life of the grey, miserable countryside".[28] Naum Gabo, an avant-garde artist of the period, provides an important insight into the ideology of the avant-garde: "...though not denying the values of naturalistic art in its application to propaganda (such as posters, films, book illustrations, etc.) [the avant-garde] nevertheless laid special stress again on the absolute values of the basic elements of art and their intuitive power to influence human psychology and so mould the spiritual life of society; [they] also laid special stress on bringing art again into the daily life of the masses by incorporating it in the design of everyday things."[29] Tugendxol'd observed that this idea of merging art and life – perhaps the great passion of the age – was "new and profoundly revolutionary. It is not for nothing that it so gripped the minds of our avant-garde artists that they...were ready in the name of art 'to put to the wall' even art itself".[30]

26 Osip Brik, "V porjadke dnja", *Iskusstvo v proizvodstve*, No. 1 (1921), 8.
27 See M. Averincev, "Xudožestvennaja žizn' provincij", *Iskusstvo*, No. 7 (1919), 7.
28 "Xudozestvennaja promyšlennost'", *Xudožestvennaja žizn'*, No. 1 (1919), 21. See also D. Arkin, "Veščnoe iskusstvo", *Ibid*, No. 4-5 (1920), 5. In 1918, one critic, after observing artists painting and exhibiting their works in the streets and squares, wrote that "in one or two years one can make Russian cities unrecognizable in this way" (V. Keržencev, "Iskusstvo na ulice", *Tvorčestvo, literatura, iskusstvo, nauka i žizn'*, No. 3 [1918], p. 13).
29 Naum Gabo, "The Concepts of Russian Art", *World Review*, (June 1942), 53.
30 Tugendxol'd, 20.

Despite the radicalism of the avant-garde, this did not happen. The Section abolished the pre-revolutionary art academies; it established new and free workshops for students and formulated new artistic principles. The Section's policy was to allow art students to select their own artists and instructors for guidance, as was the case during the Renaissance. From the very beginning of his training, the student was to observe his master's technique and devices, from the grinding of colors to gradual participation in the art work itself. The Section discouraged the imitation of artistic styles; it emphasized individual invention and discovery: "One should not encourage eclecticism in the students by teaching them artistic styles as norms of art. Style should be treated exclusively as a historical fact. Each epoch advances its own complex of artistic forms..."[31] Another major aspect of this training included the student's presentation of his work to a board which would point out the strengths and weaknesses of his artistic development.[32]

In 1918, the Section reported the scope of its work in establishing student workshops and training of students. It had established six student workshops in Petrograd, five in surrounding districts, and many others were in the planning stages, even for the Red Army and Navy. As for students, four thousand one hundred twenty four students from ages nine to twenty-four were enrolled in the workshops.[33]

By 1920, the Section's drive for artistic emancipation engendered powerful opposition. The pressure for artistic continuity with past traditions mounted. The Section's radical experiments could not be fully or immediately applied in conditions still closely tied to the historical past. Means became incompatible with ends. People became indifferent, at times hostile, to the problems of artistic education; many could not, or would not, absorb the artistic principles and were suspicious of the Section's aims. Artists were "stubbornly reluctant" to be drawn into life and into the problems of training and educating students. Within the artistic bureaucracy, misunderstanding, confusion and resistance emerged on the artistic tastes and goals of the Section. Less venturesome artists felt no sense of common purpose with the avant-garde and carried out their own 'line'. The avant-garde, eager to transform life through art, was too utilitarian, abstract, and formal in their approach to art; they had no bond with, or anchor in, the past, but artistic renaissance was

[31] "Iskusstvo v trudovoj škole", 24.
[32] *Obzor dejatel'nosti izobrazitel'nyx iskusstv*, 14-16.
[33] "Xudožestvennoe vospitanie i kul'tura", 5.

"inconceivable without a solid link with traditions, with the accumulated experience of the past on the basis of a viable cooperation of generations".[34]

Other conflicts arose. Since the avant-garde had supported the Revolution, the Section tended to give priority to the purchase of their art works for showing in the newly created art museums. This naturally embittered artists hostile to the Section, who refused to cooperate with it unless assured of equal treatment. Many of these artists, initially opposed to the Revolution, gradually came to accept it as an accomplished fact.[35] They began to attack the Section's policies and the art of the avant-garde as "destructive", "bourgeois decadence", and "unintelligible". At first, Lunačarskij defended the Section. He stated that the Section would purchase the art works of all groups, but primary consideration would be given to the works of those artists who "were persecuted in the epoch of the domination of bourgeois tastes and thus not represented in our galleries".[36] Later, however, when a large majority of artists were seeking an accommodation with the regime, Lunačarskij began to favor them so as to win them over to the regime.

In this precarious situation, the avant-garde counter-attacked. They asserted that their art was a "state" and "proletarian" art. This brought forth retaliation and charges of "domination" and "dictatorship" from opponents. But these charges were "exaggerated".[37] At this point, Lunačarskij intervened. He restated his policy of impartiality to all art movements. After discussing the matter with Lenin, who wanted the avant-garde's attacks to cease, Lunačarskij wrote an article in the Cubo-Futurist newspaper, *The Art of the Commune.*[38] It would be tragic, he

[34] A. Bakušinskij, "Očerednaja zadača v dele xudožestvennogo vospitanija", *Xudožestvennaja žizn'*, No. 3 (1920), 2.

[35] Šterenburg attempted to identify these artists: "But it is no secret to anyone just who the real artist is. In the majority of cases, he is the one who does not know his craft, paints by 'inspiration,' waits months for it and at the same time does nothing else, demanding that society and now the state buy up all the products of his inspiration. The Section had to experience incredible difficulties." See *Obzor dejatel'nosti izobrazitel'nyx iskusstv*, 72.

[36] "Ot otedla izobrazitel'nyx iskusstv Narkomprosa", *Petrogradskaja pravda*, November 28, 1918.

[37] Tugendxol'd, 18. See also "Lenin i Lunačarskij", *Literaturnoe nasledstvo*, LXXX (Moscow, 1971), pp. 292, 717.

[38] This newspaper was perhaps named after an avant-garde society, *Commune des arts*, which arose during the French Revolution. One of its founders, Jacques Louis David, envisioned an artistic organization as a "free and democratic association with absolute freedom of exhibition, in contrast to the undemocratically restricted offical Salons with their academic juries" (Donald D. Egbert, *Social Radicalism and the Arts* [New York, 1970], 35-36).

remarked, if the Cubo-Futurists fancied themselves "as a state artistic school, as representatives of an official, even if revolutionary, art as dictated from above". Lunačarskij criticized the newspaper for its "destructive tendencies in relation to the past". He was disturbed by the paper's habit of speaking simultaneously in the name of a particular school as well as in the name of the regime.[39]

Lunačarskij's reproach was ineffective. In the same issue in which his article appeared, the Cubo-Futurists replied with defiance and ridicule. They took Lunačarskij to task for poetic ignorance: he had applied a 'literal' interpretation to Majakovskij's poetry, which attacked the art of the past. They also pointed out that the conflict between the Cubo-Futurists and other artistic groups concerned the latter's completely passive response to the former's efforts to create "the future art of the commune".[40] Punin defiantly observed in this same issue: "We do not need the state... because we are struggling for a socialist future unknown to the state."[41] Brik also remarked tauntingly that almost all political dictators were the "most unmitigated compromisers" in matters of cultural development.[42]

A state of uneasy tension prevailed until the end of 1920. The Section relentlessly pursued its revolutionary artistic aims. The Bolshevik regime, torn between supporting the avant-garde and their opponents, did not intervene: it would have been impractical to do so. Besides, the regime shared many of the basic policies of the Section. By the end of 1920, with the consolidation of the Revolution, Lenin was able to turn to cultural matters. He had grown suspicious of the avant-garde because of their radicalism, anarchism, and defiance. He resented their attacks on the art and literature of the past which he admired. In December 1920, Lenin identified the Cubo-Futurists with "petty-bourgeois elements" and labeled them "advocates of an idealist philosophy hostile to Marxism..."[43] He reduced their authority and, shortly after, deposed them.

With the advent of the New Economic Policy, continuity with past traditions had reasserted itself. Lunačarskij noted at a conference that "we need to create an academy which will train those who are capable

39 A. Lunačarskij, "Ložka protivojadija", *Iskusstvo kommuny*, December 29, 1918.
40 "Ot redakcij", *Ibid.*
41 Nikolaj Punin, "Futurizm – gosudarstvennoe iskusstvo", *Ibid.*
42 Osip Brik, "Dovol'no soglašatel'stva", *Iskusstvo kommuny*, January 12, 1919.
43 See "Xronika literaturnoj žizni", in *Istorija russkoj sovetskoj literatury 1917-1929*, I (Moscow, 1958), 574.

of being exponents of state policy in the realm of art".[44] But the avant-garde was not yet crushed. Šterenburg could still muse in 1921: "...our ideal is a distant star which still shines ahead, but now we must meet what the revolution demands of us."[45]

The avant-garde episode in the Bolshevik Revolution is certainly not without historical irony. When Punin pointed out in the Cubo-Futurist newspaper that Marx had anticipated the avant-garde with the injunction to change the world, he was historically justified. Like Saint-Simon, Marx looked to artists – poets, painters, muscians, writers – as the natural leaders of the "good society" because they were "best fitted to move mankind to progress by stimulating sentiment".[46] With the evolution of Marxism in the nineteenth and twentieth centuries, the notion of 'avant-garde' became associated not with artists, but with political parties, which attracted artists with notions of social elitism and who were not too reluctant to subordinate their art to political and social goals as the price for political involvement. The Bolshevik Revolution brought into sharp focus the conflict between the artistic avant-garde and the political avant-garde over the leadership of society. They debated whether the avant-garde artist could survive with the triumph of the political avant-garde (i.e. Marxism-Leninism). In the final analysis, the debate centered on differing notions of revolution; for the avant-garde, an esthetic revolution was integral to a political revolution; for the Bolshevik leaders, it was not.

Ironically, Lenin, as a Marxist, shared in theory the very notions of artistic education which the avant-garde tried to implement during the revolutionary years. "Art belongs to the people", Lenin once remarked to Clara Zetkin. "Its thickest roots must go down into the midst of the broad toiling masses. It must be understood and loved by them. It must unite the feelings, thoughts and will of these masses. It must produce artists among them and develop them."[47] In practice, however, Lenin was extremely partial to Russian realistic writers and artists and believed

44 See "Pervaja Vserossijskaja konferencija zavediuščix podotdelami iskusstv", *Vestnik rabotnikov iskusstv*, No. 4-6 (1921), 63.

45 See "Doklady po naučno-xudožestvennym voprosam", *Vestnik teatra*, No. 80-81 (1921), 9.

46 Egbert, 119.

47 Quoted in P. Reddaway, "Literature, the Arts and the Personality of Lenin", in *Lenin: The Man, the Theorist, the Leader. A Reappraisal*, L. Schapiro and P. Reddaway, eds. (London, 1967), 51-52.

that 'socialist' art could have little, if any, validity beyond a 'realistic' framework.

2. THE CREATION OF *LEF* AND FUTURIST THEORIES

In 1921, Aleksandr Voronskij was commissioned by the Party to create a literary journal – *Krasnaja nov' (Red Virgin Soil)* – and a publishing house – *Krug (Circle)*. Voronskij's major aim was to create "a united front of literary forces".[48] He was to counteract the influence of the private publishing concerns by making it attractive for fellow-travellers (i.e. non-Communist) and Communist writers to publish their works in these organs. Maguire adds:

> The plan in short was to form a 'center' that would attract the best writers, new and old, who were sympathetic, or at least not openly hostile to the Revolution; to bring them together under Party auspices, carefully blunted in order to avoid any suggestion of coercion; and gradually, through example and patient persuasion, to win them over completely.[49]

Voronskij, however, became, according to Brik, "exclusively concerned with attracting" the fellow-travellers, and was unable to devote proper attention to proletarian writers and to a "small but active group of artistic intelligentsia" whose leader was Majakovskij.[50] Consequently, the proletarian writers and the Futurists sought to create their own journals so as to challenge Voronskij's journal. It was these three groups – the fellow-travellers, the Futurists, and Octobrists – which in the main came to dominate the literary scene in the 1920's.

To be sure, there were other reasons for the Futurists' feud with Voronskij's journal. First, they believed that a 'proletarian' literature could be created, which Voronskij denied.[51] Second, by publishing their

[48] E. Dinerštejn, "Majakovskij v 'Kruge' i 'Krasnoj novi'", in *Majakovskij i sovetskaja literatura* (Moscow, 1964), 407.

[49] Robert A. Maguire, *Red Virgin Soil: Soviet Literature in the 1920's* (Princeton, 1968), 22-23.

[50] Osip Brik, "Majakovskij – redaktor i organizator", *Literaturnyj kritik*, No. 4 (1936), 128.

[51] Dinerštejn, 145. According to Voronskij, a 'proletarian' literature could not be created without the assimilation of the best of the literatures of the past. For him, literature was a reflection of universal aspirations and experiences. It was a mode of objective knowledge of reality and life in "sensible images" and capable of producing "changes in the life of the individual and in mankind as a whole" (Maguire, 197). Voronskij also emphasized the role of "immediate impressions" and "intuition" in the creative process. He believed that "If the old art had been passive, contemplative,

works in Voronskij's journal, the Futurists believed that they had lost their identity as a group and were thus unable to crystallize their views. Third, they found it difficult to agree with Voronskij's notion of art as "cognition of life". Fourth, the Futurists believed that the art of the past had no relevance or application to the special literary problems which the Revolution had introduced. Fifth, they believed that inquiries into the formal problems of art were necessary to the creation of new literary forms and modes of expression.

The Futurists described the aims of *Lef* (*The Left Front of Art*, 1923–1925) in relatively sober terms.[52] These aims are of high interest for the Futurist notions they retained rather than abandoned. The key notion of the artist as a producer was retained. Futurist art was still equated with Communist art, once the former's "valuable Communist features" were developed. The Futurists considered themselves nationally and internationally avant-garde and would maintain links with West-European avant-garde movements. They would struggle against bourgeois tastes, against Voronskij and the October group – the "compromisers" who speak in "old worn out phrases about absolute values and eternal beauties". The reexamination of Futurist art would prune it of its less valuable features – "individualistic distortion". The Futurists spoke of providing models that bare devices "for the creation of effective agitational works". Technical devices would be used even for "tendentious realism". The Futurists did not point out the nature of the relationship of the former to the latter. The struggle with "self-contained formalism" implied that the Formalist critics associated with *Lef* would not neglect the social factors of literature.[53] When one takes into account the alliance between Formalists and Futurists within *Lef*, these aims were ingeniously formulated as a compromise between them.

In the first issue of *Lef*, the Futurists amplified their views in three programmatic statements. These statements were not so much a guide to literary activity as a call for battle on many fronts. After an historical

devoid of will, it would not have compelled people to act and struggle" (quoted in Maguire, 78). As Voronskij saw it, Russian literature exerted an "honorable, beneficial, noble role in the struggle against Tsarist despotism" (quoted in Maguire, 78). For further discussion of Voronskij's literary views, see Maguire's work, which is the best study of the subject.

52 See V. Katanjan, *Majakovskij: Literaturnaja Xronika* (Moscow, 1961), 175.

53 For Boris Èjxenbaum, Formalism was "In the limits of a literary science...a revolutionary movement insofar as it frees literary science of old, obsolete tradition and compels examination anew of all basic concepts and schemes" ("Vokrug voprosa o formalistax", *Pečat' i revoljucija*, No. 5 [1924], 10).

sketch of Futurism with emphasis on its service to Bolshevism and its attempts to create a Communist art, the aim of *Lef* was to unite "the left forces" and "to explode the old", to fight "to encompass a new culture", "to agitate the masses with its art" and to struggle for an art of "life-building".[54] The Futurists called for a reexamination of tactics: they considered the classics as 'textbooks' and aids to the elimination of illiteracy, not a source for galvanizing writers. The 'new' Futurist tactic – which contradicted Party policy on assimilating the art of the past as a pre-condition of 'proletarian literature' – was to exert all efforts in "*the struggle against transferring the methods of the work of the dead to today's art*".[55]

The predominance of literary theory and manifestoes was the cardinal feature of *Lef.*[56] Theory and manifestoes seem to have served to renew and redefine the Futurist literary program and to focus on 'future' literary achievements. An analysis of *Lef's* theories will demonstrate this; it will reveal Majakovskij's basic purpose in creating *Lef* and the seeds of Futurist theory to come: "the literature of fact".

In their joint article, Majakovskij and Brik remarked that their literary practice was to erase the distinction between the language of prose, poetry, and everyday language. The word for them was the basic fact of poetry. In theory, the Futurists were to work on "the phonetic organization of language, for polyphony of rhythm, for simplification of verbal construction, for the invention of new thematic devices". They noted further that "This work represents no purely aesthetic striving, but rather a laboratory for the best expression of contemporary facts."[57] Significantly, the implicit notion here is that Majakovskij and Brik viewed Futurist art as one of evolution and a product of careful linguistic inquiry. *Lef* was an attempt to solve literary problems, a forum or meeting ground for Futurist work on poetry and linguistic and literary study. Brik seems to be right in observing that Majakovskij believed that complete unity among the Futurists was unnecessary with regard to their platform. As long as they shared common views and aims, Majakovskij thought that the Futurists should have their own journal to express

[54] "Za čto boretsja *Lef?*", *Lef*, No. 1 (1923), 6-7.
[55] "V kogo vgryzaetsja *Lef?*", *Lef*, No. 1 (1923), 8.
[56] For an account of the contents of *Lef*, see L. Švecova, "*Lef i Novyj Lef*", in *Očerki istorii russkoj sovetskoj žurnalistiki 1917-1932* (Moscow, 1966), 320-332.
[57] V. Majakovskij and O. Brik, "Naša slovesnaja rabota", *Lef*, No. 1 (1923), 40-41.

them.[58]

Brik himself wrote a manifesto which defined the Formalist position. Theoretically, he saw the poet as a kind of 'Renaissance' craftsman who undertakes a literary task with the knowledge of the demands of his clients. Brik laid heavy emphasis on the centrality of investigating "the devices of poetic craft". Echoing Šklovskij Brik noted that "The history of poetry is the history of the development of the devices of its literary formation." The Formalists, as Brik saw it, were the most qualified educators of the proletariat for "answering the problems of the day" and for "overcoming the traditions of bourgeois literature".[59] The role of the Futurists was "technical", not ideological:

OPOJAZ [The Society for the Study of Poetic Language] will help proletarian art not by vague discussions about the new 'proletarian spirit' and 'Communist consciousness', but by precise technical knowledge of the devices of contemporary poetic art.[60]

As for other Futurists, Čužak called for an end to Voronskij's notion of literature as 'cognition of life' because it could not build life but only reflect it passively. For Čužak, the art of the past merely raised problems without ever solving them. His key notion was that art should be "life-building" *(žiznestroenie)* and linked to "the processes of production" so as to create "barter values in the light of the future".[61] To the realization of these notions Čužak never addressed himself.

The gap between Futurist theory and practice soon dissatisfied the impatient and dogmatic Čužak. He saw the urgent necessity of defining the nature of Futurist art. He admitted that he himself was not clear on this score.[62] In his view, the Futurists needed an art that would do more than "agitate". They needed "models", and the designation of "concrete tasks". He was also certain that Majakovskij's *Pro èto (About This)*, with its lyricism and focus on the "daily grind" and "philistinism" was not the

58 Brik, "Majakovskij – redaktor i organizator", 135.

59 Osip Brik, "Tak nazyvaemyj formal'nyj metod", *Lef*, No. 1 (1923), 213. The notion of the "social command" originated with the Futurists. Erlich notes that "The slogan was subsequently appropriated by the critical hacks of the *On Guard* faction and thus became associated with the political regimentation of literature. To the *Lef* spokesman, however, 'social command' connoted not so much direct Party controls over writers, as the spontaneous response of the poet to the social needs of his epoch or of his class" (*Russian Formalism: History-Doctrine*, 2nd, rev. ed. [The Hague, 1965], 112). See also Edward J. Brown, *Russian Literature Since the Revolution* (New York, 1963), 59-60.

60 Brik, "Tak nazyvaemyj...", 215.

61 N. Čužak, "Pod znakom žiznestroenija", *Lef*, No. 1 (1923), 34, 37.

62 N. Čužak, "K zadačam dnja", *Lef*, No. 2 (1923), 151.

model. In effect, Čužak was strongly implying that Majakovskij had to avoid writing on these themes.[63]

A parallel discussion on Formalist theory at this time was developed in Tynjanov's study of the evolution of literary genres. This study is important for an understanding of the Futurist-Formalist theory of 'literature of fact' and invites brief discussion. For Tynjanov, literary evolution was apparently a series of 'shifts' of genres from the 'periphery' to the 'center' and vice-versa as a result of social changes. Expanding on Šklovskij's theory of the 'canonization of minor genres', Tynjanov noted that "In the epoch of the decline of any literary genre", non-fictional genres shift to the center.[64] He demonstrated that in the eighteenth century the writing of letters, diaries, memoirs and petitions was greatly influenced by the prose style of the time. These genres in turn became "literary facts".[65] As an example, Tynjanov pointed to Karamzin's *Letters of a Russian Traveler* and the subsequent evolution of the ordinary letter reflecting artistic style *(bytovoe pis'mo)* in A. Turgenev's and P. Vjazemskij's time.[66] Tynjanov's analysis of literary genres from a *contemporary perspective* strongly suggested that contemporary literature had to draw on non-fictional genres to solve the 'crisis' or decline of the novel. Notably, in that same year Tynjanov wrote that "The novel finds itself in an impasse; what is needed today is a sense of a new genre, i.e. a sense of decisive novelty in literature. Anything less than that is merely a half-measure."[67]

In summing up the 1917-1925 period of Russian Futurism, one might note that the Futurists often disagreed about the nature of art and often

[63] Čužak, "K zadačam dnja", 152. In another article, Čužak noted that Futurism was confused between art as production and "vulgar lyricism". His remark was most likely aimed at Majakovskij. See N. Čužak, "Pljusy i minusy", *Lef*, No. 3 (1923), 32.
[64] Ju. Tynjanov, "O literaturnom fakte", *Lef*, No. 2 (1924), 103. This article was reprinted in his *Arxaisty i novatory* (Leningrad, 1929).
[65] Tynjanov, 110.
[66] Tynjanov, 111.
[67] Quoted in Erlich, *Russian Formalism...*, 149. Interestingly, there was considerable discussion at this time about the crisis of the novel. Osip Mandel'stam remarked in 1923 that the novel dealing with "the fate of one man or a whole group of men" was at an end. He also suggested that the novel would no longer "shape and educate the minds of contemporaries" ("Konec romana", in his *Sobranie sočinenij v dvux tomax*, II [New York, 1966], 308-309). See also Viktor Šklovskij, "Sovremenniki i sinxronisty", *Russkij sovremennik*, No. 3 (1924), 235-247 and N. Aseev, "Konec belletristiki", *Pečat' i revoljucija*, No. 7 (1922), 68-80.

expressed contradictory views in the course of developing their theories and in view of changing circumstances. They basically agreed, however, that the artist had to play a new and active role in society and that art had to be directly related to it. Despite their disagreements, therefore, this notion was the dynamic that yoked the Futurists and was largely the viability and the inner consistency of their movement. When seen from this perspective, the Futurist movement becomes intelligible.

3. CRITICISM OF THE FUTURISTS

The Futurists were soon criticized from many quarters. Trotsky's criticism was very likely the most objective and comprehensive.[68] Perhaps the unofficial cultural spokesman for the Party until 1925, Trotsky saw the Futurists not as 'revolutionaries', but as "Bohemian nihilists". He pointed out that the Bolsheviks were traditionalists and Marxists for whom "the Revolution appeared as the embodiment of a familiar tradition, internally digested".[69] They thus could not erase the cultural traditions of a thousand years as the Futurists wanted to do. For Trotsky, this was an essential psychological difference between a political revolutionary and "revolutionary innovators of form".[70] The latter, moreover, were not "part of the revolutionary tradition" because they merely "fell into" the Revolution.

Trotsky went on to note, however, that Futurism could undergo a "rebirth" and contribute to the creation of a new art. He saw several independent and at times contradictory elements in Futurism – Formalism, Marxism, Trans-Sensism. The Futurists, Trotsky was sure, would abandon the latter because it would only eviscerate poetry. As for his positive assessment of the aims of Futurism, Trotsky wrote: "The problems raised by the theorists of the 'Lef' group about art and a machine industry, about art which does not embellish life, but forms it, about conscious influence upon the development of language and systematic formation of words, about biomechanics as the education of the activities of man in the spirit of the greatest rationality, and therefore

[68] See also V. Polonskij, "Zametki o žurnalax", *Pečat' i revoljucija*, No. 4 (1923), 291-302; V. Polonskij, "Zametki o žurnalax", *Pečat' i revoljucija*, No. 5 (1923), 323-330; V. Poljanskij, "O 'levom fronte' v iskusstve", *Pod znamenem marksizma*, No. 4-5 (1923), 197-209; A. Lunačarskij, "Kak nexorošo vyxodit", *Pravda*, December 7, 1923; L. Sosnovskij, "Želtaja kofta iz sovetskogo sitca", *Pravda*, May 23, 1923.

[69] Leon Trotsky, *Literature and Revolution* (New York, 1957), 131.

[70] Trotsky, 132.

of the greatest beauty – are all problems which are extremely significant and interesting from the point of view of building a Socialist culture."[71] Then Trotsky continued with this negative criticism: "Unfortunately, the 'Lef' colors these problems by a Utopian sectarianism. Even when they mark out correctly the general trend of development in the field of art or life, the theorists of 'Lef' anticipate history and contrast their scheme or their prescription with that which is. They thus have no bridge to the future. They remind one of anarchists who anticipate the absence of government in the future, and who contrast their scheme with the politics, parliaments and several other realities that the present ship of State must, in their imagination, of course, throw overboard. In practice, therefore, they bury their noses before they have hardly freed their tails."[72]

To be sure, Trotsky's literary views were an extension of his historical and political views. As a convinced Westerner, he believed that a 'Socialist art' could have no validity or authenticity if it did not assimilate or develop within the framework of West-European and Russian literatures, just as the Bolshevik revolution had no validity without corresponding revolutions in the West. He thus saw the literature of the period as a "transition" to "Socialist art": "Revolutionary art which inevitably reflects all the contradictions of a revolutionary social system, should not be confused with Socialist art for which no basis has as yet been made. On the other hand, one must not forget that Socialist art will grow out of the art of this transition period."[73] Trotsky did not satisfactorily point out how this was to happen, because he apparently did not expect to see the fruition of that art in his own lifetime.

Trotsky believed, however, that the Futurists were right in their prognosis that art would merge with life, with "production" and "collective group life",[74] Trotsky's own vision of 'Socialist art' was in almost striking agreement with the artistic notions of the Futurists: In the "classless society", Trotsky observed, "Art then will become more general, will mature, will become tempered, and will become the most perfect method of the progressive building of life in every field."[75] This seems to echo Čužak. Trotsky added that in the future "The wall between art and industry will come down. The great style of the future will be

[71] Trotsky, 134.
[72] *Ibid.*
[73] Trotsky, 229.
[74] Trotsky, 136.
[75] Trotsky, 230.

formative, not ornamental. Here the Futurists are right."[76]

Finally, Trotsky was perhaps compelled to conclude, in effect, that the Futurists were ahead of their time. In presenting their views as an "ultimatum", he noted, the Futurists lacked historical perspective and were denying art the useful role of "picturing and imaging knowledge". The problem of the Futurists, Trotsky remarked further, was that their searchings outstripped their findings, which was why the Party could not canonize their searchings. However serious the Futurists were in their Marxian pursuits, Trotsky added, their immediate task was to give practical expression to their theories of the new art.[77]

4. THE CRISIS AND DISSOLUTION OF *LEF*

In January, 1925, the Odessa Futurists with the support of Čužak called for a conference of the "left workers of art" in Moscow. This conference proved to be a direct challenge to Majakovskij's leadership of *Lef*. The Odessa Futurists maintained that *Lef* did not represent "the left front of art" because its literary practice contradicted its principles and because it lacked a unified organization with a clear direction. To be sure, this was Čužak's argument against *Lef* in *Lef*. In their view, the *Lef* group under Majakovskij "could not in any way claim hegemony" of the whole of the *Lef* movement. Although some believed that *Lef* needed a new leadership, Majakovskij remained its leader. *Lef*, however, was now for the Odessa Futurists "without any guiding significance".[78]

In his speech at the conference, Majakovskij pointed out that Čužak wanted "complete agreement on all questions" concerning "the creation of precise formulas for all our work, a precise unconditional implementation of certain directives".[79] Majakovskij "categorically" protested against this organizational plan. He noted that the word "Lef" was chosen as a general word, not so much to designate Futurists or Constructivists but to imply that literary "groups of the most different shades could mechanically unite in this *Lef*". Majakovskij continued by saying that "To unite them chemically according to Čužak is impossible until we smash the very atom of contemporary artistic life."[80] Majakovskij

[76] Trotsky, 249.
[77] Trotsky, 139-140.
[78] Brik, "Majakovskij – redaktor i organizator", 139.
[79] Majakovskij, XII, 275.
[80] Majakovskij, XII, 276.

thus rejected a "monolithic organization" of Futurists and proposed that the two principles of *Lef* be: (1) "a federative union with absolute freedom of corporations" and (2) "a solid material base". In conclusion, Majakovskij remarked that *Lef* would remain a union of left front workers who would pursue unflinchingly the principles of the "old Futurists".[81]

The opportunity for this, however, never came. Shortly after this conference, *Lef* ceased publication. Majakovskij's efforts to attract new writers and poets to *Lef* – Zelinskij, Kirsanov – were too late to stem its declining circulation.[82] The "Achilles heel of *Lef*", as Polonskij observed, was its "reluctance to be content with the role of the poetic vanguard of the revolutionary intelligensia, a vanguard which possessed a high degree of craftsmanship".[83]

5. *NEW LEF* AND THE 'LITERATURE OF FACT'

Before discussing the final 'phase' of Russian Futurism, one must stress one fundamental development in the literary setting after *Lef* ceased publication. This was the Party resolution of July, 1925, which largely shaped the literary development and controversies until 1930 and perhaps after. On the one hand, its aim was to check the raging literary disputes and to reject attempts to commit the Party to the program of any one literary group *for the moment:* "Everything compels the assumption that a style corresponding to the epoch will be created, but it will be created by different methods, and the solution of this problem has not yet begun. Any attempt to bind the Party in this direction in the present phase of the country's cultural development must be rejected."[84] On the other hand, the Party specifically committed itself to the *future* creation of the "hegemony of proletarian literature".[85] This implied that the Party in the immediate future would abandon its policy of "free competition of

81 Majakovskij, XII, 277-278. In January, 1923, Majakovskij wrote to Čužak: "Remember that the aim of our alliance is *communist art*...a sphere which is still vague, which does not lend itself yet to precise definition or theorizing; a sphere where practice, intuition are way ahead of the most imaginative theoretician. Let us work together on this without imposing anything on each other, possibly by perfecting each other, you with your knowledge, we with our taste" (Majakovskij, XIII, 61).

82 *Lef's* circulation in 1923 was five thousand. By 1925 it had declined to fifteen-hundred.

83 Polonskij, *Očerki literaturnogo dviženija...*, 144.

84 Quoted in Polonskij, 243.

85 Quoted in Polonskij, 242.

various groups and tendencies" and impose a "proletarian" ideology on all writers. What is more, as it happened, the Party called upon literature to take part in socialist reconstruction.

This resolution, which seems to have added fuel to the literary controversies that followed, was certainly one reason for the Futurists to create *New Lef* (which began publication in 1927).[86] Another basic reason was their firm conviction that the 'imaginative' literature of the past could not be artificially transplanted to the revolutionary era. The Futurists and Formalists consequently advocated a 'literature of fact', which became the theoretical and practical core of *New Lef*. This literary theory created a solid alliance between the Futurists and Formalists and had its roots in previous Futurist-Formalist theory. It was now competitively and polemically ranged against the prescriptive slogans of RAPP (The Russian Association of Proletarian Writers) – "psychologism", "study the classics", "for the living man", "tear off the masks". Moreover, it was also an attempt to create new literary genres to reflect the revolutionary era. This, it was believed, would make the writer an active participant in the events of his time.

As Brik saw it, the Russian intelligentsia developed to a high degree "its ability to experience imaginary [*vymyšlennyj*] facts and events" because it was alienated for a long time from all forms of "practical work".[87] Brik went on to suggest that the "active" Soviet intelligentsia was not and could not be seriously involved in the problems raised by "imaginative literature" because it already knew the solutions in "reality". Only problems raised in a "real" form, Brik noted, could be of interest to the Soviet intelligentsia. Brik also observed that a "fixation and montage of facts" would create a more lasting impression on the reader than "imaginative literature".[88]

From the perspective of literary evolution, the Futurists and Formalists believed that the Bolshevik revolution marked a radical break with prerevolutionary literature and acted as a brake on the course of literary evolution.[89] This largely explained the crisis of the 'novel' and its frag-

[86] Majakovskij noted that "Politically, *Lef* shares the platform of RAPP. Why doesn't *Lef* merge with it? The difference is in the formal approach to literature" (XII, 495).

[87] N. Čužak, "Pisatel'skaja pamjatka", in *Literatura fakta. Pervyj sbornik materjalov rabotnikov Lefa*, N. Čužak ed. (Moscow, 1929), 12.

[88] Osip Brik, "Bliže k faktu", in *Literatura fakta...*, 82.

[89] Interestingly, in 1924 Èixenbaum observed that there was a change in the literary tastes of the Russian readers and that literature had to find a new reader: "Russian literature had its loyal reader for a long time: 'the Russian intelligentsia'. This reader

mented and documentary character in the early 1920's. "The novel exists", Šklovskij noted, "but exists like the light of a dying star."[90] This meant, for Šklovskij, that the "traditional psychological novel", with its fable *(fabula)* formulae, was inapplicable to the shaping of new literary material of the revolutionary epoch: fact and reporting.[91] For Brik, the Bolshevik revolution had ushered in a completely new constellation of thematic problems which past literary methods and devices could not solve. Brik suggested that the writer-craftsman was an instrument or agent for the regeneration and continuation of a literary process which in turn shapes his use and selection of literary methods and devices. The writer, according to Brik, was merely executing, as it were, a historical-literary injunction in response to the demands of a specific literary situation. Brik explained:

Every work of art is the result of a complex interrelation of individual elements of creative art. The author's role is to use these elements and to combine them into a definite artistic product. These elements, of which the art work is created, are external to, and independent of, the author; the author only more or less successfully uses them for his work.

In every given epoch there is a certain quantity of artistic methods and devices available for creative use. A change in these methods and devices does not depend on the author's will, but is the result of the evolution of creative art.[92]

Armed with this determinism, Brik made a critical dissection of RAPP's literary notions and slogans,[93] as exemplified in a highly representative

no longer exists because there is no intelligentsia itself, at least in the old meaning of the word" ("V ožidanii literatury", *Russkij sovremennik*, No. 1 [1924], 280).

90 Viktor Šklovskij, "Togda i seičas", in *Literatura fakta...*, 125.

91 Viktor Šklovskij, "Prestuplenie èpigona", in *Literatura fakta...*, 130.

92 Osip Brik, "Učit' pisatelej", in *Literatura fakta...*, 181.

93 RAPP's literary theory had a good deal in common with that of Voronskij's, especially with regard to the importance of "immediate impressions", "sensible images", and "intuition" in artistic creation. RAPP believed that literature should depict life "realistically" in its forward development and "should discover and reveal the inherent contradictions in society and in man himself" (Edward J. Brown, *The Proletarian Episode in Russian Literature 1928-1932* [New York, 1953], 74). As for RAPP's slogans, "study the classics" meant to master Tolstoj's method of psychological realism and description of human behavior. "Tear off the masks", a slogan borrowed from Lenin's writings on Tolstoj, meant the "unmasking of enemies, the freeing of the citizenry from the vestiges of the capitalist past..." (Herman Ermolaev, *Soviet Literary Theories 1917-1934: The Genesis of Socialist Realism* [Berkeley, 1963], 69). "For the living man" meant "showing forth the complex human psyche, with all its contradictions, elements of the future, both conscious and subconscious" (Quoted in Brown, *The Proletarian Episode...*, 78). RAPP also stressed the centrality of ideology in literature and was willing "to make literature serve immediate political aims, all of which accounted for the narrowness and the dogmatism of their literary theories" (Ermolaev, 72).

work of that group: Fadeev's *The Rout* (1927). Brik's aim was to demonstrate that the methods and techniques of the literary 'past' were inapplicable to a new literary and social era which demanded for its expression the creation of new literary techniques.

As Brik saw it, Fadeev was not concerned in his work with an objective presentation of the civil war or, more importantly, with the struggle and the external activities of the partisans which would arouse contemporary interest in them, but with their psychological conflicts and experiences.[94] This aspect of Fadeev's work clearly reflected the influence of Tolstoj, whom Fadeev admittedly read and studied in accordance with RAPP's criteria.

Brik, however, went on to note with insight that Čexov's influence, not Tolstoj's, was far more pervasive in Fadeev's work. This influence could be seen in the clash between two dominant types of Čexovian characters in Fadeev's novel: the clash between 'weak-willed' and 'strong-willed' characters. Brik saw this clash as the 'basic theme' of Čexov's stories and elaborated: "The meaning of this theme is that there are people who are adjusted to life and people who are unadjusted. Adjustment, however, is made at the price of lowering one's intellectual level. To be adjusted to life, one must be more crude, more obtuse, more straightforward. Usually Čexov does not show us the internal side of those who are adjusted to life. He presents them as an external force, while he presents the unadjusted, intellectual people with all the inner details of their inner life."[95] The "unadjusted", "weak-willed" character in Fadeev's novel became Mečik, a "negative type", who plays "a central role in the whole novel and...determines the whole compositional structure and style of the novel".[96] Opposed to Mečik were Morozka and Baklanov, who were adjusted, crude, and obtuse.

Brik continued his dissection by pointing out that Fadeev had made extensive use of Čexov's stylistic devices, such as the phrases "for some reason", "somewhere", "he felt like", "it seemed to him". For Čexov, these verbal devices were central to the characterization of the 'weak-willed' and 'unadjusted' characters so as to "strengthen the impression of [their] vague [*smutnyj*] state".[97] Fadeev, however, by using Čexov's character types also necessarily used his verbal phrases to characterize the partisans. This led to a bizarre result: the partisans had no notion of

94 Osip Brik, "Razgrom Fadeeva", in *Literatura fakta...*, 89.
95 Brik, "Razgrom Fadeeva", 91.
96 "Razgrom Fadeeva", 91-92.
97 "Razgrom Fadeeva", 92.

the aim or "cause" of their struggle, which Brik saw as the major shortcoming of Fadeev's novel:

An extraordinarily absurd story is the result. Our proletarian literature, in desiring somehow to get away from a poster portrayal of an active part of our society, is trying to present that part in a so-called 'living' portrayal. A living portrayal boils down to the point where they are beginning to speak about people not in clear and direct language, but in a cloudy and vague one when describing, in the main unconsciously, the movements and experiences of these people. It turns out that 'some' people 'for some reason' proved to be outstanding figures in a cause whose meaning they do not know and do not understand. The formula turns out to be: 'He may be a drunkard and a thief, but he is nevertheless a builder of socialism.'

It seems to our proletarian writers that the point of showing the living man lies precisely in the contradiction between the results of men's actions and their inner substance.[98]

Brik concluded by emphasizing the necessity of a "cause", for showing the role of active men "in our cause". What this cause was Brik did not say.[99]

RAPP's literary notions were critically examined from other perspectives by other Futurists and Formalists. Percov observed that RAPP merely added several slogans to Voronskij's notion of art as cognition of life.[100] Percov pointed out that RAPP's insistence on the centrality of Communist ideology in literary creation ignored the view that ideology itself was not the material of art. Ideology functioned rather as a catalyst and existed 'immanently' in literary technique. "We are against 'thesis' literature as we are against literature which 'tears off the masks'."[101] Percov debated both the value and possibility of having the classics of the nineteenth century rewritten. He believed that RAPP's uncritical regard for, and dependence on, the classics were an implicit confession that the proletarian writers lacked the technique and knowledge of literature as a craft. It was a non-sequitur, Percov remarked, that a "critical study" of the Russian classics would bestow "independence" on proletarian literature. RAPP simply believed that the study of the "realists" would produce "realists".[102]

98 "Razgrom Fadeeva", 92-93.

99 In support of Brik's article on Fadeev's novel, Trenin, a young Formalist critic, adduced a cogent array of examples from Čexov's and Tolstoj's works to point out their parallels with Fadeev's work. See V. Trenin, "Intelligentnye partizany", in *Literatura fakta...*, 95-98.

100 Percov, *Literatura zavtrašnego dnja*, (Leningrad, 1929), 107.

101 Percov, 95.

102 Percov, 99-102.

Tret'jakov ridiculed RAPP's expectation of a "Red Tolstoj". He considered such a possibility a "fantastic belief", as preposterous as the appearance of a "proletarian czar".[103] For Tret'jakov, the novel of Tolstoj's time could not compete with the mass circulation of the contemporary newspaper, which had supplanted the novel as an 'instructive' organ. One of the tasks of the Futurists was to train Soviet people to read the newspaper. Another was to have writers work for newspapers and have them adjust their craft to its requirements. Tret'jakov passionately believed that the newspaper would one day reach such a state of development that it would "become completely the narrative literature *(èpos)* and Bible of our time".[104] Not *War and Peace*, but contemporary reality was the new 'novel' of the age in which the readers and writers were the *dramatis personae*. "There is no need to wait for Tolstojs, for we have our own narrative literature. Our narrative literature is the newspaper."[105]

For the Futurists and Formalists, 'imaginative literature' could not objectively or factually reflect the events of the day because they believed that it was a 'distortion' of reality. They thus saw in newspapers, diaries, sketches, feuilletons, biographies, memoirs and travelogues the solution to literary crisis of the post-revolutionary period and the key to the "writer's immediate role in the construction of our times...and the relation of all his writings to concrete needs".[106] They believed that 'fact', peculiar to those genres, was the most effective and objective source of knowledge about those events and apparently necessary for arousing a

[103] S. Tret'jakov, "Novyj Lev Tolstoj", in *Literatura fakta...*, 29.
[104] Tret'jakov's call for the writer's work for newspapers apparently coincided with the decline of the 'thick' journals: "A growing daily press gradually took over most of the reportorial functions that had been fulfilled in the old chronicles and surveys. The various departments of the newspapers offered much the variety as the journals, but in a far more accessible form" (Maguire, *Red Virgin Soil...*, 378).
[105] Tret'jakov, "Novyj Lev Tolstoj", 29. It is of no minor significance, to be sure, that several leading members of RAPP, who comprised the Litfront, shared the Futurists' and Formalists' criticism of RAPP's literary notions and slogans. See Brown, *The Proletarian Episode...*, 150-154, I. Bespalov, "Protiv gramotnosti", *Pečat' i revoljucija*, No. 9 (1929), 17-24, and N. Stepanov, "V zaščitu izobretatel'stva", *Zvezda*, No. 6 (1929), 185. Notably, the Litfront also supported the Futurist-Formalist notion of 'literature of fact'. See *Literaturnaja èntsiklopedija*, VI (Moscow, 1932), 349-350. According to Brown, "The demand that various styles and tendencies be allowed to develop freely within RAPP is one of the cardinal points in the Litfront program" (*The Proletarian Episode...*, 159). The Futurists were undoubtedly aware of this and were therefore quite reluctant to join RAPP even after Majakovskij had joined it.
[106] N. Čužak, "Literatura žiznestroenija", in *Literatura fakta...*, 60.

new 'perception' of reality. To this notion, craftsmanship and the autonomy of the writer, not ideology, were central.[107]

For Čužak, "any historically necessary form" was first factually oriented and then functioned as parody. Devices, when applied to factual materials, would create new literary forms. "Only a decisive transition to new, rationally effective devices", he noted, "will save our literature from decay."[108] Čužak was unable to say whether devices themselves would 'distort' factual material. He believed that a factual representation of reality, directed to the mass readers, would contribute to its transformation. A revolution of literary forms had to attend, as he saw it, the cultural revolution, which he interpreted as a "*revolution of consciousness above all*".[109] Majakovskij, too, spoke of the "sum of devices" and "skills" as methods in creating the cultural revolution. Invention and the testing of new literary methods – these were the "salient features" of the Futurists.[110]

Šklovskij saw in factual materials the creation of new literary forms by experimenting with literary genres, a kind of prelude to a new literature. "Literature needs concreteness and cross-breeding with the new life for the creation of a new form."[111] Šklovskij noted further, echoing Mandelštam:

> I am convinced that the old form – the form of individual destiny, the threading of incidents by means of a glued-together hero – is now unnecessary. The new form will temporarily consist of creating an orientation toward material. This new form, the form of the serious feuilleton and newspaper sketch, does not yet exist.
>
> Travelogues, autobiographies, memoirs are the surrogate form for the new pre-literature. For the present, no one needs big novels, epic canvases. These are a kind of aluminum wagons which are issued at a time when one must build a steel and aluminum automobile. The literature of tomorrow will differ not thematically, but thematically and formally from the literature of today.[112]

The Futurists and Formalists, however, were not very clear about the methodology of the 'literature of fact'. Čužak frankly admitted that it was lacking, but would be forthcoming. Literature for him simply had to

107 See Edward J. Brown, *Russian Literature...*, 60.
108 Čužak, "Pisatel'skaja pamjatka", 28.
109 Čužak, "Literatura žiznestroenija", 64.
110 Majakovskij, XII, 401-402.
111 Viktor Šklovskij, *Gamburgskij sčët* (Leningrad, 1928), 84, and his *Tret'ja fabrika* (Moscow, 1926), 84-85.
112 Šklovskij, *Gamburgskij sčët*, 109.

be concrete, real, and aimed at "organizing society".[113] Brik noted that facts and descriptions of events ought to be presented from a "definite viewpoint".[114] Šklovskij noted that the contemporary writer, unlike the writers of the past, was at a disadvantage because he was unable to learn the craft of literature from his contemporaries. He thus suggested that writers take other jobs and professions so as to find material and acquire technical skills in writing.[115]

As to why the Futurists and Formalists lacked a methodology, Erlich observes:

> Clearly, in the Formalist responses to contemporary literature, the diagnosis mattered more than the prescription, the will to change was more crucial – and more widely shared – than the commitment to a particular set of innovations. Whatever the nature or direction of the literary 'upheaval' championed at the moment, the emphasis of Formalist criticism was invariably on a bold and uninhibited search for novelty; its watchword – 'inventiveness'...
>
> If the Formalist's insistence on 'decisive novelty' encouraged the quest for unorthodox and 'difficult' modes of expression, his emphasis on the uniqueness of literary art provided the theoretical basis for a vigorous, if short-lived, campaign against the political regimentation of literature.[116]

If the Futurists and Formalists lacked methodology, they did not lack models, some of which were Tynjanov's *Kjuxlja*, Majakovskij's *How I Wrote Esenin*, Šklovskij's *Sentimental Journey* and *The Third Factory*, Boris Kušner's *103 Days in the West*, and Reed's *Ten Days That Shook the World.*[117]

By 1930, RAPP, with Party support, gained the upper hand over the Futurists and Formalists. Majakovskij now could no longer resist the pressure to surrender to RAPP's literary organization and leadership.[118] In the main this marked, to be sure, the dissolution of the Futurists and Formalists as a group and the apparent erosion of their opportunity to

113 Čužak, "Pisatel'skaja pamjatka", 109.

114 Osip Brik, "Protiv tvorčeskoj ličnosti", in *Literatura fakta...*, 75.

115 Viktor Šklovskij, "O pisatele i proizvodstve", in *Literatura fakta...*, 189-193. According to Šklovskij, the significance of the "formal method" was that art was viewed as production (*Tret'ja fabrika*, 65).

116 Erlich, *Russian Formalism...*, 149-150.

117 See for example, Čužak, "Literatura žiznestroenija", 61-62.

118 See Majakovskij, XII, 426. "The negative attitude of the leaders of RAPP toward Majakovskij is the most glaring example of their failure to appreciate a genuine and original artist whose creative 'line' did not happen to agree with their own" (Brown, *The Proletarian Episode...*, 147). See also Edward J. Brown, "The Year of Acquiescence", in *Literature and Revolution in Soviet Russia 1917-1962*, 48-50.

develop a 'literature of fact'. Averbax, RAPP's leader, considered the Futurist-Formalist notion of the writer as a craftsman a serious threat to its organization and leadership because it placed the writer above "collective collaborative work" and "hindered the development of literature".[119] Averbax saw in the "facts of social life" the basis of artistic representation.[120] He noted that RAPP's literary method was concrete evidence that the "future belonged to this particular literary school". Once all writers, he went on, whatever their differences and orientations, "united under RAPP's leadership, literature would quickly result in an unprecedented blossoming" and in the appearance of "Shakespeares".[121]

According to Fadeev, the burden of the Futurists' theory of fact was the negation of art and the elimination of the "concrete man" in literature. Fadeev pointed out that facts had to be filtered through "class psychology" and interpreted. The Futurist emphasis on fact meant that they lacked "a unified world view" and hence were unable to interpret reality. Ideology for the Futurists, Fadeev noted, consisted in form. Only proletarian literature, Fadeev went on, armed with Marxism, was able to "tear off all the masks" and reveal "the objective laws of development" and "the true essence of phenomena in images".[122]

6. CONCLUSION

Until its dissolution in 1930, Russian Cubo-Futurism never lost sight of the principles that inspired it. Arising as a radical break with literary traditions and as an attack on literary tastes and idols, it committed itself to a search for new poetic forms and linguistic innovation. The notion of a literary crisis often attended that search and was perhaps shaped by it. The artistic milieu of the prerevolutionary era – Symbolism, Cubism – contributed significantly to the shaping of the principles of Futurism. These principles became a condition of the existence of Futurism and, one might add, almost an end in themselves.

[119] See V. Kaverin, "Neskol'ko let", *Novyj mir*, No. 11 (1966), 137. See also I. Grossman-Roščin, "Prestuplenie i nakazanie", *Na literaturnom postu*, No. 22 (1928), 24.

[120] See L. Averbax, "Novyj lef", in his *Kul'turnaja revoljucija i voprosy sovremennoj literatury* (Moscow-Leningrad, 1928), 115-133.

[121] See Kaverin, 137.

[122] A. Fadeev, "Stolbovaja doroga proletarskoj literatury", in his *Sobranie sočinenij v pjati tomax*, V (Moscow, 1960), 23-31.

During the 1920's, the Futurists did not abandon these principles. They allied themselves with Bolshevism because they projected onto it their own social and politically anarchic revolt, which was apparently an extension of their esthetic revolt. Hence the equation of Futurist art with proletarian art. The Bolsheviks, however, became suspicious of the Futurists' idealism, their emphasis on creative innovation, their notion of the artist as a producer and skilled craftsman,[123] and their efforts to integrate him into society. When the Bolsheviks realized that the Futurist notion of factual literature would free the writer "from the obligation to produce ideologically tendentious 'artistic literature'",[124] they rejected the Futurists. This seems to point up one of the paradoxes of Russian Futurism during the 1920's: it was intensely political and yet deemphasized the role of ideology in art, especially in the 'literature of fact'.

The "literature of fact", Drozda observes, was "part of the artistic process of its time"; and however one-sided and exaggerated, it was of genuine and considerable significance in view of the mass eclectism that ensued in Soviet literature.[125] The emphasis on fact, the Futurists and Formalists believed, would mark an important step in orienting the Soviet reader to a new view or 'perception' of reality and contribute or lead to its transformation.[126] They believed, moreover, that literature should accommodate itself to literary evolution and be integrated into life.[127] The 'literature of fact' was essentially the Futurist-Formalist response, as it were, to the Party's call for a "style corresponding to the epoch", a mode of writing which they considered was shaped by the course of literary evolution. In other words, in advocating a factual literature, the Futurists and Formalists saw historical precedents for it. Unlike RAPP, they were not saying what literature ought to have been, but what kind of literature was possible within the framework of literary evolution (i.e. in view of the literary trends of the 1920's). Given the circumstances of the late 1920's, their perspective on the nature and direction of literature was perhaps much more sophisticated and 'radically' realistic than that of other literary groups, especially of RAPP.

The 'literature of fact' was the Futurists' and Formalists' last and

123 This point is well made by Krystyna Pomorska, *Russian Formalist Theory and Its Poetic Ambiance* (The Hague, 1968), 92-93.

124 Brown, *Russian Literature...*, 60.

125 M. Drozda, "Osip Brik jako kritik", *Československa rusistika*, No. 1 (1967), 16.

126 See V. Šklovskij, *Žili-byli* (Moscow, 1964), 375.

127 See R. Grebeničkova, "Literatura faktu a teorie romanu", *Československa rusistika*, No. 3 (1968), 162-167.

perhaps desperate attempt to be, as they wrote, "useful to our Soviet youth, which frankly considers itself the engine of socialistic construction, but which because of its inexperience has become a prisoner of ill-suited and alien literary devices. We want to warn it against mindless imitation of obsolete forms of literary craftsmanship, once we have directed its thinking to a quest for its own literary paths which stem organically from the demands of the revolutionary epoch."[128] The 'literature of fact' was also, as Erlich notes, the Futurists' "perfect example of the integration of literature with life".[129]

[128] See *Literatura fakta...*, 5. The notion that the artist should take an active and leading role in the shaping of society was advanced by Saint-Simon and Marx. Egbert points out that "Under [Soviet] socialist realism...artists play a thoroughly subordinate role in clear contrast to that position as leaders of society ascribed to them by Saint-Simon and his followers. And it is a role that also contrasts with the conception of artistry held by the young Marx..." ("The Idea of 'Avant-garde' in Art and Politics", 355).

[129] Erlich, *Russian Formalism...*, 121.

VIII

RUSSIAN AND ITALIAN FUTURISM

1. SOME SIMILARITIES AND THE PROBLEM OF 'INFLUENCE'

Russian Cubo-Futurism and Italian share many characteristics. Both felt a deep gap between poetry and urban or industrial society and, programmatically, sought to make the former reflective of the latter's technique, speed, and tempo. This basic similarity, however, points up a basic difference between the two movements. Poetically, the Russian Futurists reacted pessimistically towards, and violently against, industrial society because of its threat to human values and its dehumanization of man. The Italian Futurists, on the other hand, viewed industrial society optimistically and wanted to glorify it poetically. The negation by both movements of past culture and literature followed from their felt gap between poetry and modern industrial society. Moreover, both movements partly derived their poetic theories from painting. Both saw the need of experimenting with language, to make it more pliable and to liberate it from the fetters of conventional meanings and grammatical rules. Both movements were nationalistically oriented,[1] and last, but not least, they both embraced totalitarian regimes. Many of these characteristics, of course, are common to many of the literary avant-garde movements of Western Europe of this century.

When dealing with Italian and Russian Futurism, the problem of the former's influence on the latter almost inevitably arises. The topic thus far has not been very productive. For almost fifty years, literary historians have argued and discussed the problem without any conclusive results. In his history of Russian Futurism, Markov, a leading authority on it, notes that the "question of direct Russian borrowings from Marinetti remains to be explored". He goes on to say, after pointing out several

[1] For Italian Futurism, see Rosa Clough, *Futurism: The Story of a Modern Art Movement* (New York, 1961), 16.

aspects of Russian Futurism which are reminiscent of Marinetti (e.g. various typefaces, whistles, mathematical symbols, musical notations, destruction of syntax, glorification of intuition), that to "prove that all these similarities are the result of direct borrowing is not so easy".[2] The Italian scholar Colucci, in his recent study, rightly concluded that the influence of Italian Futurism on Russian Futurism was above all theoretical.[3] His other conclusions are moot: that Marinetti's treatises and those of the figurative arts profoundly influenced Majakovskij's lyric poems and Kručënyx's "poetic conception"; that the Italian literary manifestoes "were like the skeleton around which was formed the living substance of poets like Majakovskij..."[4]

Colucci's observations on the theoretical influence of Italian Futurism, however, find solid support from the Russian Futurists themselves. In 1927, Osip Brik frankly admitted that the Futurists borrowed a number of slogans from the Italian Futurist manifestoes. He gave these borrowings as examples, among others: "We want to sing the love of danger, the habit of energy and rashness"; "The main element of our poetry will be courage, audacity, and revolt"; "Beyond struggle beauty does not exist".[5] The Italian Futurist manifestoes did, then, serve as a source of identity for the Russian Futurists, provided them with an urban esthetics (to which they paid lip service) and provided them in 1913 what they lacked in the 1910 *Sadok sudej:* a manifesto of protest, shock, and rejection of the past. After 1913, such manifestoes became an almost permanent feature of the Russian Futurism.

Beyond the realm of theoretical or manifesto influence, however, the problem of further influence does not appear to merit serious consideration. As Markov suggests, to pinpoint precisely the Italian influence on Russian Futurism, or to find 'clear-cut' examples of that influence, is difficult.[6] Influence-hunting in this case runs the almost inevitable risk of imputing to the Italian Futurists poetic elements in Russian Futurism which were part of the Russian literary tradition, or elements common to the age, or both. The problem of influence often tends to be one of coincidence.

There are other difficulties to the problem. Notably, the most significant

[2] Vladimir Markov, *Russian Futurism: A History* (Berkeley, 1968), 162.
[3] Michele Colucci, "Futurismo russo e futurismo italiano: Qualche nota e qualche considerazione", *Richerche slavistica*, No. 12 (1964), 176.
[4] *Ibid.*
[5] Osip Brik, "My – futuristy", *Lef,* No. 8-9 (1927), 50-52.
[6] Markov, 162.

achievements of the Russian Futurists were in poetry, not in the figurative arts.[7] The converse is true for Italian Futurism, which produced no poet comparable to the stature of Majakovskij and Xlebnikov.[8] This almost necessarily precludes a fruitful poetical comparison of the two movements. Furthermore, if we examine, as Colucci admonishes, the two movements "in their spiritual roots, in their deepest *raison d'être*", one cannot say that both movements shared the same views about man's future in industrial society, with which they hoped to come to grips. But then so did other avant-garde movements attempt the same (e.g. the Surrealists).

The difficulty of pinpointing the precise poetic influence of Italian Futurism on Russian Futurism does not preclude, however, a useful comparison of the theoretical foundations of the two movements. This comparison, seen through a discussion between two Futurist theoreticians, Bendikt Livšic and Marinetti, will illuminate the basic poetic orientations of Russian and Italian Futurism.

After Marinetti arrived in Russia in January 1914, the Cubo-Futurists naturally wanted to deny any connection with Italian Futurism, however obliquely. They wrote a letter to a newspaper and asserted that modern Russian literature was the product of the historically distinct formation of the Russian language, and therefore independent of any Gallic influences. Shortly after, however, Majakovskij, whose own theoretical statements reflected the esthetics of the Italian Futurists, changed his view. In a letter to a newspaper, he observed that the Cubo-Futurists were "united by a hatred for the past, but men of different temperaments and characters". He saw a literary parallelism between Russian and Italian Futurism, although he denied that the former was a continuation *(preemstvennost')* of the latter. For Majakovskij, Futurism was a "social movement born of the big city, which itself is destroying all national boundaries. The poetry of the future will be cosmopolitan."[9] To be sure,

[7] This is not to say, however, that the figurative arts did not have some influence on Russian Futurist poetry. For example, Colucci notes that one of Majakovskij's early poems "follows point by point – transformed poetically, of course – a manifesto by Russolo" (168). Colucci goes on to say that "Majakovskij was purely, totally futurist, in the Italian sense of the word, for not more than a year, but that without Italian futurism, without papers like the 'Manifesto tecnico della pittura', all of his work from 'Vladimir Majakovskij' to 'The Cloud in Trousers', from '150,000,000' to 'At the Top of My Voice' would be inconceivable stylistically" (172). Such statements are not particularly useful or constructive, however extreme and contradictory.

[8] See Colucci, 164. "The best works left to us by Marinetti and his followers remain the manifestoes they signed – significant fact – composed most often in French" (Renato Poggioli, *The Theory of the Avant-garde* [Cambridge, 1968], 228).

[9] See N. Xardžiev, "Kommentarij: Zabytye stat'i Majakovskogo", in *Literaturnoe*

this was basically an esthetic principle of Italian Futurism.

In his conversation and public talks, Marinetti was critical of the theory and practice of the Russian Futurists. He considered their neologistic experiments as "plusquaperfutism", and Xlebnikov's poetry as "the language of a pre-historical period". Marinetti remarked to Kul'bin, a Russian painter, that the Cubo-Futurists were too abstract, while the Italian Futurists were earthbound, which was a mark of both their strength and weakness.[10]

Attention will now be directed to the theoretical aspects of Russian and Italian Futurism as discussed and defined by Livšic and Marinetti in 1914.

Marinetti: ...we both have a common enemy – *passéism* – and we must act jointly. *Passéism* in Italy and Russian *passéism* – with us one can only use this term conventionally – are quite different things...The yoke of the past, which is your major tragedy, is almost unknown to us; it is, after all, directly proportionate to the quantity of national genius, embodied in works of art. In Russia there were no Michelangelos, but Opekušins, Antokol'skijs, Trubeckojs – are they obstacles to anyone? Moreover, is this really Russian art? And Puškin?

Livšic: We do have Xlebnikov. For our generation he is the same as Puškin was for the 19th century, the same as Lomonosov was for the 18th century. ... (Here Livšic points out that his explanation of Xlebnikov's significance for Russian poetry is unconvincing to Marinetti, who remarks suddenly:)

Marinetti: No, the creation of new words is still not everything... Look at us, we have shattered the syntax. We are using the verb only in the infinitive; we have abolished the adjective, eliminated punctuation marks...

Livšic: Your struggle is superficial. You are struggling with separate parts of speech and are not even trying to penetrate beyond the plane of etymological categories... You don't want to see in a grammatical sentence only the external form of logical reasoning *(suždenie)*. All the arrows which you are aiming at the traditional syntax are missing the mark. Despite your innovations, the connection of the logical subject with the predicate remains firm, for from the viewpoint of this connection, it makes no difference by which part of speech the aspects of logical reasoning are expressed.

---

nasledstvo, II (Moscow, 1932), 157.

10 *Ibid.*

Marinetti: Are you denying the possibility of shattering the syntax?

Livšic: Not at all. We are only asserting that by those means which you, the Italian Futurists, are limiting yourselves to, one cannot achieve anything.

Kul'bin: (in support of Livšic) We have advanced the notion of trans-sense as the basis of irrational poetry.

Marinetti: Trans-sense? What is that? But, after all, this is not my "words in liberation". Are you familiar with my technical manifesto on literature?

Livšic: Of course. But I think that you are contradicting yourself.

Marinetti: (heatedly) How?

Livšic: By the way you recite!... What aim are you seeking by an amorphous mass of words which you call "words in liberation"? To cancel out the mediating function of reason with the greatest amount of disorder, isn't that so? There is quite a difference, however, between a typographical outline of your "Tsang Tumb Tuuum" and uttering it aloud.

Marinetti: Many of my listeners at home who have read my book have said the same thing.

Livšic: That only confirms the idea that I'm trying to express to you. Have you tried to realize how the difference between your writing of your "words in liberation" and your reading can be explained? I just heard your declamation and thought: is it worth destroying – even as you do it – the traditional sentence so as to restore it anew, by returning to it the logical predicate taken from it by suggestive moments of gesture, mimicry, intonation, sound imitation?

Marinetti: But do you know that Boccioni carves one and the same thing from various material: marble, wood, bronze?

Livšic: Oh, that's not the same thing in the least. In my view, a work of art is complete only when it is self-contained, when it does not seek an object beyond itself. Poetry is one thing, and declamation is another...

Marinetti: (interrupts) Declamation! That's not the point. It is only a transitional stage, a temporary substitution for syntax which has functioned up to now as an interpreter and guide. When we succeed in putting into common use what I call the "wireless imagination", when we are able to discard the first series of analogies so as to be limited only to the second – in a word, when we lay the firm foundations for a new intuitive perception of the world in which reason will take the place of what resembles it, a more than modest place, there won't be any question about declamation.

Kul'bin: (attempts to speak) Bergson...

Marinetti: Bergson is irrelevant here. So you haven't read my "Supplement to the Technical Manifesto of Futurist Literature"? While disclaiming any influence of Bergson's philosophy, I point out in the manifesto that even in 1902 I took as the epigraph to my poem "The Conquest of the Stars" the passage from the "The Conversation of Monos and Una", where Poe, in comparing the poetic inspiration with the cognitive capabilities of reason, gives unconditional preference to the first. Why [excitedly] is it impossible to utter "intuition" and Bergson's name emerges immediately? One could think that before him only a pure rationalism existed in the world. ... (Here Livšic allows Marinetti to 'make short work' of Bergson, since there were no Bergsonians in Russian Futurism, according to Livšic)

Marinetti: (continues) Intuition! Who said that one can draw a sharp boundary between intuition and rational perception? I never maintained that! On the contrary, the relativity of both conditions, mutually intersecting each other at every moment, is indisputable for me. The ideal poetry which we allow ourselves to dream about at the present and which is nothing other than the inseparable link in the "analogies of the second order", will be completely irrational. For this, however, one still has to overcome a great deal: to eliminate all psychology from literature, to substitute it with the lyrical obsession with essence...

Livšic: You say obsession with essence. But if this is not a poetic metaphor, you should be aware that in this regard the priority belongs to us, to those whom you regard as Asiatics... Obsession with essence is not enough in itself. To realize it in a work of art requires above all the existence of the feeling for material... But in the West this is precisely what is lacking: the West does not sense material as the organic substance of art. This can be corroborated by dozens of examples. For the last forty years there is certainly no lack of them.

Marinetti: The liberation of art, however, for you, in Russia, began under the influence of the French...

Livšic: To the West we are not opposing Russia, but the whole of the East, of which we are only a part... Have you really forgotten of the time when the names of Hokusai and Utamaro were no less popular in Paris than Claude Monet or Renoir? And *pointillé?* It is usually considered as the daughter of the impressionistic 'comma', and as the grandchild of Delacroix's broad brush stroke. But is it really no closer to a mosaic, which contains all the properties of *pointillé* including the vibration of light which is achieved with the aid of gold plates? It is not for nothing that *pointillé* in the person of Sinjak led to a blind alley, but for us, in Russia, *pointillé* continued its life like an organic cell, splitting, broadening and transformed into stained-glass panels by Vladimir Burljuk. Have you seen Jakulov's paintings? Do you know that his revolving sun disk is a year older than Deloneevskij's *simultanéité?*

Marinetti: You are talking only about painting...

Livšic: Because it is, like sculpture and music, the international language of art. Do you believe that the case is different with poetry? Unfortunately, Xlebnikov for you is merely a name: he is utterly untranslatable in those very works where his genius is expressed with the greatest force. Rimbaud's most daring ventures are baby talk in comparison with what Xlebnikov is doing, by shattering the millennial linguistic stratification and by fearlessly plunging into the articulatory chasm of the primordial word.

Marinetti: (shrugs his shoulders) Why is this archaism necessary? Is it really capable of expressing the whole complexity of the tempo of contemporary life?

Livšic: Your question is extremely characteristic. It is only added proof of (your) indifference to material, an indifference which you are vainly attempting to conceal by loud phrases about the lyrical obsession with material. In fact, in the name of what do you propose to eliminate punctuation marks? In the name of the beauty of speed, isn't that so? Well, we, excuse me, don't give a rap for this beauty. While lying in a bunk of a sleeping car, we do not at all want to feel that we have been transferred into space. Maximum comfort, for which contemporary technology is striving, just consists in easing every jolt, toss, and other 'beauties' of speed as much as possible. Does the possession of a woman really give you pleasure only when you are having sexual intercourse with the object of your admiration? We call this debauchery.

Marinetti: You Russians are lazy and sedentary. This is perhaps a truly Eastern feature...

Livšic: We are more consistent than you. Five years ago we abolished punctuation, but we didn't do that so as to replace it with a new punctuation, to say to a point, which only slackens your notorious tempos... By this method we emphasize the continuity of the verbal mass, its elemental cosmic essence. The only obsession with essence that is available to the poet is the obsession with the material of his

> art, an immersion in the element of the word. This is not archaism, but the practice of cosmology, which does not admit of itself any dimension in time.[11]

The discussion, although it did not end on a very happy note or find Marinetti and Livšic in agreement on principles, seems to have a certain value in shedding some light on the theoretical poetics of Russian and Italian Futurism.

[11] As rendered by Benedikt Livšic, *Polutoraglazyj strelec* (Leningrad, 1933), 222–228.

IX

FRENCH SURREALISM AND RUSSIAN FUTURISM

1. SOME COMPARISONS AND DIFFERENCES

As two major avant-garde movements of this century, the similarities between Russian Cubo-Futurism and French Surrealism are striking. They invite investigation of the significance of the former for the latter, their shared hopes and aspirations and their commitment to a distorted version of Bolshevism. Having common origins in Symbolism and Cubism and primarily poetic movements, both arose as a radical revolt against literary conventions, reputations, and traditions and as a vehement protest against the cultural and moral disintegration of 'bourgeois' society. Both sought the "philosopher's stone" for man's revenge on "things".[1] Their overwhelming passion for scandal, action, negation, shock and demonstration often concealed their 'positive' aim: "to transform the world" and "to change life".[2] As political anarchists, the Surrealists and Futurists eagerly embraced and served Bolshevism because they saw it as the destruction of 'bourgeois' society and the fulfillment of their cultural and spiritual revolution. For them, Bolshevism became a means to their own cultural and esthetic revolt; for the Bolsheviks, the avant-gardists became a means to further their political ends.

The major similarities, to be sure, do not end here. Both movements saw poetry as a means of liberating and transforming mankind. The Russian Futurists saw in poetry the advent of new social orders which they opposed to the society which they abominated. The Surrealists certainly extended this aim, gave it depth or 'inwardness' and democratized it. Although both movements saw poetic creation as largely rooted in linguistic processes – independent of reason and logic – which nourished

1 Maurice Nadeau, *The History of Surrealism* (New York, 1965), 163.

2 Breton once observed: "'Transform the world', Marx said, 'Change life', Rimbaud said – these two watchwords are for us one and the same" (quoted in Nadeau, 195).

and governed poetic content, this notion served as the source and inspiration more of Surrealism than of Futurism.

In contrast, the Surrealists believed that, since rational human activity had led to a morally outrageous and culturally inferior social order, man's exploration of his dreams, of hallucinatory, and hypnotic states, and of irrational subconscious processes would reveal the basic answers to human and social problems. As Breton defined it, Surrealism was

> Pure psychic automatism by which one intends to express, either verbally or in writing, or otherwise the real function of thought. Thought dictated in absence of all control ruled by reason, and beyond all esthetic or moral preoccupation... Surrealism is based on the belief in the superior reality of certain forms of associations heretofore neglected, in the omnipotence of the dream and in the disinterested play of thought. It tends to destroy definitively all other psychic mechanisms, and to substitute itself for them in resolving the major problems of life.[3]

The correspondence between two worlds, which the poet bridges, is Surrealism's deep and subtle link with Symbolism. For the Surrealists, poetry was a new mode of knowledge and discovery, an opportunity for penetrating and tapping the unconscious; and because this 'mystical' activity was common to all men, as Eluard pointed out, the Surrealists "aim to reduce the differences between men and thus refuse to serve an absurd order based on inequality, deceit and cowardice".[4] Paradoxically, the probing of the irrational provided the key to a 'rational' social order.

The very nature of the Surrealists' social objectives and their belief in the fundamental 'rationality' of 'bourgeois' society were partly responsible for their being attracted to Bolshevism and their ultimate political commitment to it. In a conversation with Lunačarskij, the Soviet Commissar of Education, in 1923, Aragon and Breton expressed their violent hostility towards bourgeois society whose most abominable and stifling feature, they noted, was its dull, dry, cold and narrow rationalism and belief in reason as the basic principle of the universe. For the Surrealists, this rational principle merely masked a tremendous and arcane spontaneity which only the 'principle of intuition' could penetrate and which the artist could grasp by "seeing things in their surrealist significance". The Surrealists also saw that they must revolt against bourgeois society "so as to topple the kingdom of the bourgeoisie and at the same time the kingdom of reason; so as to restore the great kingdom

[3] André Breton, "Manifeste du Surréalisme (1924)", in his *Manifestes du Surréalisme* (Paris, 1962), 40.

[4] Quoted in Claude Mauriac, *André Breton* (Paris, 1949), 17.

of the life of spontaneity; so as to dissolve the world in the true music of an existence of intensity". For this reason, the Surrealists valued the Asian continent because it was unsullied by European rationalism. Aragon and Breton called upon the Soviets to lead Asia to the destruction of bourgeois pseudo-culture even if this meant the destruction of the Surrealists themselves, so long as reason and the "all-strangling principle of bourgeois" were also destroyed in the onslaught.[5] They noted elsewhere:

Logical Europe crushes the mind endlessly between the hammers of two terms; it closes and opens man's mind. Now, however, the strangulation is at its crisis; we have suffered too long under the harness. Man's Mind is greater than the mind, the metamorphoses of life are numerous. Like you, we reject progress. Come, demolish our homes.[6]

The Surrealists' notion of the aims of the Bolshevik revolution represented the very antipode of Lunačarskij's – and Lenin's and Trotsky's – understanding of it. Lunačarskij observed that it required a considerable effort to overcome the Surrealists' "amazement and even indignation" when he remarked that they were absolutely mistaken about the aims of the Revolution. He viewed it not as "any Asiatic mystical metaphysics", but as an extension of reason guided by, and committed to, Western civilization, whose best fruit was Marxism, the apogee of dialectical reason, a higher form of science which Bolshevism intended to bring to the West.[8]

2. THE SURREALIST POLITICAL COMMITMENT AND 'PROLETARIAN' LITERATURE

The Surrealists' commitment to Bolshevism in 1925 gave new momentum, vitality, and solidarity to their movement, as it had to the Futurists in

[5] Anatolij Lunačarskij, "Aleksandr Blok", in his *Sobranie sočinenij v vos'mi tomax*, I (Moscow, 1966), 488.

[6] "Lettre aux écoles du Bouddha", *La révolution surréaliste*, No. 3 (April 1925), 22. In another context Breton and the Surrealists wrote to the French Ambassador to Japan in 1925: "We wish with all our might that the revolutions, the wars, the colonial insurrections will annihilate this Western civilization, the evil of which you defend as far as the Orient; and we call the destruction of this state of affairs the one our minds would be most likely to accept" (quoted in Mauriac, 14).

[7] "Essentially the [Bolshevik] Revolution means the people's final break with the Asiatic, with the Seventeenth Century, with Holy Russia, with ikons and with roaches. It does not mean a return to the pre-Peter era, but on the contrary, it means a communion of the entire people with civilization and a reconstruction of the material foundations of civilization in accordance with the interests of the people" (Leon Trotsky, *Literature and Revolution* [Ann Arbor, 1960], 94. Sidney Monas writes that

1917. Like the Futurists, the Surrealists believed that Bolshevism mirrored their own 'surreal' and cultural revolution.

In an almost ecstatic review of Trotsky's biography of Lenin, Breton remarked that Bolshevism, as an organized political system, had manifested its superiority by consummating a vast social upheavel in a relatively brief period. He suggested that the Surrealists' commitment to Bolshevism was necessary if they seriously expected to achieve their cultural and spiritual objectives. For Breton, the Bolsheviks were the supreme revolutionary avatars who had reached "the acme of their Destiny" by executing their revolutionary will. As he saw it, the Bolsheviks had not abandoned their aims of extending their revolution to Western Europe, but would immediately respond to the revolutionary call.[9] In that event, Breton and the Surrealists apparently assumed that they would become the new cultural arbiters, a role which 'bourgeois' society, they felt, had denied them.

Curiously enough, except for Lunarčarskij's and Trotsky's encouragement,[10] the Surrealists' commitment to Bolshevism created suspicion and even hostility in the French Communist Party, which was an obedient servant of the Comintern. Their bourgeois origins, their Bohemianism, their refusal to submit to Party work and strict discipline and to abandon their poetic aims and notions, and their passion for dissent and protest, aroused suspicion and doubt in the Party about the Surrealists' reliability or loyalty as Party members. It is not surprising that relations between them remained tense. But even though the Party distrusted the Surrealists, it considered their attacks on 'bourgeois' society useful to its cause.[11]

Political commitment soon posed a test for the Surrealists as the

---

the founding mission of Bolshevism "was world revolution and the total transformation of man" ("Engineers or Martyrs: Dissent and the Intelligentsia", *Problems of Communism*, September-October 1968, 5).

[8] Lunačarskij, 489.

[9] André Breton, "Leon Trotsky: Lénine", *La révolution surréaliste*, No. 5 (October 1925), 28. See also in the same issue "La révolution d'abord et toujours", 31-32. Breton, for example, seriously entertained the extension of the Bolshevik revolution to France. David Caute observes that Breton "longed to see the Cossacks watering their horses on the Concorde" (*Communism and the French Intellectuals 1914-1960* [New York, 1964], 94).

[10] Lunačarskij, for example, observed that the "Surrealists have rightly understood that the task of all revolutionary intellectuals under a capitalist regime is to denounce bourgeois values. Their efforts deserve to be encouraged" (quoted in Robert S. Short, "The Politics of Surrealism, 1920-1936", *Journal of Contemporary History*, No. 2 [1966], 18).

[11] See Short, 10-14.

Bolsheviks began to mobilize West European intellectuals for revolutionary struggle. For what was at stake was the very integrity of Surrealist art as a means of discovery in the face of the Party's efforts to transform it into an instrument of political propaganda and to create a 'proletarian' literature in France, the Soviet Union, America and other countries.[12]

In 1928, the French Communist Party assigned the novelist Henri Barbusse the task of creating a weekly cultural review called *Monde*,[13] which received the heavy financial support of the Comintern. The purpose of the review was to attract and win over Leftist writers and intellectuals, to counter the hostility of the general press and professional organizations towards them, and to replace and counter *Clarté*,[14] which Barbusse had lost to the Trotskyists after it had initially been a Party organ. Another purpose of *Monde* was to create a 'proletarian' literature in France, or to urge "intellectuals to lead the communist movement toward a new, popular art which would come with the liberation of the masses..."[15]

The notion of a 'proletarian' literature met with the firm, violent resistance of the Surrealists. In reply to an inquiry by *Monde*, Breton simply did not envisage the possibility of creating in France an art that would express the aspirations of the proletariat. He believed that a writer, shaped by bourgeois society, was unable to interpret those aspirations. That a writer could have some notion of them Breton did not deny.

12 In America, the notion of 'proletarian' literature apparently first arose in 1921, when Michael Gold urged writers to immerse themselves in the life of the masses as a solution to their isolation. He defined 'proletarian' literature thus: "The Revolution, in its secular manifestations of strike, boycot, mass-meeting, imprisonment, sacrifice, agitation, martyrdom, organization, is thereby worthy of the religious devotion of the artist. If he records the humblest moment of that drama in a poem, story or picture or symphony, he is realizing Life more profoundly than if he had concerned himself with some transient personal mood." See "Towards Proletarian Art", *Liberator*, February 1921, 22. For an excellent treatment of this in America, see James B. Gilbert, *Writers and Partisans: A History of Literary Radicalism in America* (New York, 1968), 75-85.

13 Interestingly, the editorial board of *Monde* consisted of A. Einstein, M. Gorkij Upton Sinclair, M. Ugarte, M. de Unamuno, L. Bazalgette, M. Morhardt and Leon Werth.

14 In 1921, Barbusse organized *Clarté* as a "Center of International Revolutionary Education" committed to the creation of a new social order arising from the "radical destruction of the capitalist system" and assured by the "dictatorial preponderance of the class heretofore exploited and despoiled". Barbusse called this an "intellectual" task. When Max Eastman of *Liberator* objected, Barbusse replied that for him there was no distinction between intellectuals and proletarians. See his "In Defense of *Clarté*", *Liberator*, October 1921, 30.

15 Caute, 102. See also Jacques Fauvet, *Histoire du parti communiste français*, I (Paris, 1964), 100-101 and Roger Garaudy, *D'itinéraire d'Aragon* (Paris, 1961), 217.

Sincerity and sensibility were critical factors, too. But not unlike the Russian Futurists and Formalists, Breton saw the writer's work as a product of literary evolution and of "dialectical materialism", which determined its validity within that evolution. To reject this determinism, Breton suggested, would be anti-Marxian. Breton saw the rise of a 'proletarian' literature only with the rise of proletarian culture.[16] As to when that would happen, Breton cited Trotsky:

> Vague theories of proletarian culture, conceived by analogy and antithesis with bourgeois culture, are the result of comparison between proletariat and bourgeoisie, comparisons to which the critical mind is completely alien. It is certain that a moment will come in the development of the new society when economy, culture, have the greatest freedom of progressive movement. But we can only make fancy conjectures about this. In a society that will be pruned of the crushing worry of daily bread, where communal laundries will wash well everybody's good linen; where the children, all the children, well fed, healthy and gay, will absorb the elements of science and art, as well as the air and sunlight; where there will no longer be any useless mouths; where the liberated egoism of man – a formidable power – will tend only to knowledge, to the transformation and improvement of the universe. In that society, the dynamism of culture will not be comparable to anything that we have known in the past. But we shall reach it only after long and painful transition which is almost completely before us.[17]

One of the basic appeals of Trotsky's remarks to Breton was obviously the notion of the cultural transformation of society.

There were other replies to *Monde's* inquiry. The Surrealist Benjamin Péret was more violent than Breton. Péret argued that 'proletarian' literature could not exist because the proletariat had more immediate tasks to fulfill. He then scornfully questioned Barbusse's sincerity in raising the inquiry and disparaged his talent as a novelist. Péret concluded: "All these men here, limited, weak hypocrites, allow each moment to pass in hope of rising up to the rich and honorable. All this would be perfect and just if they did not try to control the liberal anger of the proletariat which they pretend to guide and represent."[18]

For Lucien Sablé, the inquiry ignored the flexibility and complexity of Marxist thought. Like Breton and the Futurists, Sablé noted that art was the product of many determinants, a reflection of the life of a given historical period. He thus wondered if 'proletarian' art would differ from 'non-proletarian' art, as if 'proletarian' chemistry and physics would

16 André Breton, "Seconde manifeste", in his *Manifestes du Surréalisme*, 186-187.
17 Breton, "Seconde manifeste", 188.
18 "Notre enquête sur la littérature prolétarienne", *Monde*, November 17, 1928, 6.

differ from other forms. Sablé believed that the most immediate mission of the proletariat was revolutionary action, of which to him it seemed incapable. Finally, he wondered if literature would be the principal mode of future artistic expression.[19]

For the Surrealists, literary developments in Russia of the late 1920's were also cause for alarm and subsequent disillusionment with Bolshevism. The Russian Association of Proletarian Writers (RAPP), with Party backing, had gradually eliminated and persecuted other literary groups and individual writers. As it assumed dictatorial power, RAPP dogmatically insisted on the immediate creation of a 'proletarian' literature and culture, whose elements, it claimed, prevailed even in bourgeois society.[20]

Majakovskij's suicide in 1930, partly a protest against RAPP and the increasing regimentation of Soviet life, demonstrated to the Surrealists that the "atmosphere in Russia was profoundly uncongenial to poetry and spiritually barren..."[21] Majakovskij and the Russian Futurists represented for the Surrealists artists of a 'post-revolutionary' situation in which the Surrealists hoped to find themselves in the future.[22]

To be sure, the Surrealists were not unaware of the bitter literary struggle that the Futurists waged against RAPP in the late 1920's. The Futurists considered the writer a 'craftsman' and 'producer' whose work was not unlike other forms of work; they wanted the writer to work for journals, newspapers, factories, to write sketches, diaries, reports and memoirs – in short, to write a 'literature of fact' that was in their view far more directly relevant to, and reflective of, the problems of the day than 'imaginative' literature. They believed that 'imaginative' literature was an intrinsically solitary art form that alienated the writer from the

19 *Ibid.* A number of Americans also replied: Stark Young, Theodore Dreiser, Sherwood Anderson, Eugene Jolas, Harriet Moore, Michael Gold, and Floyd Dell. See *Monde*, November 24, 1928, 12.

20 Herman Ermolaev, *Soviet Literary Theories 1917-1934: The Genesis of Socialist Realism* (Berkeley, 1963), 58.

21 Short, 18.

22 "Majakovskij's poems are in themselves a definition, an affirmation of the poet's place in a new order" (Elsa Triolet, *Majakovskij: Vers et proses de 1913 à 1930* [Paris, 1932], 9). See also her "Majakovskij et nous", *Poésie*, No. 38 (1947), 8-34. Triolet, the wife of Louis Aragon, was also the sister-in-law of Osip Brik, the chief theoretician of Russian Futurism during the 1920's. One should also note here that Majakovskij was given a reception by the Surrealists on his arrival in Paris in 1927. In one of his travel sketches, Majakovskij remarked that the Surrealists were a vigorous group, but wondered if they had a literary 'program'. He also noticed a similarity between the poetry and manifestoes of early Russian Futurism and those of the Surrealists, thus suggesting that the Surrealists were still in a 'pre-revolutionary' situation. See his "Ezdil ja tak", in his *Polnoe sobranie sočinenij*, VIII (Moscow, 1958), 334.

building of 'socialism' and, as Kušner observed, from "direct and immediate participation in political and cultural work".[23]

The Surrealists naturally tended to identify the fate of the Russian Futurists with their own; and this identity can be clearly seen in an article on Majakovskij by the Futurists Neznamov and Katanjan, which was translated into French and which appeared in the Surrealist journal.[24] Neznamov and Katanjan pointed out that for Majakovskij poetry was synonymous with life and struggle. In freely choosing to write for the Revolution, Majakovskij became a 'proletarian' poet not by using the proletariat as a poetic theme, but by taking up its cause: "He learned how to test his works on the masses. He understood that the problem of the masses is actually not only the problem of audience, but also a literary problem, not only the problem of fulfilling a task, but a formal problem as well. This is to say that not being satisfied *to learn to write for the masses*, he learned how to do it with the highest possible value, and this at the expense of his own heart." Finally, Majakovskij took part in the events of his time as an individual actor whom the Revolution had lost. Why Majakovskij was lost they did not really explain.

Breton, however, offered an ingenious and penetrating vindication, if not explanation, of Majakovskij's suicide. For Breton, Majakovskij's suicide stemmed from the contradiction or conflict between his desire to be a revolutionary poet and his desire to realize his personal 'destiny', in his case to find love or to overcome the pain of unrequited love to which no true revolutionary is immune. Put differently, Majakovskij's desire to find love in the 'present' was much greater than his desire to create for the 'future' of the proletariat. The irreconcilability of his conflict led to suicide. Majakovskij, however, did not betray the Revolution to which he was intellectually committed; rather he was himself betrayed by his desire to love, which Breton saw as characteristic of the 'human condition'. This irrepressible desire to love, which precluded a 'sentimental' commitment to the Revolution, marked the greatness of Majakovskij as a revolutionary poet.[25] By the same logic, to be sure, Breton was perhaps unwittingly providing a justification for the Surrealists' intellectual, but not 'sentimental' commitment to the Revolution.

23 Boris Kušner, "Pričiny otstavanija", *Krasnaja nov'*, No. 11 (1930), 132.
24 P. Neznamov and V. Katanjan, "C'est justement cela un poète prolétarien", *Le Surréalisme au service de la révolution*, No. 1 (July 1930), 16-22.
25 André Breton, "La barque de l'amour s'est brisée contre la vie courante", *Le Surréalisme au service de la révolution*, No. 1 (July 1930), 16-22. The title of Breton's article, translated from the Russian, was a line in Majakovskij's 'suicide' poem.

Majakovskij's suicide also raised the problem of 'proletarian' literature. Breton concluded:

More than ever, now that Majakovskij is dead, we refuse to register the weakening of the spiritual and moral protest which he took up. We deny, and will continue to do so, the possibility of a poetry or an art susceptible of accommodating itself to extremist simplification – "à la Barbusse" – of ways of thinking and feeling. We have yet to be shown a 'proletarian' work of art. The enthusiastic life of the struggling proletariat, the stupefying and shattering life of the mind surrendered to its own beastly aspects. As far as we are concerned, it would be an extremely vain wish to want to participate in only one of these dramas. Expect no concession from us in this realm.[26]

As Breton's remarks suggested, 'proletarian' art had no relation to the struggling proletariat. That it was the 'external' variant of Soviet 'socialist realism' which the Party adumbrated in the late 1920's, is not unlikely. The very notion of 'proletarian' literature was a contradiction in terms since the proletariat possessed no discrete or definable culture of its own. As Philip Rahv perceptively observed, 'proletarian' literature had no relation even to revolutionary thought. The principal implication that it entailed for the artist was his alliance with the proletariat and his recognition of the class struggle as the basic fact of social life, thus yoking art and politics. Moreover, 'proletarian' literature made no distinction between "the politics of writing in a *generic* and *normative* sense and the politics of an individual writer in a particular historical period; and...it fails to define in what way a writer's alliance with the working class is or is not an alliance with a particular party of that class".[27] Class and Party here were synonymous. To weld the artist to the Communist Party as a political functionary and to write 'Party' or 'Party-minded' literature was the real meaning of 'proletarian' literature. One should add that in this scheme of things only the Party could evaluate the correct – or to use a Soviet term, 'progressive' or 'non-progressive' – orientation of the artist's political outlook, an orientation subject to the changes in Party line, to which that outlook would have to conform.[28] Hence the writer's relinquishment of his artistic freedom. There was no basic distinction, then, between 'proletarian' literature and Soviet 'socialist realism'.

The Russian Futurists and French Surrealists realized the consequences

[26] Breton, "La barque de l'amour...", 22.

[27] Philip Rahv, "Proletarian Literature: A Political Autopsy", *Southern Review*, No. 4 (1939), 619.

[28] Rahv, 621.

of 'proletarian' literature for their art: it threatened with a utopian mythology and banal schematism the tension between their political and artistic commitments.

3. CONCLUSION

Many intellectuals and writers of the 1920's and 1930's, outraged by social and cultural decay and by the injustices of modern industrial society, turned to communism for salvation, for some political banner that would liberate them from their bewilderments,[29] but they never seriously pondered the tragic consequences of the destruction of a society that sanctioned their assaults against it. To this extent, they were politically naive. These assaults, moreover, were often of an emotional nature; as the French writer Roger Vailland put it: "We were Trotskyists really, forever talking about the 'permanent revolution,' unemployed intellectuals, more keenly aware of the emotional aspects of rebellion than of revolution."[30]

The reasons for the writer's and intellectual's commitment to communism were surely many. The evidence adduced here seems to indicate that one of the dominant reasons was that communism held out the vision of a literary and cultural regeneration that would attend revolutionary struggle and change, with the profoundly appealing prospect of the writer's and intellectual's active and leading role in it, however mythically heroic.

The literary and cultural aims of the Surrealists and Russian Futurists could not, in the final analysis, be reconciled with the political, organizational, material and institutional aims of Bolshevism.[31] Bolshevism and 'proletarian' literature offered the Surrealists and Futurists two unacceptable alternatives: "the alternative of supporting a revolutionary regime through esthetic conformity (that is, through ceasing to exist) or attempting to revolutionize (themselves) without any prospect of changing life, in view of the superior forces of the 'professional revolutionists.'

[29] William Philips and Philip Rahv, "Literature in a Political Decade", in *New Letters*, Horace Gregory ed. (New York, 1937), 170.

[30] Quoted in Caute, 96. Clifford Browder observes that Breton's "conversion to Marxism was another instance of a strong subjective enthusiasm, an adherence less intellectual than emotional in nature" (*André Breton: Arbiter of Surrealism* [Geneva, 1967], 123).

[31] See Monas, 5 and Short, 21.

Either of these choices could only lead to the end of avant-gardism."[32] Hence the inevitable break with Bolshevism that followed.[33] The apparent dilemma of many avant-garde literary movements is that they cannot remain 'revolutionary' by being apolitical. Yet political commitment or involvement is at once their salvation and bane.

32 Harold Rosenberg, "Collective, Ideological, Combative", *Art News Annual*, No. 34 (1968), 78.

33 Majakovskij's suicide in 1930 largely led to the dissolution of the Futurist group. For the Surrealists' break, see Short, 19.

SELECTED BIBLIOGRAPHY

FUTURIST ANTHOLOGIES, MANIFESTOES, AND PERIODICALS

"Čitatel'", *Novyj Lef*, No. 1 (1927), 1-2.
"Kogo predosteregaet *Lef?*", *Lef*, No. 1 (1923), 10-11.
"*Lef* k boju", *Lef*, No. 3 (1923), 3.
Lef: Žurnal levogo fronta iskusstv (1923-1925).
Majakovskij, V. and Brik, O., "Naša slovesnaja rabota", *Lef*, No. 1 (1923), 40-41.
Novyj Lef: Žurnal levogo fronta iskusstv (1927-1928).
Pervyj žurnal russkix futuristov, No. 1-2 (Moscow, 1914).
Poščëčina obščestvennomu vkusu (Moscow, 1912).
Rykajuščij Parnas (St. Petersburg, 1914).
Sadok sudej, No. 1 (Moscow, 1910).
Sadok sudej, No. 2 (St. Petersburg, 1913).
Sojuz molodëži (St. Petersburg, 1913).
Troe (St. Petersburg, 1913).
"V kogo vgryzaetsja *Lef?*", *Lef*, No. 1 (1923), 8-9.
"Za čto boretsja *Lef?*", *Lef*, No. 1 (1923), 1-7.

WORKS OF EARLY FUTURISTS

Burljuk, David, *K 25-ti letiju xudožestvenno-literaturnoj dejatel'nosti* (New York, 1924).
—, *Entelexizm* (New York, 1929).
—, "Tri glavy iz knigi 'Majakovskij i ego sovremenniki'", *Krasnaja strela* (New York, 1932).
—, *Mayakovsky* (= *Color and Rhyme*, No. 31) (1966).
Burljuk, David and Marussy, *Two Months in Our Native Country* (= *Color and Rhyme*, No. 40) (1959).
—, *Fifty Years With Mayakovsky* (= *Color and Rhyme*, No. 49) (1961).
—, *Hilea: 1907-1913* (= *Color and Rhyme*, No. 57) (1965).
Kamenskij, Vasilij, *Put' èntuziasta* (Moscow, 1931).
—, *Žizn' s Majkovskim* (Moscow, 1940).
Kručënyx, Aleksej, *Čort i rečetvorcy* (Moscow, 1913).
—, *Tajnye poroki akademikov* (Moscow, 1913).
—, *Vozropščem* (Moscow, 1913).
—, *Golodnjak* (Moscow, 1922)
—, *Zaumniki* (Moscow, 1922).
—, *Apokalipsis v russkoj literature* (Moscow, 1923).
—, *Faktura slova* (Moscow, 1923).

—, *Fonetika teatra* (Moscow, 1923).
—, *Sdvigologija russkogo jazyka* (Moscow, 1923).
—, *Lef-agitki Aseeva, Majakovskogo, Tret'jakova* (Moscow, 1925).
—, *Na bor'bu s xuligantstvom v literature* (Moscow, 1926).
—, *Novoe v pisatel'skoj texnike* (Moscow, 1927).
—, *15 let russkogo futurizma* (Moscow, 1928).
Majakovskij, Vladimir, *Polnoe sobranie sočinenij v dvednatcati tomax* (Moscow, 1939).
—, *Polnoe sobranie sočinenij*, 13 vols. (Moscow, 1955-1961).
Xlebnikov, Velimir, *Sobranie proizvedenij*, 5 vols. (Leningrad, 1929-1933).
—, *Izbrannye stixotvorenija* (Moscow, 1936).
—, *Neizdannye proizvedenija* (Moscow, 1940).
Xlebnikov, V. and A. Kručënyx, *Slovo kak takovoe* (Moscow, 1913).
"Zabytye stat'i Majakovskogo", *Literaturnoe nasledstvo*, Vol. 11 (Moscow, 1932), 117-164.

WORKS ABOUT FUTURISM AND FUTURISTS

Aksenov, I., "K likvidacii futurizma", *Pečat' i revoljucija*, No. 3 (1921), 82-97.
Almanax s Majakovskim (Moscow, 1934).
Aseev, N., "Organizacija reči", *Pečat' i revoljucija*, No. 6 (1923), 71-78.
—, *Dnevnik poèta* (Leningrad, 1929).
—, "Velimir", *Literaturnyj kritik*, No. 1 (1936), 185-192.
Averbax, L., "Novyj lef", in his *Kul'turnaja revoljucija i voprosy sovremennoj literatury* (Moscow-Leningrad, 1928), 115-133.
—, "Preodolenie otstavanija ili likvidacija iskusstva?", *Na literaturnom postu*, No. 12 (1931), 1-5.
Bebutov, G., *Gimnazičeskie gody Vladimira Majakovskogo* (Tbilisi, 1946).
Bespalov, I., "Put' Majakovskogo", *Pečat' i revoljucija*, No. 3 (1930), 5-7.
Bobrov, S., "Buka russkoj literatury", *Pečat' i revoljucija*, No. 3 (1923), 252-254.
Bowra, C. M., "The Futurism of Vladimir Mayakovsky", in his *The Creative Experiment* (London, 1949), 94-127.
Brik, L., "O Majakovskom", *Novyj mir*, No. 11-12 (1942), 240-246.
—, "Predloženie issledovateljam", *Voprosy literatury*, No. 9 (1966), 203-207.
Brik, Osip, "Sosnovskomu", *Lef*, No. 3 (1923), 4.
—, "Tak nazyvaemyj formal'nyj metod", *Lef*, No. 1 (1923), 213-215.
—, "V proizvodtsvo", *Lef*, No. 1 (1923), 105-108.
—, "Ot kartiny k sitcu", *Lef*, No. 2 (1924), 27-31.
—, "My – futuristy", *Novyj Lef*, No. 8-9 (1927), 49-52.
—, "Ne teorija, a lozung", *Pečat' i revoljucija*, No. 1 (1929), 25-30.
—, "Majakovskij – redaktor i organizator", *Literaturnyj kritik*, No. 4 (1936), 112-146.
Čeremin, G., *Rannij Majakovskij* (Moscow-Leningrad, 1962).
Čiževskij, D., "Poèzija russkogo futurizma", *Novyj žurnal*, No. 73 (1963), 132-169.
Clough, Rosa, *Futurism: The Story of a Modern Art Movement* (New York, 1961).
Čukovskij, K., *Lica i maski* (St. Petersburg, 1914).
—, *Futuristy* (Petersburg, 1922).
—, "Majakovskij", in his *Sobranie sočinenij*, Vol. II (Moscow, 1965), 346-371.
Čužak, N., "K zadačam dnja", *Lef*, No. 2 (1923), 145-152.
—, "Pljusi i minusy", *Lef*, No. 3 (1923), 28-33.
—, "Pod znakom žiznestroenija", *Lef*, No. 1 (1923), 12-39.
Čužak, N., ed., *Literatura fakta: Pervyj sbornik materialov rabotnikov lefa* (Moscow, 1929).
de Courtenay, Baudouin, "K teorii 'Slova kak takovogo' i 'Bukvy kak takovoj'",

Izbrannye trudy po obščemu jazykoznaniju, Vol. II (Moscow, 1963), 243-246.
Dreier, Katherine, *David Burliuk* (New York, 1944).
Drozda, V., "Osip Brik jako kritik", *Československa rusistika*, No. 1 (1967), 13-18.
Družin, V., "Velimir Xlebnikov", *Zvezda*, No. 3 (1930), 226-227.
Dymsic, A., ed., *V. Majakovskij* (Moscow-Leningrad, 1940).
Folejewski, Zbigniew, ed., "Futurism East and West", *Yearbook of Comparative and General Literature*, Vol. XIV (1965), 61-64.
Folejewski, Zbigniew, "Majakovskij and Futurism", *Comparative Literature Studies* (Special Advance Issue, 1963), 71-78.
Gofman, V., "Jazykovoe novatorstvo Xlebnikova", in his *Jazyk literatury* (Moscow, 1936), 185-240.
Gold, Michael, *David Burljuk: Artist-Scholar, Father of Russian Futurism* (New York, 1944).
Gollerbax, E., *Poèzija Davida Burljuka* (New York, 1931).
Gorlov, N., "Lef preodolevajuščij slovo i slovo preodolevajuščee Lef", *Lef*, No. 3 (1923), 17-21.
—, *Revoljucija i futurizm* (Moscow, 1923).
Gric, T., "Rifma Majakovskogo", *Literaturnyj kritik*, No. 3 (1939), 155-164.
Grossman-Roščin, I., "Tezisi o tvorčestve Vladimira Majakovskogo", *Oktjabr'*, No. 5-6 (1930), 243-257.
Gukovskij, G., "O stile Majakovskogo", *Zvezda*, No. 7 (1940), 165-171.
Holoquist, Michael, "The Mayakovsky Problem", *Yale French Studies: Literature and Revolution*, No. 39 (1967), 126-136.
Humesky, Assya, *Majakovskij and His Neologisms* (New York, 1964).
Ivanov-Razumnik, R., "Duša futurizma", *Kniga i revoljucija*, No. 7 (1921), 16-22.
—, "Futurizma i 'vešč'", *Kniga i revoljucija*, No. 8-9 (1921), 22-28.
—, *Vladimir Majakovskij* (Berlin, 1922).
Jakobson, Roman, *Novejšaja russkaja poèzija* (Prague, 1921).
—, "O pokolenii, rastrativšem svoix poètov", in *Smert' Vladimira Majakovskogo* (Berlin, 1931), 7-45.
Joll, James. "F. T. Marinetti: Futurism and Fascism", in his *Three Intellectuals in Politics* (New York, 1960), 133-178.
Kalinin, F., "O futurizme", *Proletarskaja kul'tura*, No. 7-8 (1919), 41-43.
Kamenskij, Vasilij, *Junost' Majakovskogo* (Tbilisi, 1931).
—, *Put' èntuziasta* (Moscow, 1931).
Katanjan, V., *Majakovskij: Literaturnaja xronika*, 4th ed. (Moscow, 1961).
Kovalenko, S., "Dvadcat' let raboty Majakovskogo", *Voprosy literatury*, No. 4 (1963), 95-108.
Kožinov, V., "Dostoevskij ili geroi Dostoevskogo?", *Voprosy literatury*, No. 9 (1966), 208-209.
Kušner, B., "Organizatory proizvodstva", *Lef*, No. 3 (1923), 97-103.
Literaturnaja ènciklopedija, Vol. VI (Moscow, 1932), 341-351.
Literaturnoe nasledstvo: Novoe o Majakovskom, Vol. LXV (Moscow, 1958).
Livšic, Benedikt, *Polutoraglazyj strelec* (Leningrad, 1933).
Lunačarskij, Anatolij, "Kak nexorošo vyxodit", *Pravda*, December 7, 1923.
—, "Eščë o Puškine", in his *Sobranie sočinenij*, Vol. I. Moscow, (1963), 36-42.
—, "Ložka protivojadija", in his *Sobranie sočinenij*, Vol. II (Moscow, 1963), 206-208.
Majakovskij i sovetskaja literatura (Moscow, 1964).
Majakovskomu. Sbornik vospominanij i statej (Leningrad, 1940).
Markov, V., "O Xlebnikove: Popytka apologii i soprotivlenija", *Grani*, No. 22 (1954), 126-145.
—, *The Longer Poems of Velimir Khlebnikov* (Berkeley, 1962).
—, "The Province of Russian Futurism", *The Slavic and East European Journal*,

VIII, No. 4 (Winter, 1964), 401-406.
—, *Russian Futurism: A History* (Berkeley, 1968).
Mathauser, Z., "Ruskij kubofuturismus, jeho determinace a transcendence", *Československá rusistika*, No. 4 (1967), 208-214.
Mil'kov, V., "Tradicii i novatorstvo v poèzii Majakovskogo", *Oktjabr'*, No. 4 (1955), 17-80.
Mixajlov, A., "Protiv recidivov lefovščiny", *Na literaturnom postu*, No. 6 (1931), 30-34.
Myškovskaja, L., "Po voprosam poètiki Majakovskogo", *Krasnaja nov'*, No. 4 (1934), 185-198.
Nemcinova, O., "Jazyk V. V. Majakovskogo", *Russkij jazyk v škole*, No. 2 (1950), 32-40.
Pasternak, Boris, "Černyj bokal", in his *Sočinenija*, Vol. III (Ann Arbor, 1961), 147-152.
Percov, V., *Literatura zavtršnego dnja* (Leningrad, 1929).
—, *Naš sovremennik* (Moscow, 1940).
Percov, V. and N. Serebrjannyj, eds., *Majakovskij: Materialy i issledovanija* (Moscow, 1940).
Poljanskij, V., "O 'levom fronte' v iskusstve", *Pod znamenem marksizma*, No. 4-5 (1923), 197-209.
Polonskij, Vjačeslav, "Lef ili Blef", in his *Na literaturnye temy* (Moscow, 1927), 7-22.
—, *O Majakovskom* (Moscow, 1931).
Pomorska, K., *Russian Formalist Theory and Its Poetic Ambiance* (The Hague, 1968).
Postupal'skij, I., *Literaturnyj trud D. Burljuka* (New York, 1930), 6.
—, "Xlebnikov i futurizm", *Novyj mir*, No. 5 (1930), 187-196.
Šapirštejn-Lerc, Ja., *Obščestvennyj smysl russkogo literaturnogo futurizma* (Moscow, 1922).
Sel'vinskij, I., "Vstreči s Majakovskim", *Oktjabr'*, No. 9 (1963), 137-152.
Šklovskij, V., "O poèzii i zaumnom jazyke", *Poètika*. Petrograd, (1919), 13-26.
—, *O Majakovskom* (Moscow, 1940).
—, "O kvartire Lefa", in his *Žili-byli* (Moscow, 1964), 370-389.
Sosnovskij, L., "Želtaja kofta iz sovetskogo sitca", *Pravda*, May 23, 1923.
Spasskij, Sergej, *Majakovskij i ego sputniki* (Leningrad, 1940).
Stahlberger, Lawrence, *The Symbolic System of Majakovskij* (The Hague, 1964).
Surma, Jurij, *Slovo v boju: Estetika Majakovskogo i literaturnaja bor'ba 20-x godov* (Leningrad, 1963).
Švecova, L., "*Lef i Novyj Lef*", in A. Dement'ev, ed., *Očerki istorii russkoj sovetskoj žurnalistiki 1917-1932* (Moscow, 1966), 311-344.
Tarasenkov, A., "Literatura fakta", *Pečat' i revoljucija*, No. 8 (1929), 106-110.
Timofeev, Leonid, *Poètika Majakovskogo* (Moscow, 1941).
—, "Ob izučenii stixa Majakovskogo", *Literatura v škole*, No. 3 (1953), 22-37.
Timofeeva, V., "O jazyke Majakovskogo", *Zvezda*, No. 6 (1952), 148-158.
—, *Jazyk poèta i vremja: Poètičeskij jazyk Majakovskogo* (Moscow-Leningrad, 1962).
Trenin, V., *V masterskoj stixa Majakovskogo* (Moscow, 1937).
Trenin, V. and N. Xardžiev, "Majakovskij i 'satirikonskaja poèzija'", *Literaturnyj kritik*, No. 4 (1934), 117-139.
—, "Retuširovannyj Xlebnikov", *Literaturnyj kritik*, No. 8 (1934), 142-150.
—, "Poètika rannego Majakovskogo", *Literaturnyj kritik*, No. 4 (1935), 171-189.
Tret'jakov, Sergej, "Tribuna Lef", *Lef*, No. 3 (1923), 154-164.
Triolet, Elsa, *Maiakovskii: poète russe* (Paris, 1945).
Tschižewskij, Dmitrij, ed., *Anfänge des russischen Futurismus* (Wiesbaden, 1963).
Tynjanov, Jurij, "O Xlebnikove", in his *Arxaisty i novatory* (Leningrad, 1929), 581-595.
Vel, "V. Xlebnikov – osnovatel' budetjan", *Kniga i revoljucija*, No. 9-10 (1922), 20-25.
Vinokur, G., "Futuristy – stroiteli jazyka", *Lef*, No. 1 (1923), 205-213.
—, "Xlebnikov", *Russkij sovremennik*, No. 4 (1924), 222-226.

—, "Rečevaja praktika futuristov", in his *Kul'tura jazyka*, Moscow, (1929), 301-319.
—, *Majakovskij – novator jazyka* (Moscow, 1943).
V. Majakovskij v vospominanijax sovremennikov (Moscow, 1963).
Volp'e, C., "Stixotvorenija Velimira Xlebnikova", *Literaturnoe obozrenie*, No. 17 (1940), 33-47.
Xajlov, A., "Periferijnye žurnaly", in A. Dement'ev, ed., *Očerki istorii russkoj sovetskoj žurnalistiki 1917-1932* (Moscow, 1966), 463-507.
Zakrževskij, A., *Rycari bezumija: futuristy* (Kiev, 1914).
Žirmunskij, Viktor, "Review of Roman Jakobson, *Novejšaja russkaja poèzija*", *Načala*, No. 2 (1919), 213-215.
—, "Vokrug 'Poètiki' Opojaza", in his *Voprosy teorii literatury* (The Hague, 1962), 337-356.
—, "Stixosloženie Majakovskogo", *Russkaja literatura*, No. 4 (1964), 3-26.
Živ Kručënyx: Sbornik statej (Moscow, 1925).

WORKS ON LITERARY CRITICISM, THEORY, HISTORY, AND LITERARY JOURNALS

Adrianov, S., "Kritičeskie nabroski", *Vestnik Evropy*, No. 10 (1910), 386-398.
Aseev, Nikolaj, "Konec belletristiki", *Pečat' i revoljucija*, No. 7 (1922), 68-80.
Asmus, V., "V zaščitu vymysla", *Pečat' i revoljucija*, No. 11 (1929), 11-31.
—, "Filosofija i èstetika russkogo simvolizma", *Literaturnoe nasledstvo*, Vol. XXVII-XXVIII (Moscow, 1937), 1-53.
Belyj, Andrej, "Venok ili venec", *Apollon*, No. 11 (1910), 1-10.
—, *Na perevale: Krizis žizni* (Petersburg, 1918).
—, *Stixotvorenija i poèmy* (Moscow-Leningrad, 1966).
Berdyaev, N., "Russkij duxovnyj renessans načala XX v. i žurnal *Put'*," *Put'*, No. 49 (1935), 3-22.
—, *The Destiny of Man*, trans. by N. Duddington (London, 1954).
—, *The Meaning of the Creative Act*, trans. by D. A. Lowrie (London, 1954).
Berger, John, *The Success and Failure of Picasso* (Baltimore, 1965).
Bespalov, I., "Protiv gramotnosti", *Pečat' i revoljucija*, No. 9 (1929), 17-24.
Block, H., "The Alleged Parallel of Metaphysical and Symbolist Poetry", *Comparative Literature Studies*, No. 1-2 (1967), 145-159.
Bobrov, S., "Metod i apologet", *Pečat' i revoljucija*, No. 5 (1924), 16-19.
Bowra, C. M., *Poetry and Politics 1900-1960* (London, 1966).
Brjusov, Valerij, "Novye tečenija v russkoj poèzii", *Russkaja mysl'*, No. 3 (1913), 124-133.
—, "Novye tečenija v russkoj poèzii", *Russkaja mysl'*, No. 8 (1913), 71-81.
—, "God russkoj poèzii", *Russkaja mysl'*, No. 5 (1914), 25-31.
—, "Včera, segodnja i zavtra russkoj poèzii", *Pečat' i revoljucija*, No. 7 (1922), 38-68.
—, "Sredi stixov", *Pečat' i revoljucija*, No. 1 (1923), 70-78.
—, "Sud akmeista", *Pečat' i revoljucija*, No. 3 (1923), 96-100.
—, "O rifme", *Pečat' i revoljucija*, No. 1 (1924), 114-123.
Brown, Edward, J., *The Proletarian Episode in Russian Literature 1928-1932* (New York, 1953).
—, *Russian Literature Since the Revolution* (New York, 1963).
Bugaev, B. [A. Belyj], *Simvolizm* (Moscow, 1910).
Carr, Edward, H., *The Bolshevik Revolution 1917-1923* (*A History of Soviet Russia*), Vol. I (London, 1950).
—, *Socialism in One Country* (*A History of Soviet Russia*), Vol. I (New York, 1958), 3-68.

Chvatik, K., "K voprosu o xudožestvennom avangarde", *Československa rusistika*, No. 4 (1967), 193-196.
Dikušina, N., "Literaturnye žurnaly 1917-1928 gg.", in *Istoria russkoj sovetskoj literatury*, Vol. I (Moscow, 1958), 490-527.
Donald, D. Egbert, "The Idea of 'Avant'garde' in Art and Politics", *The American Historical Review*, LXXIII, No. 2 (December, 1967), 339-366.
Donchin, Georgette, *The Influence of French Symbolism on Russian Poetry* (The Hague, 1958).
Èjxenbaum, Boris, *Anna Axmatova: Opyt analiza* (Petersburg, 1923).
—, "Vokrug voprosa o formalistax", *Pečat' i revoljucija*, No. 5 (1924), 1-12.
—, "V ožidanii literatury", *Russkij sovremennik*, No. 1 (1924), 280-290.
—, *Literatura, teorija, kritika, polemika* (Leningrad, 1927).
—, *Skvoz' literaturu* (The Hague, 1962).
Erlich, Victor, "Russian Poets in Search of Poetics", *Comparative Literature*, IV (1952), 54-74.
—, *Russian Formalism: History and Doctrine*, 2nd, rev. ed. (The Hague, 1965).
Ermolaev, Herman, *Soviet Literary Theories 1917-1934: The Genesis of Socialist Realism* (Berkeley, 1963).
Eršov, L., *Russkij sovetskij roman* (Leningrad, 1967).
Evgen'ev-Maksimov, V., *Očerki istorii novejšej russkoj literatury* (Moscow-Leningrad, 1927).
Fadeev, A., "Stolbovaja doroga proletarskoj literatury", *Sobranie sočinenij*, Vol. V (Moscow, 1960), 7-37.
Fanger, Donald, *Dostoevsky and Romantic Realism* (Cambridge, 1965).
Florovskij, Georg, *Puti russkogo bogoslovija* (Paris, 1937).
Fowlie, W. *Rimbaud* (Chicago, 1966).
Fyodorov, N., "The Question of Brotherhood or Relatedness, and of the Reasons for the Unbrotherly Dis-Related, or Unpeaceful State of the World, and of the Means for the Restoration of Relatedness", *Russian Philosophy*, J. M. Edie et al. eds., Vol. III (Chicago, 1965), 16-54.
Gastev, A., "Rost Proletkul'ta", *Proletarskaja kul'tura*, No. 9-10 (1919), 30-34.
Gibian, George, ed., "The Grotesque in Russian and Western Literature", *Yearbook of Comparative and General Literature*, XIII (1964), 56-59.
Gofman, V., "Jazyk simvolistov", *Literaturnoe nasledstvo*, Vol. XXVII-XXVIII (Moscow, 1937), 53-102.
Gorodeckij, Sergej, "Nekotorye tečenija v sovremennoj russkoj poèzii", *Apollon*, No. 1 (1913), 46-50.
Gray, Camilla, *The Great Experiment: Russian Art 1863-1922* (New York, 1962).
Grossman-Roščin, I., "Prestuplenie i nakazanie", *Na literturnom postu*, No. 22 (1928), 13-24.
Gumilëv, Nikolaj, "Pis'ma o russkoj poèzii", *Apollon*, No. 8 (1910), 59-64.
—, "Nasledie simvolizma i akmeizm", *Apollon*, No. 1 (1913), 42-45.
Gura, V., "Stanovlenie žanra romana v sovetskoj literature načala 20-x godov", *Problemy realizma*, Volgoda, (1966), 38-65.
Hayward, M. and L. Labedz, eds., *Literature and Revolution in Soviet Russia 1917-1962* (London, 1962).
Holthusen, Johannes, *Russische Gegenswartsliteratur: 1890-1940*, Vol. I (Bern, 1963).
Istorija russkoj sovetskoj literatury v trëx tomax, 1917-1920, Vol. I (Moscow, 1958), 528-722.
Ivanov, Vjačeslav, *Borozdy i meži* (Moscow, 1916).
Izdebskij, V., *Salon: Katalog internacional'noj vystavki kartin.* (Odessa, 1910).
Jakobson, Roman, *O češkom stixe, preimeščestvenno v sopostavlenii s russkim* (Prague, 1923), 100-115.

—, "Closing Statement: Linguistics and Poetics", in *Style in Language*, T. A. Sebeok, ed. (Cambridge, 1964), 35-377.

Jennings, L. B., *The Ludicrous Demon: Aspects of the Grotesque in German Post-Romantic Prose* (Berkeley, 1963), 1-27.

Judd, Hubert, "Baudelaire's Revolutionary Poetics", *Romanic Review*, XLVI, No. 1 (February, 1955), 164-177.

Kahler, Eric, "The Transformation of Modern Fiction", *Comparative Literature*, No. 2 (Spring, 1955), 121-128.

—, *The Tower and the Abyss* (New York, 1957).

Karlinsky, S., *Marina Cvetaeva: Her Life and Art* (Berkeley, 1966).

Kaverin, V., "Neskol'ko let", *Novyj mir*, No. 11 (1966), 132-158.

Kayser, W., *The Grotesque in Art and Literature*, trans. by U. Weisstein (Bloomington, 1963).

Kochan, Lionel, *Russia in Revolution 1890-1918* (London, 1966).

Kogan, P., "O formal'nom metode", *Pečat' i revoljucija*, No. 5 (1924), 25-32.

—, *Literatura velikogo desjatiletija* (Moscow-Leningrad, 1927).

Kuzmin, Mixail, "O prekrasnoj jasnosti: Zametki o proze", *Apollon*, No. 4 (1910), 5-10.

Lampert, Eugene, *Nicolas Berdyaev and the New Middle Ages* (London, 1949).

Lehmann, A., *The Symbolist Aesthetic in France 1885-1895* (London, 1950).

Ležnev, A., *Literatura revoljucionnogo desjatiletija 1917-1927* (Xar'kov, 1929).

Lossky, N., History of Russian Philosophy (New York, 1951).

Maguire, Robert A., *Red Virgin Soil: Soviet Literature in the 1920's* (Princeton, 1968).

Makovskij, Sergej, *Portrety sovremennikov* (New York, 1955).

—, *Na parnase 'serebrjannogo veka'* (Munich, 1962).

Mandelštam, O., "Burja i natisk", *Sobranie sočinenij v dvux tomax*, G. Struve and B. Filippov, eds., Vol. II (New York, 1966), 381-393.

—, "Konec romana", *Sobranie sočinenij v dvux tomax*, G. Struve and B. Filippov, eds., Vol. II (New York, 1966), 308-311.

Markov, Vladimir, "On Modern Russian Poetry", *Modern Russian Poetry*, Vladimir Markov and Merrill Sparks, eds. (London, 1966), li-lxxx.

Marx, Karl, *Economic and Philosophic Manuscripts of 1844* (Moscow, 1961).

Men'šutin, A. and A. Sinjavskij, *Poèzija pervyx let revoljucii* (Moscow, 1964).

Merežkovskij, Dmitrij, *Nevoennyj dnevnik 1914-1916* (Petrograd, 1917).

Monas, Sidney, "Poets and Literary Men of Russia", *Massachusetts Review*, VVI (Spring, 1964), 578-583.

Muchnic, Helen, *From Gorky to Pasternak* (New York, 1961).

Orlov, V., "Na rubeže dvux epox: Iz istorii russkoj poèzii načala našego veka", *Voprosy literatury*, No. 10 (1966), 111-143.

Pasternak, Boris, *I Remember: Sketch for an Autobiography*, trans. by M. Harari (New York, 1959).

Plexanov, Georgij, *Literatura i èstetika*, Vol. II (Moscow, 1958), 475-488.

Poggioli, Renato, *The Poets of Russia 1890-1930* (Cambridge, 1960).

—, "The Artist in the Modern World", in his *The Spirit of the Letter: Essays in European Literature* (Cambridge, 1965), 323-342.

Polonskij, Vjačeslav, "Zametki o žurnalax", *Pečat' i revoljucija*, No. 4 (1923), 291-292.

—, "Zametki o žurnalax", *Pečat' i revoljucija*, No. 5 (1923), 323-330.

—, *Očerki literaturnogo dviženija revoljucionnoj epoxi* (Moscow-Leningrad), 1929.

Rader, M., "Marx's Interpretation of Art and Aesthetic Value", *British Journal of Aesthetics*, No. 3 (1967), 237-249.

Sajanov, V., *Sovremennye literaturnye gruppirovki*, 2nd ed. (Leningrad, 1930).

Sklovskij, Viktor, "Sovremenniki i sinxronisty", *Russkij sovremennik*, No. 3 (1924), 235-247.

—, *Tret'ja fabrika* (Moscow, 1926).

—, *Gamburgskij ščët* (Leningrad, 1928).
—, "Žili-byly", *Znamja*, No. 9 (1961), 176-187.
Spender, Stephen, "Writers and Politics", *Partisan Review*, XXXIV (Summer, 1967), 359-381.
Stepanov, N., "V zaščitu izobretatel'stva", *Zvezda*, No. 6 (1929), 182-192.
Struve, Gleb, *Russian Literature Under Lenin and Stalin* (Norman, 1971).
Tal'nikov, D., "Literaturnye zametki", *Krasnaja nov'*, No. 11 (1928) 259-281.
Tomaševskij, B., *Stilistika i stixosloženie* (Moscow, 1959).
—, *Stix i jazyk: Filologičeskie očerki* (Moscow-Leningrad, 1959), 61-68, 115-129.
Trotsky, Leon, *Literature and Revolution* (New York, 1957).
Turbin, V., *Tovarišč Vremja i Tovarišč Iskusstvo* (Moscow, 1961).
Tynjanov, Jurij, "O literaturnom fakte", *Lef*, No. 2 (1924), 100-116.
"Uroki 'litfronta'", *Literatura i iskusstvo*, No. 3-4 (1930), 5-8.
Vinokur, G., "Jazyk našej gazety", *Lef*, No. 2 (1924), 117-140.
Vinogradov, V., "Ponjatie sintagmy v sintaksise russkogo jazyka", *Voprosy sintaksisa sovremennogo russkogo jazyka*, ed. V. Vinogradov (Moscow, 1950), 206-212.
Zavalishin, Viacheslav, *Eearly Soviet Writers* (New York, 1962).
Zelinskij, K., *Na rubeže dvux èpox* (Moscow, 1959).
Zenkovsky, Vasily, *A History of Russian Philosophy*, trans. by G. Kline, Vol. II (New York, 1953), 588-604.
Žirmunskij, Viktor, *Nemeckij romantizm i sovremennaja mistika* (Petersburg, 1914).

INDEX

Academy of Verse, 22
Acmeism, 15, 16, 36, 90
Anderson, Sherwood, 159 n
Andreev, Leonid, 36, 40
Annenskij, Innokentyj, 22
Antokol'skij, Mark, 148
Apollo (*Apollon*, Acmeist journal), 15, 22
Arcybašev, Mixail, 36
Art (*Tvorčestvo*, Futurist journal), 77
Aragon, Louis, 109, 154, 155, 159 n, 160, 160 n
Art of the Commune (*Iskusstvo kommuny*, Futurist newspaper), 123
Aseev, Nikolaj, 77, 90, 112
Asmus, V., 31 n
Avant-garde (avant-gardism), 9, 145, 154, 163; in Majakovskij's poetry, 56, 68, 72; characteristics of, 109
Avant-garde, Russian artistic, chapter on, 114-126; composition of, 116; theories and programs of, 117-122, opposition to, 118, 122-123; deposition of, 124; historical significance of, 125
Averbax, Leopold, 142
Axmatova, Anna, 15

Bal'mont, Konstantin, 20, 40, 101
Babel', Isaak, 90
Barbusse, Henri, 157, 157 n, 158
Baudelaire, Charles, 56, 73
Bazalgette, L., 157 n
Bebel, A., 79
Belyj, Andrej (Boris Bugaev), 29, 30, 31, 37 n, 40, 41, 42, 44, 55 n, 101, 109; relationship of, to Russian Futurism, 31 n
Benois, A., 68
Berdjaev, Nikolaj, 53 n
Bergson, Henri, 150
Beskin, E., 102
Blok, Aleksandr, 17, 22, 30, 40, 44, 56, 84
Boccioni, Umberto, 149
Bolshevism (Bolsheviks), 124, 125, 128, 143, 153, 154, 155, 156, 162, 163; Futurist commitment to, 116, 143, 154, 155-156; Surrealist commitment to, 154, 155-156
Breton, André, 109, 153 n, 154, 155, 156, 156 n, 157, 158, 160, 160 n, 161
Brik, Lilja, 76
Brik, Osip, 10, 76, 116, 118, 119, 120, 124, 126, 128, 129, 135, 136, 137, 138, 146, 159 n
Brjusov, Valerij, 17, 30, 36, 40, 56, 66 n, 70, 74, 83, 83 n, 108 n, 111
Browder, C., 162 n
Brown, Edward J., 139 n
Bunin, Ivan, 40
Burljuk, David, 10, 17, 17 n, 18, 22, 34, 35, 35 n, 36, 41, 80, 99, 105, 106, 108, 111, 112; chapter on, 67-78; early life and artistic activities of, 67-68; role of, in organizing Futurism, 69; esthetics of, 70-72; poetry of, 72-75, poetic devices of, 73; poetic influences on, 73; poetic themes of, 73; influence of, on Majakovskij's early poetry, 75-76; departure of, from Russia, 77; activities of, during 1920's, 77-78
Burljuk, Nikolaj, 17, 17 n, 35
Burljuk, Vladimir, 17, 17 n, 151

Caute, David, 156
Centrifuge (Futurist group), 23
Chagall, Marc, 116
Clarté (French journal), 157
Colucci, Michele, 146, 146 n, 147 n
Comintern, 156
Communist Party, French, 156, 157
Communist Party, Russian, 37, 79, 141,

143, 156, 159, 161
Company of 41 Degrees (Futurist group), 86
Corbiére, Tristan, 17, 74
Cubism, 32 n, 33, 36, 43, 68, 71, 80, 111, 116, 142, 153
Čexov, Anton, 137, 138
Čukovskij, Kornej, 94, 95, 101, 109
Čužak, Nikolaj (Nasimovič), 77, 129, 130, 130 n, 132, 133, 134 n, 140

Delacroix, F., 151
Dell, Floyd, 159 n
Denike, A., 21
Deržavin, Gavril, 33
Dostoevskij, F., 43, 82, 108
Dreiser, Theodore, 159 n
Drozda, M., 143

Efrejmin, L., 100 n
Egbert, Donald, 144 n
Ego-Futurists, 23 n
Eluard, Paul, 109, 154
Einstein, Albert, 157 n
Engels, F., 79
Erlich, Victor, 129 n, 144
Evgen'ev-Maksimov, V., 112
Evreinov, N., 45
Èfros, Avram, 114
Èjxenbaum, Boris, 92, 111, 127 n, 135 n

Fadeev, Aleksandr, 137-138, 142
Fëdorov, Nikolaj, 43, 49, 49 n, 52, 53, 53 n
Fellow-travellers (literary group), 126
Florovskij, Georg, 53 n
Folejewski, Zbigniew, 10, 31 n, 66
Formalism (Formalists), Russian, 112, 113, 127, 127 n, 139, 139 n, 140, 141, 143, 158; literary theories of, in 1920's, 129-131; alliance of, with Russian Futurism, 135
Futurism, Italian, 42; relationship of, to Russian Futurism, 145-152
Futurism (Futurists), Russian: formation of, 16-18; early period of, in historical perspective, 108-113; as a unified movement, 108; links of, with modern avant-garde, 108-109; anarchist strain in, 109; social revolt of, 110; alliance of, with Russian artistic avant-garde, 116, 117; postrevolutionary activities of, 114-144; continuity in, 142; relationship of, to Italian Futurism, 145-152; relationship of, to French Surrealism, 153-163; *see also* chapters on Xlebnikov, Majakovskij, Burljuk, Kručënyx, Kamenskij

Gabo, Naum, 121
Gippius, 109 n
Gold, Michael, 157 n, 159 n
Gollerbax, E., 72
Express Gončarova, Natalja, 67
Gor'kij, Maksim, 19, 40, 76, 157 n
Gorlov, N., 95
Gorodeckij, Sergej, 15, 16, 21, 86 n
Gumilëv, Nikolaj, 15, 16, 21, 22, 29, 61
Guro, Elena, 17, 17 n, 68
Gusman, B., 100

Hokusai, K., 150

Ivanov, Vjačeslav, 20, 21, 22, 29, 31, 71, 86 n, 109
Ivanov, Vsevolod, 90
Ivanov-Razumnik, R., 110

Jack of Diamonds (*Bubnovyj valet;* art group), 18, 71
Jakobson, Roman, 24, 30, 60, 61
Jakulov, Georgij, 151
Jolas, Eugene, 159 n

Kamenskij, Vasilij, 10, 16, 17, 21, 22, 68, 90, 108, 111, 112; chapter on, 98-107; early life and activities of, 98-100; poetic theory and practice of, 100-105; notion of the poetic word, 100-101; orientation of poetry, 101-102; major poetic theme of, 102; orientation of, to folklore, 104; post-revolutionary activity of, 106-107
Sten'ka Razin, 99
Heart of the People is Sten'ka Razin, The (Serdce narodnoe – Sten'ka Razin), 102, 104
This Also is a Biography (Èto i est' biografija), 107
Career of an Enthusiast, The (Put' èntuziasta), 107
Kandinskij, Vasilij, 68, 114, 116
Karamzin, Nikolaj, 130
Katanjan, Vasilij, 160
Keep, John, 103 n
Kirsanov, S., 134
Kručënyx, Aleksej, 10, 18, 34, 35, 42, 100,

101, 108, 112, 146; chapter on, 79-97; early life and activities of, 79-90; relationship of, with Xlebnikov, 80; notion of trans-sense language, 81-82; theory and practice of trans-sense language, 82-91; critical reaction to the use of trans-sense language in poetry, 91-96; role of, in Russian Futurism, 96-97
Declaration of Trans-sense Language (Deklaracija zaumnogo jazyka), 86, 91
Declaration of the Word as Such (Deklaracija slova kak takovogo), 35
Game in Hell, A (Igra v adu), 80, 81
"dyr bul ščyl," 93, 96
Word as Such, The (Slovo kak takovoe), 3
Kul'bin, Nikolaj, 21, 68, 148, 149, 150
Kušner, Boris, 117, 141, 160
Kuz'min, Mixail, 15, 22, 22 n

Larionov, Mixail, 67
Lef (*The Left Front of Art*, Futurist journal), 77, 90, 106; formation of, 126-127; Futurist theories in, 127-129; criticized by Trotsky, 131-133; crisis in, 133; dissolution of, 134; reorganization of, into *New Lef*, 135; opposition in, to RAPP, 135-139
Lenin, Vladimir, 103 n, 123, 124, 125, 155, 156
Leonov, Leonid, 90
Lermontov, Mixail, 82, 83, 98
"Literature of fact," 107, 159; discussion of, 139-141, 143-144
Litfront (literary group), 139 n
Livšic, Benedikt, 31 n, 34, 36, 96, 108, 147; discussion with Marinetti, 148-152
Lomonosov, Mixail, 33, 101
Lozanova, A., 103
Lunačarskij, Anatolij, 115, 116, 117, 117 n, 123, 124, 154, 155, 156, 156 n

Maguire, Robert, 126
Majakovskij, Vladimir, 10, 17, 18, 35 n, 36, 69, 71, 74, 75, 76, 77, 79, 80, 96, 101, 105, 108, 109, 110, 111, 112, 116, 119, 124, 126, 128, 129, 133, 139 n, 140, 141, 146, 147, 159, 159 n, 160, 160 n, 161, 163 n; chapter on, 38-66; early life and activities of, 38-40; esthetics of, 42-43; early poetry of, 43-55; influence on early poetry, 43; development and maturity of major poetic theme, 43-54; view of the Bolshevik revolution, 55; poetic devices of, 56-66; grotesque depiction of city, 56-58; neologisms of, 58; declamatory nature of poetry, 59-60; poetic meters of, 60-61; stress and intonational character of poetry, 61-63; poetic rhymes of, 63-66; suicide of, 160-161
About This (Pro èto), 129
Cloud in Pants (Oblaka v štanax), 43
From Street to Street (Iz ulicy v ulicu), 64
How to Write Poetry (Kak sdelat' stixi), 59
Morning (Utro), 63
Open Letter to Workers (Otkrytoe pis'mo rabočim), 54
Vladimir Majakovskij: A Tragedy (Vladimir Majakovskij: Tragedija), 43, 45
War and the Universe (Vojna i mir), 44, 48, 50, 51, 53
"Making it strange," *(ostranenie)*, 32, 111
Makovskij, Sergej, 22 n
Malevič, Kazimir, 105, 116, 118 n
Mallarmé, Stephane, 74
Mandel'štam, Osip, 15, 21, 130 n
Marc, F., 68
Marinetti, Filippo, 145, 146, 147; discussion with Livšic, 148-152
Markov, Vladimir, 9 n, 26, 31 n, 32, 33, 34, 35, 81, 102 n, 112, 145, 146
Marx, Karl, 79, 120 n, 125, 144 n
Marxism, 39, 39 n, 41, 125
Matjušin, Mixail, 17 n, 20, 21, 68
Men'šutin, A., 102, 103 n
Merežkovskij, D., 36
Mezzanine of Poetry (poetic group), 23
Michelangelo, 148
Monas, Sidney, 155 n
Monde (French journal), 157
Monet, Claude, 150
Moore, Harriet, 159 n
Morhardt, M., 157 n

Nekrasov, Nikolaj, 98
Neologism, poetic, 24, 31; in Xlebnikov's poetry, 23-24; in Majakovskij's poetry, 58
Newspaper of the Futurists (Gazeta futuristov), 77

Neznamov, P., 77, 160

Octobrists (proletarian literary group), 126, 127
Opekušin, A., 148
OPOJAZ (Society for the Study of Poetic Language), 129

Pasternak, Boris, 39, 96
Percov, Viktor, 138
Péret, Benjamin, 158
Piksanov, N., 104
Plexanov, G., 79
Poggioli, Renato, 108
Polonskij, Vjačeslav, 57, 116, 134
Pomorska, Krystyna, 143 n
Pound, Ezra, 109
Punin, Nikolaj, 116, 118, 124, 125
Puškin, Aleksandr, 78, 82, 83, 84, 86, 89, 94, 98, 103, 108, 148

Rahv, Philip, 161
RAPP (Russian Association of Proletarian Writers), 135-136, 139 n, 141, 142, 143, 159; literary notions of, 136 n, 137; Futurist criticism of, 137-139
Razin, Stepan, historical account of revolt, 102-103; folklore on, 103-104; role in Kamenskij's poetry, 104-105
Red Virgin Soil (Krasnaja nov'), 126
Reed, John, 141
Remizov, Aleksej, 20
Renoir, Jean, 150
Revolution, Bolshevik, 10, 54, 55 n, 77, 78, 86, 102 n, 103, 103 n, 104, 112, 126, 155, 155 n, 160
Rhyme, poetic, in Majakovskij's poetry, 63-66
Rimbaud, A., 17, 73, 74
Rolland, M., 17

Sablé, Lucien, 158-159
Sadok sudej (A Trap for Judges), 17, 23, 98, 146
Saint-Simon, 125
Scales, The (Vesy, Russian Symbolist journal), 19
Schmeman, Alexander, 110 n
Sejfullina, Lidija, 90, 91
"Self-sufficient word," 18
"Shift," poetic, 32, 33, 111
Sinclair, U., 157 n
Sinjavskij, Andrej, 102, 103 n
Slap in the Face of Public Taste, A (Poščečina obščestvennomu vkusu), 18, 34, 73, 96
"Social command," 129, 129 n
"Socialist Realism," 161
Sokolov, B., 104
Sologub, F. (Teternikov), 36, 40
Spasskij, Sergej, 36, 76
Stepanov, Nikolaj, 17, 27, 30
Studio of Impressionists (Studija impressionistov), 23
Surrealism (Surrealists), French, 11, 147; relationship of, to Russian Futurism, 153-163; defined by Breton, 154; reaction of, against bourgeois culture, 154-155; commitment of, to Bolshevism, 155-157; reaction of, against proletarian literature, 157-161
Symbolism (Symbolists), Russian, 15, 16, 17, 28, 29, 30, 32, 33, 36, 43, 44, 68, 70, 73, 74, 83, 84, 90, 92, 101, 102, 104, 107, 108, 109, 110, 111, 142, 154
Šklovskij, Viktor, 34, 76, 92, 93, 111, 116, 130, 136, 140, 141, 141 n
Šterenburg, David, 116, 117, 117 n, 123 n, 125
Ščerba, L., 62

Tatlin Vladimir, 105, 116
Tolstoj, Lev, 78, 82, 136, 137, 138, 139
"Trans-sense language" *(zaumnyj jazyk)*, 82, 86, 88, 90, 91, 106, 111; Xlebnikov's theory of, 23, 29, 81; Kručënyx's theory of, 81, 83, 85, 85 n; Kručënyx's poetic use of, 86-88; critical discussion of, 91-96
Trenin, Vladimir, 61, 74, 138 n
Tret'jakov, Sergej, 77, 92, 139
Triolet, Elsa, 159 n
Trotsky, Leon, 94, 117, 155, 156, 158; view of Futurism in 1920's, 131-133
Tugendxol'd, Jakov, 114, 121
Trubeckoj, Pavel, 148
Turgenev, A., 130
Tynjanov, Jurij, 35 n, 111, 130, 141

Ugarte, M., 157 n
Unamuno, M. de, 157 n
Utamaro, K., 150

Vailland, Roger, 162
Vinokur, G., 61, 93, 94
Vjazemskij, P., 130

Voronskij, Aleksandr, 126, 126 n, 127, 127 n, 136 n, 138

Werth, Leon, 157 n

Xardžiev, Nikolaj, 22, 34, 74
Xlebnikov, Velimir, 10, 17, 18, 42, 68, 69, 80, 81, 86 n, 94, 99, 99 n, 101, 102, 108, 109, 110, 112, 148, 151; chapter on, 19-37; early life and activities of, 19-20; syncretism of, 21; influences on early poetry, 22; linguistic theories of, 23-24, 28-29; neologisms of, 23-24; historical theories of, 25; poetic devices of, 30-32; poetic orientation of, 29; relationship of, to Futurism, 34; concept of Futurism, 36; relationship of, to Symbolism, 37-38
Crane, The (Žuravl'), 23, 29-34
Czar's Bride, The (Carskaja nevesta), 23
Forest Maiden, The (Lesnaja deva), 27
Game in Hell (Igra v adu), 80-81
I and È (I i È), 27
Incantation by Laughter (Zakljatie smexom), 23
Marie Vetsera (Maria Večora), 27
Numbers (Čisla), 28
Otter's Children, The (Deti vydry), 27, 34
Scratch on the Sky, A (Carapina po nebu), 34
Sinner's Temptation (Iskušenie grešnika), 21
Things Were Much Too Blue (Byli vešči sliškom sini), 20
War in a Mousetrap, The (Vojna v myšelovke), 34
World Harmony (Ladomir), 28
"*Zangezi*," 34
"*Zoo*," *(Zverinec)*, 23

Yeats, William Butler, 109
Young, Stark, 159 n

Zakrževskij, V., 92
Zavališin, V., 49 n
Zelinskij, F., 22, 134
Zetkin, Clara, 125
Žirmunskij, Viktor, 61, 93, 97, 111